W9-BZX-292

Pothole Confidential

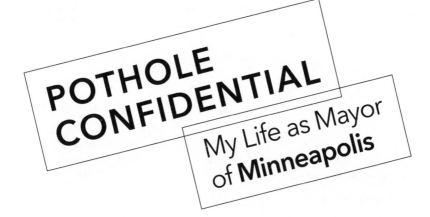

# POTHOLE CONFIDENTIAL

## My Life as Mayor of Minneapolis

# R.T. RYBAK

UNIVERSITY OF MINNESOTA PRESS

*Minneapolis*

*London*

Published by the University of Minnesota Press
111 Third Avenue South, Suite 290
Minneapolis, MN 55401-2520
http://www.upress.umn.edu

Printed in the United States of America on acid-free paper

The University of Minnesota is an equal-opportunity educator and employer.

22   21   20   19   18   17   16        10   9   8   7   6   5   4   3   2   1

Library of Congress Cataloging-in-Publication Data
Names: Rybak, R.T.
Title: Pothole confidential : my life as mayor of Minneapolis / R.T. Rybak. Other titles: My life as mayor of Minneapolis
Description: Minneapolis : University of Minnesota Press, [2016] | Includes bibliographical references and index.
Identifiers: LCCN 2015050084 | ISBN 978-0-8166-9940-7 (hc)
Subjects: LCSH: Rybak, R.T. | Mayors–Minneapolis–Minnesota–Biography. | Minneapolis (Minn.)–History. | Minneapolis (Minn.)–Politics and government. | Minneapolis (Minn.)–Biography.
Classification: LCC F614.M553 R93 2016 | DDC 977.6/053092–dc23
LC record available at http://lccn.loc.gov/2015050084

*To Megan, who lived a life she wouldn't have chosen*
*so we could make other lives a little better*

# Contents

## Start in the Middle

SHILOH TEMPLE WAS COMMON GROUND. In the complex world of north Minneapolis—where years of high crime, high poverty, and high drama spawned so many factions—the thriving church located in a former Kodak plant was a safe spot for everyone.

I was there in June 2006 to celebrate the life of Brian Cole. A few nights earlier the eighteen-year-old high school basketball star with a wide network of friends left a party and was standing under a tree to get out of the rain. Someone in a passing SUV opened fire and killed Brian. The gang member who took the shot apparently was looking for someone else. Now a few hundred of us were inside Shiloh Temple International Ministries on West Broadway Avenue trying to make sense of why a good kid in the wrong place at the wrong time was dead because somebody thought he was somebody else.

There were moving eulogies from the podium, which would have had even more impact if there hadn't been so much more drama in the pews. Warring gangs that made Brian their innocent victim had been trading shots and threats since the shooting, and there was real concern the funeral would be disrupted. That never happened, but something more moving did take place.

As the service wound down, people were invited to pay their last respects to Brian, who was lying in an open casket at the front of the church. I was seated behind the casket near the altar and watched for more than an hour as one person after another leaned over his body. I forced myself to stay focused on each of those faces coming to terms with the death of their friend. Was this finally going to be the death that would keep kids from killing kids? I came to the cold realization that I didn't see anger, I didn't see swagger, I just saw deep, deep pain on one face after another.

That pain was even harder to witness because those faces were so young. It was absolutely clear from people's expressions that they knew how deeply wrong Brian's death was, but I also saw a hopeless recognition that no one knew how to stop the killings from happening again. Even more devastating, I was the mayor and I didn't know how to stop them either.

I didn't know how intensely I was concentrating until I left the church. As I got into my car, the horror on those faces—their hopelessness and mine—all came together. All the pain I had seen came crashing in on me. As Mark Klukow, the police officer who was with me, drove away, I began to cry almost uncontrollably and couldn't stop.

What Klukow knew, and I had forgotten, was that this was not my last stop of the day. I stared out the window, too full of grief to say anything, as he drove across Minneapolis to the Green Institute. He handed me my talking points as I got out of the car, but before I could look at them a very relieved event organizer appeared, said the speeches were just starting, and pulled me on the stage.

"In honor of Energy Independence Day we will have Mayor Rybak wear this three-cornered hat and sign a Declaration of Energy Independence!" So there I stood, fresh from a heart-wrenching funeral, dressed like Paul Revere, struggling to ad-lib a few lines about alternative energy.

There were three more stops before I got home.

By this point I had been mayor for five years, accustomed to days when I careened from one world to another, from one emotion to another. I didn't know I would be mayor for seven more years, and I didn't know the war against the violence that took Brian Cole's life would continue for years until we finally started to win. I didn't know the I-35W bridge would collapse during rush hour one August afternoon—and be rebuilt. Or that north Minneapolis would be hit by, and rebound from, a devastating tornado. I didn't know I would help set off a real estate boom on the east side of downtown, perform historic same-sex marriages, help start a beer brewing boom, find ways to repave miles of streets, and much more.

It was, however, already clear that the job I had wanted for most of my life was more rewarding than, and completely different from, what I had expected. I also knew the job was changing me as much as I was changing the city.

Those teenagers saying farewell to Brian Cole in his casket were in grade school when I took office and would be adults before the end of my last term. I can't know how they turned out, but I will never forget their faces.

# The Beginning

JIM KAAT WON THE GAME two nights ago, and an ailing Camilo Pascual pitched a gem last night. I had won Game 1, pitching a shutout and hitting that home run, so I was dog tired. But it was the 1964 World Series, and there was no other choice: I had to pitch on only three days' rest.

So that's how I found myself in the ninth inning of a pitcher's duel with Juan Marichal. I knew there was almost nothing left in my aching right arm. My fastball just struck out Willie McCovey, but with a 3–2 count on Willie Mays I had to go with the curve Camilo taught me. We were one strike away. I snapped my wrist as the ball left my fingers—and a helpless Mays missed strike three. Metropolitan Stadium erupted as I tried to take in the reality of having led the Twins to a world championship. As teammates rushed the mound in celebration, I heard a familiar voice in the background.

"R.T., look what you've done to the house!" Lois Marcus, my mother's best friend from across the alley, shook me out of my fantasy World Series and back to my yard in southwest Minneapolis. She pointed to the marks my wet tennis balls were making on the back wall, as hour after hour I threw and caught them, threw and caught them in an ongoing world of make-believe where I took my rightful place as the true star of the invincible Minnesota Twins.

Lois went into the house with my mom, and I went back to something most would call "a game" but I called "my life." I know I went to school in those days, and Cub Scouts and camp, but most of what I remember was preparing for my future as a Twin. It was inevitable. If I wasn't throwing the ball against the house, I was listening to the Twins on WCCO Radio and imagining broadcast legend Halsey Hall's phlegmy voice making a habit of calling out my name.

Baseball made so much sense to me then. You won; you lost. The game started, finished, then you played again. It was so much cleaner than the ambiguity of real life, at least until I found another game that seemed to fit those clean parameters: politics.

THE SAME YEAR I HELPED the Twins win the 1964 series, my mom sent my brother and sister and me out with literature for Barry Goldwater. I was not quite nine years old but I had already sold Christmas wreaths door to door for Cub Scouts, so putting a political brochure in someone's door seemed a reasonable activity. Goldwater was crushed in the election, but the blowout didn't dampen my enthusiasm one bit.

In the next few years I had very little time for my homework but found plenty of time to read *Time* and *Newsweek* every week, and watch the evening news religiously. I may not have been the smartest kid in my class, but I knew far more about politics than almost anyone my age. It would probably be more accurate to say I spent far more time than anyone I knew finding the news that justified why I should be a Republican. By the time the next election came around, I was spending Saturdays taking the bus to Hennepin and Seventh to volunteer at Richard Nixon's headquarters.

I picked my candidates like most kids: by listening to my parents, and my mother was definitely a Republican at the time (like so many moderate Republicans from those days, she is a Democrat today). I supported my candidates like I supported the Twins: with fierce loyalty.

My obsession with politics, even at such a young age, overwhelmed anything I could possibly learn in school, and my grades showed it. I really didn't care. Twins stars and famous politicians got honorary degrees, after all.

Later in my life people would say one of my greatest assets was that I had so much energy, but during those years in school I didn't know what to do with the wave after wave of adrenaline. Being in constant motion can be very helpful when you are a mayor with a limitless number of things to do, but it didn't serve me well in school, where increasingly I became the disruptive force in the classroom. The worse that got the less I learned, and the less I learned the less I paid attention.

I recall this pattern now with a huge sense of gratitude that my mother never gave up on me and that the cocoon of a school my parents sacrificed a lot to send me to gave me second and third and fifth and hundredth chances. Years later I would also get another insight into my experiences when I was at Generation Next, immersed every day in issues of race and education. I know now that if you took all the facts of my behavior in school—distraction, disruption, bad grades—and changed the color of my skin, the result would have been far different. People would have given up on me earlier and more quickly labeled me a failure, and, worst of all, I probably would have heard all these messages and given up on myself as well. Reflecting back on my years at Breck taught me the true meaning of gratitude and the true meaning of privilege.

There were plenty of people who didn't give up on me but one I remember best was Steven Kingsbury, a new teacher who came to my school in 1968. Kingsbury was just out of college, he was decidedly not a Republican—something I figured out easily when I saw a book on his shelf titled *Teaching as a Subversive Activity.*

Kingsbury challenged everything I thought, *hard.* I fought back even harder. In the spring of 1968, he assigned us a paper about how we would vote in that year's presidential election and I ripped into a stirring defense of Richard Nixon. A few days later, as he handed back our graded papers, I looked at the cover and knew my teacher had made a mistake. He had given me an A. I had never gotten an A on anything. I walked up to his desk to see if he had indeed made a mistake. He looked me in the eye and said, intensely, "You have something to say. Keep saying it."

To this day I remember everything about that moment, about how the A looked on the paper, about the look in Kingsbury's eye and exactly what he said. More than four decades later that remains one of the most important moments in my life. It is one of the reasons I can stand up today and say what I think, and one of the reasons why I try with almost every group of kids I talk to, to tell at least one of them—especially a kid with the guts to challenge the mayor—that they have something important to say.

WHETHER HE KNEW IT OR NOT, Steve Kingsbury helped change the way I looked at myself, but he didn't change my politics. That started to happen that same summer when one hot night I sat up with my mom watching the Democratic National Convention. Chicago had broken out in chaos with police beating and teargassing the young protesters. Nothing made much sense that year, especially the assassinations of both Martin Luther King Jr. and Bobby Kennedy. This was way beyond anything that could fit into my crisp Nixonian fantasy world.

With riots in the streets, a strange subplot developed inside the convention hall. Reform Democrats nominated an obscure African American state representative from Georgia to be vice president. Julian Bond never really had a chance, but I was mesmerized. With chaos and lowball politics swirling all around him, Bond was smart, rational, and inspiring. Why couldn't someone like that be president? Why should his race matter? (Three and a half decades later I would be asking the same questions after another candidate inspired me at another Democratic Convention. Julian Bond was my first Barack Obama.)

Bond got me thinking, and so did the horrible scenes I saw on TV from Chicago. I knew something was very wrong. I knew especially that the war was wrong, and I began to realize that politics was about far more than winning and losing. Unlike baseball, there were issues that had a huge impact on people's lives. Winning still mattered—but I began to understand there had to be a *reason* to win.

I had already decided years earlier that I was planning to run for office someday myself, probably for mayor of Minneapolis, and now I developed the political version of those fantasy World Series games. Instead of throwing tennis balls against the back of the house, I listened to every political debate, every news show interview, and I talked back to the TV as if I were the candidate. Just like my fantasy World Series, in my mind, I won every one of those debates.

Through the rest of the 1968 election, I somehow convinced myself to keep working for Nixon. I bought the idea that he could actually end the war. I didn't see a better alternative. But I started to question everything I had believed. It wasn't completely clear to me at the time—I was still protecting my political loyalties to Republicans, the same way I protected my loyalty to the Twins—but I now see that the late sixties was when I shifted how I looked at the world, just like so many others during that time.

My final days as a Republican were in May 1970. I had an internship working in the Minnesota Republican Party headquarters in Pentagon Office Park in Edina. My job was to cut out articles from the paper and glue them into a scrapbook to circulate around the office.

That was the month of the Kent State massacre. Dutifully clipping those articles day after day, reading every word while I glued them into the scrapbook, I was completely stunned that something like this could happen to people who weren't that much older than me. And for what? A war no one believed in? Kill kids in your own country and thousands more on secret bombing missions? Strangely, my short time at Republican headquarters ended up being a radicalizing immersion in the news that showed me a lot had to change.

At the end of the month, I closed that scrapbook and along with it, the chapter in my life as a Republican.

# No Longer a Game

MY FATHER DIED in October 1965.

About a year and a half earlier he had suffered a serious heart attack as well as a stroke that had left his left side paralyzed and his mental capacity seriously altered. He returned home from the hospital and subsequent therapy depleted, dependent, and, on many levels, a different person. He was needy, deeply emotional, and unable to track most conversations. All that was clearly understandable to another adult, but as a ten-year-old, I alternated from wanting to get away, to pretending it wasn't happening, to being incredibly embarrassed when anyone else was around.

In a remarkable sign of strength that still amazes me decades later, my mother took care of him, and us, and went to work running his drugstore at Chicago and Franklin in south Minneapolis. For more than a year she somehow balanced everything, trying every way possible to make this seem normal to my brother and sister and me. Then one Sunday morning we came home from church and she told us our father had died.

The father I remember was gone years before, and, as much as we missed him, I knew even when I was ten years old that the very ill, very depleted shell of the man my father used to be was dying. This was not a shock. Not only did I know it, I realized the adults around us knew it, too, and I was baffled that not one of them seemed to acknowledge this very obvious reality.

I'm sure it's confounding to figure out what to say to a kid whose parent has died, but it seemed the adults were all playing some sort of dishonest game of pretending this was a sudden turn of events. Everything I remember about that time I perceived as a young kid who felt he was being treated like a fool. I couldn't tell why I experienced huge waves of anger. I would later learn that it's a natural part of coming to terms with the death of someone so close to you, but I remember very clearly making a commitment to myself at the time that I would never be so fake when I talked to people about death.

That is the tape that played back in my head, years later, when I was mayor and trying to comfort people who had experienced the death of someone near to them. I knew firsthand what it was like to feel patronized at a time like that, even by people who I am sure were well-meaning. I was absolutely not going to be the mayor, or person, who couldn't offer anything deeper than pat phrases.

I JUST WANTED LIFE to move on to a new normal, and my mom did everything possible to make that happen. She fixed up the basement of the drugstore as a kind of living room where we could come after school. Today I understand the store was in a tiny, grungy building but it didn't feel like it then at all, because my mother had taken a dank basement and made it a home—rug on the floor, lamps, a television. Every day after school Mr. Palmer, the deliveryman, brought us to the store where we went to the basement and did our homework before going to the Chef Café next door to have dinner. After dinner, we'd come back to the store and watch TV until my mom closed the store at 8:00 P.M. Sometimes on the way home we drove to a few houses to deliver prescriptions. We did it all over again the next day.

The Phillips neighborhood around the store was rapidly deteriorating in those days; it was especially dangerous given my parents' business was a drugstore with narcotics. The Chef Café on East Franklin Avenue was surely not a great restaurant to be eating in every night. To my mother's enormous credit I saw it very differently: it was the closest thing I could imagine to the perfect "Ozzie and Harriet" family scene. We were together, we had structure, we weren't distracted—and we absolutely knew we were loved. It was also the only time before I went to college that I had anything resembling good grades.

I also saw something that had a profound impact on the politics I would later try to practice. Starting each day in a comfortable middle-class neighborhood, we would spend the day at a private school where almost everyone had more money than we did (especially after my father got sick). But after leaving Breck School for the day, my siblings and I would spend the evening in a neighborhood where I got my first view of real poverty. People who came into the store, who ate with us in the Chef

Café, whose houses we saw when we delivered prescriptions, had dramatically less than we did.

Spending the day with people who had so much more, and then the evening with people with so much less, I came away with the strange gift of understanding my privilege. That growing understanding, as well as being raised by a mother who gave my siblings and me a deep sense that we should do something to make things around us better, is how I began to see politics as not just a game but primarily as a way to fix the world around me. It is almost certainly how, at the age of thirteen, I got the very unusual idea that I wanted to be mayor of Minneapolis.

The not-so-perfect-life-that-felt-perfect at the drugstore didn't last much longer for our family. Crime in the neighborhood was getting worse quickly, and there were a number of robberies at the drugstore—thankfully when we kids weren't there. My mother, however, was held up at gunpoint two nights in a row. As she lay on the floor during the second robbery, the robber put a gun to her head and demanded all the narcotics in the store. She told him she didn't have any because they were all taken in the robbery the day before. He didn't believe her; the gun clicked and she remembers praying, "God, get me up off this floor and I'll sell the damn store." Just then she remembered that an article about the previous day's holdup was taped to the counter. She told the robber—he read it, believed her, and left.

My mother knew she had to sell the store, but there was a serious consequence. She had never gone to college and was determined, no matter what, that her children would. She and my father had put a large share of what they had into sending us to Breck, a very good private school. If she didn't have the store, she would have to take us out of Breck—a move that would, in her mind, make it harder for us to get to college.

The next day, following another article in the paper about her getting held up two days in a row, she got a call from Canon Douglas Henderson, the headmaster of Breck. "Are you going to sell that store or let your kids be orphans?" he asked. He offered her a job running the school bookstore and offered us scholarships. She took the job and spent summers getting a B.A. and a master's degree. She went on to be Breck's college counselor for more than twenty years, helping hundreds of kids get their own degrees. Years later she drove our own kids, Charlie and Grace, and their cousin Tori, to Breck every day while they talked about—from first grade on— where they would go to college. (She would get to see all three graduate.)

I continued to struggle in school, but people around me noticed after my father died that I began to change dramatically. I began developing the hyperactive, hypersocial personality that, for better or for worse, became my trademark as mayor.

It was especially strange because people who knew my father described him pretty much the same way. People who knew him in his prime describe him as being a more extreme version of what I would become. They said he would glad-hand his way around his store like, well, a politician. Super social. Constant motion, in six directions at once. Sounds very familiar.

I couldn't have learned it from him; he was sick so often when I was growing up that I barely knew him. I just take it as real proof that whatever we are, we are partly just born that way.

We also learn our behavior, and I grew up learning a remarkable, ongoing lesson from my mother. No matter what hit us, she handled it, and almost always while creating a sense of security for our family. No matter what I would face, as mayor or in other parts of my life, I knew from an early age what real leadership looked like.

# Going to School, *Not Necessarily at School*

IN THEORY I went to Breck School. In reality I poured myself into every part of the school, except that nagging part about "classes." I'm not proud that I spent a remarkable lack of time and focus on the thing I was supposed to be doing at school, especially considering the sacrifices my mother made to give me the privilege of going to Breck. Some of my biggest regrets are what I lost by not being focused in high school: I never mastered a second language, never let myself believe I could understand subjects like biology and physics that would fascinate me as I got older. It's still humiliating that most of my time there I had a reputation—which I believed as well—that I just wasn't all that smart.

I directed almost all the energy I would have put into my classes into treating Breck as a kind of civic vocational school. By the time I graduated I was editor of the newspaper, played football and baseball, was president of my class almost every year except when I was the first junior ever elected president of the student body. I started a kazoo band and a lot more. If you've seen Wes Anderson's movie *Rushmore,* you get the idea.

The more I did, the more confidence I had that there was a lot more going on inside my head than others (often including myself) gave me credit for. I thought about that many times over the years, especially when I visited alternative schools that found a way to reach students who had given up on school, and often themselves. I tried to find the students who may have checked out but still had a spark I could help light.

WHILE I WAS IN HIGH SCHOOL I was also becoming even more involved outside school in local and national politics, especially when I found the first candidate who deeply inspired me. George McGovern may have lost

the 1972 election in the biggest blowout in the history of presidential elections, but he meant an enormous amount to me and still does. I heard him
speak deeply about the inequities I had seen as a kid, and he saw the United
States' relationship with the rest of the world in the moral terms we were
so hungry for during the Vietnam War. More than anything, I was drawn
to someone who called on the country to be a truer version of itself.

I connected with McGovern as a seventeen-year-old more deeply than
any candidate I would find until Barack Obama. I put everything I could
into his campaign and was crushed when he lost, but came away determined that I would find, and become, someone who tried to make us bigger not smaller.

McGovern was also right about what was wrong with Richard Nixon—
and when Watergate began to unfold I saw the impact that could be made
by Bob Woodward, Carl Bernstein, and other journalists. By the time I
was ready to go to college, I had formed a very concrete goal for myself.
First, I would become a reporter for the *Minneapolis Star Tribune,* covering
primarily architecture and city planning. Then I would become mayor of
Minneapolis. In retrospect that was an absurdly specific life plan at such
an early age, but in a circuitous way, that's exactly what I did. But first, I
had to get into college.

I ALWAYS THOUGHT that the fact I got into Boston College was proof
that college admissions offices don't read every transcript. However it was
that I got there, Boston College ended up being the perfect spot for me.
I designed my own double major: political science and communications,
with a minor in urban affairs.

Unlike high school I poured myself into classes, which now seemed so
much more relevant to what I needed to learn for the life I was designing.
I was so focused, I finished most of the major and minor courses by the
end of my junior year. This meant I spent my senior year broadening my
brain, taking fascinating classes in architecture, art history, physics, theol-
ogy, and English literature.

I could feel my brain growing in every direction. It was becoming clear
that I didn't always think about issues in a conventional way, but, unlike
high school, now I was seeing that was one of my greatest assets.

School was finally having a real impact on me, but my real laboratory
was Boston. Every Saturday, and many afternoons after classes were finished, I would take the trolley into the city and walk. Hour after hour after

hour. I studied which streets and stores were successful and which weren't, how transit affected neighborhoods, how people spent time in public places, what brought poor and middle-class people into the same place and what kept them apart. Near the end of most of those days I would make my way to Cambridge and end my time in the Harvard Book Store looking at books about architecture and city planning. Some of my favorite moments to this day are the hours I spent at that bookstore, after walking through Boston, seeing big ideas for other cities and planning what I would do in Minneapolis.

(This wasn't the first time I learned about cities by walking around them for hours. Growing up, my mother had taught my brother and sister and me to take the bus to downtown Minneapolis. Unlike the kids who grow up dependent on parental car pools, we had the freedom to spend pretty much every Saturday exploring downtown Minneapolis. I did the same every spring vacation when we visited my grandparents in my mom's hometown of San Bruno, California, just a few miles south of San Francisco. She taught us to take the bus into town there as well, just like she had done herself as a kid, apparently not fully realizing that San Francisco in the 1960s had become something really different than it was when she grew up. I wonder what my brother and I looked like: thirteen- and fifteen-year-old Minnesotans with big black glasses and buzz cuts, wandering awestruck through San Francisco, circa 1968.)

I loved Boston, but I also laughed about the insular lives my new friends from the East Coast were living. Almost none of them had any idea what a "Minnesota" was, and they assumed I came from a barren frozen farm surrounded by tipis. It turned me into a zealous salesman for Minneapolis, memorizing every person I could think of who was born there, and every product invented there. If someone made a crack about Minnesota, or even the Midwest in general, I fired back and began to develop the rap I would use as mayor as the city's hypercaffeinated pitchman. (I had to laugh a generation later when my son, Charlie, did much the same thing when he went to George Washington University in Washington, D.C., and described himself as "a Jehovah's Witness for Minneapolis.")

Those four years in Boston also taught me a lot about what can go terribly wrong in cities. The day before I started college, I turned on a local TV station and heard that forced school busing would begin the next day. Having grown up during the civil rights era, I was very used to seeing protests about racial segregation in schools, but absolutely nothing in my experience prepared me for what was about to happen in Boston. The city was, and still is, filled with strong ethnic neighborhoods whose residents fiercely protect their turf: Irish Americans in South Boston, Italian Americans in the North End, African Americans in Roxbury. This makes it convenient when you are looking for an ethnic restaurant, but the city was a powder keg when it came to implementing a busing plan that recognized "separate but equal" was definitely not equal, especially for African Americans.

The desegregation plan bused kids between these distinct neighborhoods, and Irish and Italian sections of the city exploded in opposition. Strong, proud neighborhoods were being asked to mix in ways they hadn't for generations—or ever, really. Nearly every Saturday, as I walked around the city, City Hall Plaza was filled with protesters. One Saturday it was white people. The next Saturday it was black people. This went on week after week.

There is a chilling Pulitzer Prize–winning photograph of the time when an angry crowd of white people attacked a lone black man on the plaza with a pole attached to an American flag. I walked through that plaza just a few minutes before the attack, and weekly saw scenes almost as bad.

One of the most sickening days was my first St. Patrick's Day, when I went to the famous Irish neighborhood of South Boston to see—I thought—people who loved leprechauns and drank green beer. But in the first bar we went into a very drunk and extremely angry crowd started yelling shockingly racist comments about black people in schools. When someone yelled, "Find me an [F word N word]," we got out fast. In the street outside, the famous St. Patrick's Day Parade was passing by, with a contingent from the American Nazi Party.

This was beyond anything I had ever seen and I took it out on Boston. I was there, in part, because I saw it as a Mecca for progressivism; after all, Massachusetts was the only state whose electoral votes went to McGovern. The city was a fake, I thought, parading around as a citadel of enlightenment when it was really just filled with hate and racism. I was so glad I was from a place that would never do that.

It took me awhile but I eventually realized that there were layers of complexity I didn't see. Boston, more so than almost any city, has a deep history of classism, and a desegregation plan imposed by the Yankee establishment that exempted white middle- and upper-class areas such as Brookline and Newton had deep flaws from the start. About ten years later I would read

J. Anthony Lukas's *Common Ground,* a superb book about busing in Boston that followed two white families and one black family through this period, and I came away understanding that the reality of that time was far more complex.

I also realized eventually that Minneapolis was hardly immune from much of what I saw. Our city didn't have the ethnic neighborhoods Boston had, but Minneapolis was every bit as segregated. Both cities were admirably struggling with ways to blend populations in schools, but both cities were also asking kids to do the work that adults weren't willing to do themselves.

Every city has its stage sets that are presented to the visitor, or to those who don't want to dig any deeper. Almost any city can look great on a weekend tour: the rejuvenated waterfront, "reclaimed" warehouses, pretty residential districts, great coffee shops in neighborhoods with carefully restored homes. Like the rock that never gets turned over, underneath them lies something more complex and sometimes far more disturbing.

My time in Boston taught me to turn the rock over, in other places and in my own hometown.

## For a While the Path Seemed Really Clear

---

**M**Y FIRST JOB out of college was at the *Sun* newspaper in the Minneapolis suburb of St. Louis Park. I was the editor, which was a logical title given that I was the only person on staff. I wrote almost everything, took photographs, wrote the editorials, and did the layout. On Mondays, when I laid out the paper and got it to the press, I put in an eighteen-hour day, but I loved the job. The bonus was that I was covering the same stories as reporters from the daily *Star Tribune.* I beat the daily on a few, got some attention from a few of the editors, and within a year I was hired.

This was going to be easy, I thought. I was already at the *Star Tribune* within a year, so this career path to becoming mayor was well ahead of schedule. It was all very tidy.

On my first day at the *Star Tribune* my editor asked me what I wanted to cover. I gave him a long list—city planning, politics, schools, on and on. "Anything you don't want to cover?" he asked.

"Crime," I said.

The next day I was assigned to cover crime.

From 3:00 to 11:00 P.M. five days a week, my job was to write about whatever went wrong. I scanned the police logs and tried (rarely successfully) to get the police to tell me anything about what had really happened. When there was an incident on the police scanner, I raced to the scene, tried to understand what had gone on, and then raced back to the office and usually within an hour had cranked out a story for the next day's paper.

This was a long, long way from the high-minded journalism I thought I would be practicing. At the time I was miserable—but long term it was invaluable. I saw the reality of parts of the city I never would have seen and got closer to the real gaps between the haves and have-nots, more so than at any time since my days in my parents' drugstore.

I also spent a lot of time with people in real distress—especially victims of violence and people who had lost loved ones. I learned how to talk to them, at times say something that would give them some comfort, and help them to share what they thought other people should know.

When people read about the family members of a crime victim, or see them on the news, they can't always know the backstory of how those persons in distress opened up to the journalist, who almost always was a complete stranger. That's what I learned how to do, although I hated it at the time.

A particularly heinous crime I covered involved twenty-nine-year-old Ming Sen Shiue, who in 1980 kidnapped and for seven weeks imprisoned Mary Stauffer, her daughter Beth, and Jason Wilkman, a six-year-old whom Shiue eventually beat to death. Stauffer had been Shiue's high school algebra teacher.

On the day Jason's body was found I stood outside his parents' home for half an hour, stepping away only to go to a payphone for a heated exchange with my editor, who insisted I stay there and get a comment from the family. I went over and over in my head what I could possibly say when the parents opened the door. Most of the time I tried to imagine what would have helped me when my own father died, but nothing in my own experience came close to what I expected their grief would be. Finally I went up the walk, rang the doorbell, and prayed they weren't home.

Jason's parents answered right away, probably relieved to finally know why this stranger had been standing outside their house talking to himself. I told them how deeply sorry I was, and asked if there was anything they would like people to remember about Jason. They were remarkably warm, describing their son and how their deep faith gave them an understanding that he was in a better place.

I went back down their walk feeling remarkably better, not only because I was done with this horrible assignment, but also because I saw how much of the burden had been lifted off his parents by talking about Jason. They even seemed to find it helpful to know I was going to share their comments with the thousands of readers of the *Star Tribune*.

The Shiue case was particularly gruesome, but it wasn't an isolated incident. Night after night I was out on the streets, seeing the worst thing that happened that day in Minneapolis–St. Paul. Over and over I talked to victims or their loved ones in deep distress. I sure didn't know it at the time, but my experiences gave me tremendous insight into how to comfort people at scenes of crime and violence when I was mayor.

I hated being around that much death, especially when it happened while my own grandfather, whom I loved probably even more than I did my dad, died. I am a profoundly optimistic person, but I could feel this nightly immersion in crime was tainting my view of the world. For the first time I understood the hard shell police develop when they spend years dealing with mostly the worst in people.

After I had been on the police beat a few months, one of the older homicide cops slowly began to open up to me. He had an understated Minnesotan side and a pretty hard outer layer. He would unemotionally lay out the details of how one more person had died. Nothing much shook him because he had seen it all before. Another day at the office. Until one day when it wasn't.

I walked into his office after hearing a young boy had been killed in a particularly gruesome way. The body was found on the family's front steps. The cop who had been so matter-of-fact before now was ashen. As I asked him for details he looked vacantly at me, stricken, and just said, "I have grandchildren." He walked away. Soon after I heard he had retired.

I learned there are people behind the hard crusts so many cops have to develop to survive. In some of the toughest times for victims of crime and their families, I saw over and over again that bit of humanity come through from the police officers who comforted people when they needed it the most.

It was a time when there were huge issues between the police and Minneapolis's growing gay and lesbian community. The community alleged the police weren't investigating multiple acts of gay bashing. Police also made repeated raids on gay bathhouses, even when it appeared no crimes were being committed. To some of the cops I overheard, it seemed like a bit of sport—especially the night they confiscated a giant papier-mâché penis from a bathhouse and, presumably for the humor of it, brought it back to city hall strapped to the outside of a police car. I was there the next morning to see a disgusting scene of cops parading city council members through the property room to show off the giant penis and making cracks about what the cops had done to gay people.

I kept the memory of that day for many years and felt tremendous pride as those tensions between the police and the GLBT community faded away. More and more members of the community came onto the force and then into leadership roles. I thought about those times when, in my last year as mayor, I appointed Janeé Harteau to be one of the first openly lesbian police chiefs in the country.

Police relations with people of color, especially African Americans, were another story. You can't spend so many nights at crime scenes, as I did in those days, without realizing the dramatic racial inequity in who is arrested and how they are treated. Making the issue even more complex, I was covering police stories in St. Paul at the same time, and it was clear that racial tensions within that force were nowhere as pervasive as they were in the Minneapolis department.

The inequity also became clear when I came back to the paper to file my story. Even the editors I had—generally as enlightened and open minded as you could find at that time—simply did not care as much about a crime story involving an African American person in a predominately African American part of town. I don't think it was because they were overtly racist; they just knew what everyone else knew. Crime just wasn't as newsworthy if it happened where everyone expected it would, and too many people came too willingly to expect that crime would happen in some neighborhoods.

Unlike the tensions with the GLBT community, the gaps between police and people of color did not fade away over the years. They played a major role in my time as mayor and they still exist in Minneapolis today. Those nights I covered crime—in the middle of the action but just detached enough to have perspective—would play back over and over once I was mayor. I had seen the inequity firsthand, as well as the bunker mentality police develop when they can't connect with people they are trying to protect. It was what I was thinking about when I tried, with limited success, to change department leadership and culture. It is still what I'm thinking as I see how much further we have to go.

After a couple of years on the *Star Tribune*'s crime beat I finally talked my editors into letting me write every once in a while about architecture, city planning, and commercial development. Eventually they gave me that beat full-time.

I had my flaws as a journalist—especially my lousy spelling and notoriously sloppy copy—but I developed great sources, knew the beat, and formed a deep understanding of what makes a real estate project work. Luckily, it was right as Minneapolis was undergoing a development boom, and I was on the front lines of helping readers understand how the city was changing.

One of the most important stories I covered was a renovation of Dayton's, then Minneapolis's dominant department store and a city landmark. Hearing from sources that the store was quietly planning to convert the basement into a grand food hall, I called the public relations department and told the very professional woman on the other end of the line that I knew what was going on and demanded they give me a detailed exclusive. She told me they were not ready to release anything. Arrogantly, I said I would write about it anyway and hung up. I put a small item about it in my column, which gave me my exclusive but pretty much ruined their splashy opening.

A few months later I walked up to a very attractive woman at a party. After I introduced myself, she said, "Oh, I know who you are, all right." She was the Dayton's public relations person whose opening I had messed up, and she really ripped into me. I took my licking, we wound up talking for about an hour about architecture and cities, and almost immediately I fell in love with Megan O'Hara. Thankfully she is still my wife.

# Not the Guy in the Back of the Room

---

IT TAKES A SPECIAL PERSON to be a great journalist and I met many at the *Star Tribune*. The best—reporters like Peg Meier, Steve Berg, and Doug Stone—have two core qualities: a remarkable lack of ego and the ability to stand near, but not in, the center of the action. Neither quality is my strong suit. As fun as the work was, it was becoming clear to me that I wasn't going to be happy sitting on the sidelines writing about what other people did.

That became even more apparent to me when I was covering one of the most interesting stories of my career. The Ghermezians are four very colorful brothers who in the late 1970s began working on what seemed like the crazy idea of developing a "megamall" in suburban Edmonton, Alberta—complete with amusement rides, an indoor pool, and a hockey rink. Minnesota's governor in 1983 was Rudy Perpich, who had plenty of out-there ideas of his own, and he took to the Ghermezians as if he were their long-lost fifth brother. Together, they came up with the idea to create an even grander mall in Minnesota, near the Minneapolis–St. Paul airport—the Mall of America.

Rarely do reporters get the gift of a project of this magnitude and with main characters this colorful. The governor's visions of grandeur, the Ghermezians' over-the-top claims and outlandish neckties, and a multimillion-dollar development drama set among the roller coasters. For a journalist it doesn't get much better.

I saw it differently. On a trip to Edmonton to visit the original megamall I broke off from the group to spend some time downtown. Downtown Edmonton had become a ghost town; all the life had been sucked out of it by the suburban shopping mall on steroids. That walk around town was as different as could be from the lively street scenes I had observed in San Francisco, Boston, and, increasingly, Minneapolis. Could I really be neutral covering a real estate deal that could potentially turn my own city's downtown into some kind of deserted wasteland?

When a journalist starts thinking like that he needs to get out. Fortunately, I wasn't the only person thinking like this. Minneapolis civic leaders were as freaked out about the Mall of America's impact as I was. They offered me a job as development director for the Minneapolis Downtown Council. The idea was for me to be a super-recruiter for Minneapolis, marketing the city to new businesses so that downtown Minneapolis didn't suffer the fate of downtown Edmonton.

About three minutes into the new job, it was clear I had made the right choice. I always struggled with the neutrality and studied detachment required of journalists, and it felt completely natural to finally be able to stand for something, give my opinion, and work on a cause.

With the Mall of America making such a big splash, it was a rough time to be pitching downtown Minneapolis, but for me that only made it a more exciting challenge. I built partnerships with businesses, community groups, and in city hall, and became one of the city's main pitchmen, defining a Minneapolis brand that I would refine years later as mayor.

It also quickly became clear to me that this was an ideal way to pivot from journalism into local politics. For the first time in my adult life, I could develop my own voice and take stands. I was building deep connections with political, community, and business leaders. I was finally able to go to political meetings and work on campaigns.

Everything seemed to be falling into place for my next step, which I assumed was to run for office on my way to running for mayor. A state senate seat opened up in my neighborhood and I began planning a campaign; but just as quickly a sitting state representative moved across town to run, and I saw no path to winning. That was only a temporary setback, and I started aggressively planning a series of steps that would help me run for mayor someday—the sooner the better.

Then something completely unexpected happened: I met Charlie Rybak.

When Megan was about eight months pregnant, she put my hand on her stomach to feel the foot of the baby we were about to have. It was such an astonishing moment that, years later when I would see his adult shoes, now much larger than mine, I would flash back to remembering what that tiny foot felt like inside Megan.

Charlie was born in January 1989. I can admit now that I was terrified.

As we drove away from the hospital, I looked back to see Charlie's huge, round trusting eyes. I thought to myself, "Kid, you have no idea how much I don't know!" Within days my entire perspective had changed. I fell in love with our son and with being a dad, and I realized there are many more important things in life than having your name on a lawn sign.

# *Leaning Out*

---

I HADN'T BEEN AROUND CHILDREN MUCH, so I was fascinated by watching Megan go through pregnancy. I can admit now that I was scared out of my mind. I felt completely unprepared for this unknown world. I was especially worried that because my father died when I was so young I had very little understanding of what a "dad" was supposed to do.

Eventually I would figure out that a "dad" is also a "parent," and I couldn't have had a better example than my own mom. Most important, I was married to someone who understood enough about family for both of us. Megan, one of nine kids, all of whom built their own lives around their families, led us through those first few months.

Charlie grew fast, and I changed faster. Every time I held him or looked into his eyes, I became more convinced that my perspective on what mattered was now very different. All those hours of holding a child, or watching him sleep, gives you lots of time to think, and I thought about how being a dad—something I was terrified of only a few months ago—now seemed like the most important and rewarding thing I could possibly do.

For so many years I had followed a clearly mapped out path about step A leading to step B leading to step C, leading to Dream Job of Mayor. Now each time I walked through that course in my mind, every step involved massive compromises in being the kind of dad I wanted to be.

I also thought a lot about my experience with my own dad. Like so many men of his generation, the first role of being a good father was to provide for your family, and because he did that, our family's life wasn't as hard as it could have been once he died. But when he was healthy he was working almost all the time, and he eventually worked himself to death. The net effect was that I had very few memories of him. In fact, as hard as I tried in those long hours with our new son, I could remember only one or two times when my dad and I were alone, just hanging out together. He did what he thought was best, but there was no way I was going to be that kind of dad.

Something had to give, and it was shockingly easy to realize I had to change my "Dream Job" fantasy about becoming mayor and build a whole new path.

Suddenly everything about my home life seemed completely clear—and everything about my career, for the first time in many years, was completely unclear. I kept my thoughts mostly to myself and shared them with Megan, but slowly I began asking friends for advice. One of those friends was Rip Rapson, who at the time was deputy mayor for Mayor Don Fraser. The first half of the lunch I did most of the talking, walking through this strange turn of events that made me give up what I had wanted to do for so long to be the parent I never knew I wanted to be. Rip was a good friend, and a good listener, and after getting it all off my chest I felt a lot better. Then he leaned across the table and confessed something that really took me aback: "I'm going to run for mayor."

Rarely do you get such a clear chance to make a decision about your own life and see someone close to you live the other half of what you had originally wanted. There were two doors in front of me: I chose to walk in one and my friend walked in the other.

I was very involved in the start of Rip's campaign, pulled way back, then got involved again in a campaign that was partly cathartic but mostly way too close to be comfortable. Rip is incredibly smart and was surrounded by some incredibly smart people, and his agenda was decades ahead of its time. Partnering with urbanist/writer Jay Walljasper, Rip wrote a remarkable one-hundred-page campaign book laying out a forward-looking New Urbanist agenda for equity, sustainability, and grassroots change that would deeply influence the agenda I ran on two decades later. It was also during that campaign that I got to know some of the people who would be key to my own campaigns: Walljasper and his wife, Julie Ristau, Sam and Sylvia Kaplan, Charlie Zelle, Dr. Irving and Jan Shapiro.

It was a very strange—and sometimes very uncomfortable—experience to watch my friend run for mayor. During that election, I alternatively ran to and ran away from that campaign. It was especially tough letting go of my dream while my friend was living it, but I was convinced what I was doing was right.

About a year after Charlie was born Megan got pregnant again. I remember lying in bed with Charlie one night as he went to sleep after I read him a story, and wondering how I was going to handle having another child. I looked at him sleeping and couldn't imagine possibly loving him more. I assumed there was only so much love inside a person and felt this sense of dread that now I would have to divide my compassion between two kids. I hated to think this magic time with Charlie was going to be over.

Any of those thoughts ended about two seconds after Grace was born. She had an enormous personality that lit up the room, and still does to this day. There was more than enough love to go around, and now we had this wonderful family of four.

THROUGHOUT THESE EARLY YEARS with our kids I had a series of jobs and actually did some of my most meaningful professional work.

After a couple years at the Downtown Council, I took a job at Eberhardt Commercial Real Estate, where I got both my first real private-sector experience and my real estate license. I also worked on early prototypes for a downtown Target store and an entertainment complex on Hennepin Avenue that would have been far more successful than the dumbed-down Block E that got built, and failed. That experience would come into play when I ran for mayor because I could say with authority that the Target store that was built got more city subsidy than it needed and that the Block E entertainment project the city helped build on Hennepin was doomed from the start.

A couple of years later I was having lunch with Megan's former boss at Dayton's, John Pellegrene, who was now leading marketing for Target. Pellegrene is rightfully a legend in marketing circles as the person who, more than anyone, deserves credit for changing Target's image from a cut-rate discounter into one of the world's great brands. He had brilliant ideas, but the one he told me about over lunch made no sense at first: Target had bought the naming rights to a new basketball arena in downtown Minneapolis.

"Target Center?" I said. "That sounds like a shopping mall. Why don't you call it something distinctive like Target Forum or Target Garden?"

Pellegrene explained that if the arena had a more distinctive name people would call it "The Forum" or "The Garden" and never use the "Target" part. He was right, but, more interestingly, he talked about how quickly events marketing was evolving and how Target could use its brand and customer base to create and build events. He offered me a contract to manage Target's relationship with Target Center and see what we could do to replicate the work around the country.

The idea came out of left field but quickly made sense, and I used the contract to start my own marketing consulting business. We experimented a lot as we tried to figure out cross-marketing with events, arena visibility packages, and whether any of those efforts led to people spending more money at Target stores. I was in way, way over my head and I failed a lot, but Pellegrene stuck with me. Eventually we came up with a promotional ticket strategy called TreatSeats that started with Target Center and expanded around the country, giving Target customers deals on thousands of events.

You learn a lot working closely with a true marketing genius, and much of the work I would later do to help build a "Minneapolis brand" as mayor came right from John's playbook. Even more important were the lessons I learned from Pellegrene about work–family balance. At the top of his game, under enormous pressure, Pellegrene could lead his team to produce an amazing amount of extremely high-quality work, but when anything happened with his family, everything stopped and everyone knew where his priorities were. He could talk for hours about the work on his plate, but the second the conversation turned to his family he completely lit up.

That was the first time I had ever seen a highly successful man put his family first, and it had a profound impact on me. Up to this point I had seen success as a choice between family and career, but Pellegrene illustrated that you didn't have to pick one. Much has rightfully been written about work–life balance for women, but John showed me that men could, and should, have it, too. In retrospect this is when I started to think again that eventually I could go on to be a committed father and have a demanding job like, well, mayor.

I had a few other jobs after my time at Target. I published the alternative weekly *Twin Cities Reader* for two years, was vice president of the start-up Internet Broadcasting Systems, and later worked as an independent Internet strategist helping big and small businesses build digital strategy into their plans.

All this was interesting work and I developed skills most mayors don't have. Running the *Reader* and working at Internet Broadcasting gave me management experience. The Internet strategy work helped me quickly rebuild a business plan to adapt to rapid change, which was a pivotal skill as I would later help manage the city out of a series of crises.

None of that was the least bit clear to me then, of course. At the time I saw myself as being at a great pivot where I was building a very different direction for my life. I wasn't sure where it was going to lead, but I was almost certain it wouldn't be city hall.

Megan and I converted the third floor of our house into an office, and for most of that time our kids had parents who were there when they came home from school, read to them every night, went to their games, and coached their teams. We didn't think about spending "quality time" with them. We just spent time, and loved it.

Many years later Facebook's Sheryl Sandberg wrote a book encouraging women raising children to "lean in" to their careers. This was the time when I "leaned out," completely fulfilled as we were building an amazing family.

But the itch never went away.

# *Leaning In*

SET MY OWN POLITICAL FUTURE ASIDE, but I kept working in politics. I volunteered for a number of local and national candidates, but
the campaign that would end up having the biggest impact on me long
term was when former U.S. senator Bill Bradley ran for president in 2000.
Bradley, a former NBA star, didn't get far, but he had a strong network
in Minnesota. What I didn't know at the time was that the core group I
helped run the Bradley effort with included some of the people who would
play the most significant roles in my time as mayor: Peter Wagenius, who
ran my first campaign and was my senior adviser all twelve years I was in
office, and Tina Smith, who became one of my chiefs of staff. Probably
most important, I got to work directly with Bradley's national cochair, the
late Senator Paul Wellstone, who would later make a small gesture that had
an enormous impact on my being elected mayor.

I also got involved in neighborhood politics. I served on our neighborhood board, and Megan and I started Save the Water in Minneapolis
(SWIM), a group that mobilized people around the issue of responsible
lawn care to protect city lakes.

One night Megan came home from a meeting of a new group that was
fighting a long-ignored problem that had really hurt the southern half of
Minneapolis: unchecked noise from two airplane flight paths directly over
thousands of homes. People in our part of town had fought the airport over
noise for more than two decades, and despite incredible efforts, they had
barely made a dent. The deck is stacked strongly against any community
fighting airplane noise, because in the world of aviation the airlines hold
almost all the cards. Usually people who have fought this political battle
give up, bitterly admitting that it is nearly impossible to win.

This group was different. New to political and civic issues, they were young homeowners who were free of the defeatism that had beaten down so many of us veterans. Megan told me how impressed she was with this group's energy and its catchy name, Residents Opposed to Airport Racket. What ROAR needed, she said, was some political and communications savvy. Megan convinced me to join them. That small group from ROAR would restore a lot of my faith in grassroots activism and play a big role in launching me on my path to becoming mayor.

MOST OF THE ROAR ACTIVISTS were at least twenty years younger than I, very creative, and up for almost anything. We hatched a series of publicity stunts to get attention for the cause but hit the jackpot when we decided to protest loud night flights by having a "pajama party" at the airport. The idea was to put the issue on the radar by filling the airport with people wearing pajamas.

We leafleted south Minneapolis, put creative posters on light poles, and created email lists. We went to city hall to get support and in the middle of my speech to a city council committee I unbuttoned my shirt, then unzipped my pants, and began taking off my clothes until the very nervous council members realized I was wearing pajamas underneath.

We definitely had people's attention, and we thought we had a great crowd coming, until a couple hours before the event it began to snow really hard. We assumed no one would show up. Our hearts sank thinking we had wasted all that energy and that great idea.

But as we stood in the parking lot where we were supposed to meet, a car arrived, then another, and another, and pretty soon there was a huge crowd. We went in a caravan to the airport with one local TV station covering us live from a helicopter. Once at the airport we got out of our cars and went into the terminal. As people took off their coats, you could see they had on all kinds of crazy outfits: strange pajamas, goofy bathrobes, oversized puffy slippers, hair curlers, faces covered with night cream, little kids in footie pajamas. More than a hundred of us formed a rumba line chanting things like "We-de-serve-to-sleep, hey!"

This whacked-out idea ended up at the top of every local newscast that night and suddenly catapulted ROAR and the airport issue to a whole new level. Hundreds of people joined our email list, and we became a factor in the U.S. Senate primary by forcing candidates to commit to helping us fight noise pollution.

I began writing about airport noise in a new online forum about city issues, and eventually branched out to other topics. When I wasn't writing about airport noise, I was dissecting the city's development strategies. My experience covering those issues for the *Star Tribune*, at the Downtown Council, and in commercial real estate taught me enough to believe the city was wasting many millions of dollars on excessively generous subsidies to developers. I wasn't antidevelopment; I believed Minneapolis government had a critical role in promoting growth in the city. I just didn't think the taxpayers should be chumps, and my time in development helped me see that we could get better results for less money. Minneapolis is a great city that should not be negotiating on its knees.

The online forum also introduced me to activists around the city. No one would have predicted it a few months earlier, but I was suddenly very visible among at least a group of activists and politicos. Just as I was leaning out, circumstances were leading me to lean in.

A couple of months after ROAR's pajama party I heard that Mayor Sharon Sayles Belton was going to appoint to the city's Planning Commission one of her supporters who was also a lobbyist for Northwest Airlines. I called the mayor's chief of staff to tell her this would send a very bad signal to those of us fighting airport noise. To my surprise the mayor called me back, but I was unable to convince her to reconsider. She made the appointment and our group raised a huge stink to our email list, on the online forum, and in calls to other council members.

A few weeks later the mayor's chief of staff took me out to lunch. The discussion was pretty upbeat, mostly about steps the mayor could be taking to help us fight airport noise, but near the end, the tone changed. Her chief of staff leaned across the table and said, "We've been hearing that you are thinking of running against the mayor. Well, if that's the case, bring it on."

I WAS STUNNED. Up to that point I assumed the only person who thought I could be a viable candidate for mayor was me—and even in my most delusional fantasies I would hardly admit it to myself. I suppose telling me to "bring it on" was meant to intimidate me, but to a person who had spent years suppressing a lifelong goal, it had exactly the opposite effect.

Strangely, the mayor's own chief of staff had given me the opening to finally admit to myself that I still wanted to be mayor. A few weeks later I was having dinner with my friend Dan Cunagin, who innocently asked one of those big philosophical questions: "What do you *really* want to do?" For what was, I'm sure, far longer than he hoped, I laid out that deep down I really wanted to be mayor, and I spelled out in exhaustive detail everything I would do both to get elected and once I was mayor. When I finally came up for air he waited for a minute and said, with true understatement, "I guess you thought about that."

I had absolutely thought about it and was realizing how much I had been kidding myself. I still wanted to be mayor.

Megan and I spent a few weeks talking about it, and all the flaws in the fantasy started to be clear. It got to seem ridiculous to spend all that time and effort on what would surely be a losing campaign against what I assumed was a relatively popular incumbent mayor. It was also clear that with the kids now nine and eleven years old, this was the wrong time for our family. And so grudgingly, but fairly quickly, I realized I was the wrong person to run. I should use my current visibility to put issues on the table and bide my time to run when the kids were grown.

That was my plan when I had lunch with Minneapolis City Council member Lisa McDonald, who was already well down the road to running against the mayor. I had admired a lot of McDonald's work on urban development and thought I could help push her to take on more of the airport agenda. I thought we could be partners, but the tone of the lunch was very different. Almost immediately, McDonald launched into a searing critique of the mayor's flaws and it was clear she and the mayor were involved in a growing personal grudge match that was splitting city hall.

That wasn't my fight. I had known the mayor for years, reported on her career when she was elected to the council, served on committees with her, and thought her values were in the right place. We weren't friends but I respected her. I didn't hate the mayor. I just wanted some changes.

I met next with County Commissioner Mike Opat, whose toughminded, independent voice I thought could bring some much-needed new perspective to city hall. My base in the southern part of the city could be part of a winning coalition with his base in the northern part of the city. He listened but had no interest and, significantly, reminded me he lived one block outside the city limits and had no intention of moving.

Each conversation I had with potential candidates and other activists looking for a change convinced me more that it was in fact time for a change. The challenge was that I wasn't finding anyone who fit what I was looking for.

Around that time Megan made what seemed like an offhand comment.

"If you ever did run for mayor," she said, "do you think it would be better to do it now, when the kids love being with you, or in four years, when they'll be embarrassed even to be in the front seat of the car with you?" Her question made a lot of sense.

The race still seemed like an incredible long shot, but it was also clear that winning this race wasn't the only end. Even if I did lose, which was a distinct possibility, the campaign would give me a broader platform from which to talk about the city and maybe come back in four years and win.

Megan and I tried out the idea on the kids. Over dinner one night I told them I was thinking about running for mayor. We wanted them to have as realistic a picture as we could give them, so I went into details: I wouldn't be around as much or home for dinner some nights; we wouldn't have as much money to take trips; and, what I thought would be the showstopper, I wouldn't be able to coach their teams and probably wouldn't be able to go to many of their games.

They took it all in and then very matter-of-factly told me I had to run.

Wanting to add another dose of reality, I said, "It's really a long shot, so I may lose."

"Oh, you'll definitely win, Dad," they both said, with great authority.

This officially made them the only people in town who thought that, including me.

# Back on Track

---

THERE ARE VERY FEW CLEARER EXAMPLES of raw ego than running for office. You put your name all over town—lawn signs, brochures, radio, television, and, ultimately, a ballot on which you ask people to "pick me" over someone else.

Politicians sometimes try to soften the egotism by saying they were "drafted" to run. I suppose there are some cases in which a groundswell caused someone to run in spite of herself, but it is exceptionally rare. Usually candidates who say they were "drafted" have all the sincerity of someone grudgingly saying he will eat the double chocolate cake "so the host doesn't feel bad."

In retrospect, it was a remarkable combination of arrogance and ignorance to think that I could run and win, armed with such a complete lack of the basic qualifications most people have as mayor: having never run for or held public office, having no real political base and no money.

I didn't lack confidence. In my mind I had been successful in many different sectors: journalism, many types of businesses, including real estate and city planning, the Internet, and marketing. My clients had been some fairly significant businesses and institutions, and I had pioneering experience with start-ups and the Internet. I had been a committed community activist involved in a wide range of efforts, from presidential politics to neighborhood bike lanes, and I kept my feet on the ground coaching Little League.

But this was a hard résumé to explain. My complex career could easily be seen as dabbling in a bunch of jobs, never keeping any for very long and never fully mastering any of them. Another perceived negative was that I lived in southwest Minneapolis, which had not elected a mayor in decades, partly because most of the rest of the city saw this as the most privileged part of Minneapolis.

I fully understood the absurd odds against me, but I began to see that as long as I didn't make a complete clown of myself, the worst that could happen was that I could raise some issues that needed to be out there, get known, and set myself up to win four years later.

We talked it through one night at Charlie and Julie Zelle's house with a few close friends: Linda Houden and Jerry Van Amerongen, Dan and Marnie Boivin, Rolf and Nancy Engh. For a few hours we batted pros and cons back and forth, with a lot of reality therapy that it was likely I would lose. Rolf, who had said nothing all night, finally asked the question that crystallized the whole conversation: "If you didn't do this, would you regret it for the rest of your life?" That stopped me cold because the answer was yes.

I came into that discussion the only person in the group who absolutely thought I should run. I left the only one who thought I shouldn't. In spite of my answer to Rolf's question about regret, the details of what running would mean for our family were starting to pile up.

A few nights later I couldn't sleep. Hour after hour I turned over in my head what this was going to be like for the four of us. By about 4:00 A.M. I was convinced it would be a huge mistake that would ruin our family. I thought I had done a lot in my life, some big things, some small, but there was really only one thing I had pursued with absolutely everything I had. I had been the kind of dad I wanted to be, we had built a family life with no compromises, and now I was about to ruin it all.

Like a lot of things that seem like a crisis in the middle of the night, these fears started to fade throughout the next day, but they never fully went away.

It helped that Megan didn't really didn't push one way or the other. She had gotten us into a lot of our community work, including the airport issue that I was taking on now, and had begun to appreciate how my being mayor could change what mattered.

She also had a realistic view of life in a political family. Her grandfather was a congressman from southern Minnesota in the 1950s and within her family his public role was seen as something that led to sacrifices for Megan's dad, uncle, and grandmother. Megan and I had few lofty delusions that my running for office would be an uplifting family experience. The best we hoped was that it could be done with a minimum of damage to the family.

The two other people who made it all possible were Peter Wagenius and Laura Sether. They not only encouraged me to run, they also agreed to be volunteer managers of the campaign. We met once a week at the Blue Moon café in in the Seward neighborhood of south Minneapolis.

We made the announcement in Ventura Village Food Market, the small store that occupied the space near Chicago and Franklin where my family's store had been. As I walked up to make the announcement I could have been thinking about those years ago, doing my homework in the basement of the store as I daydreamed about becoming mayor. Or I could have been thinking more about what I was going to say at the press conference. Instead, the only thing I could think about was how small the store was. Then I realized the market also included an office that was next door, so my parents' store was actually only half as large as the small space in which I was standing. I began to put things together and realized that my father, who had run the very busy Walgreen's at Ninth and Nicollet, and then his own big store with a soda fountain that was torn down for the freeway, had worked almost nonstop at those places. The result was that he had a serious heart attack. The tiny confines of the Ventura Village Market today brought home that when my parents decided to open this very small place they were probably trying to put less pressure on my dad. Ironically, only a few months after it opened, he had another heart attack and stroke that eventually killed him.

When I made the announcement my family was with me, including my mom and sister, Megan's parents and aunt and uncle. It was important to have the event in the store to remind people that in spite of my living in southwest Minneapolis I had plenty of experience in the parts of town with higher needs. The optics left something to be desired because the pictures later basically showed this unknown guy standing by the freezer case. I looked more like someone making a quick stop for some milk and eggs than a person you would trust to run your city.

My inexperience showed again when I went to City Hall to file for the election. I marched with supporters and cameras behind me to the counter where the clerk asked for my license. People watching the news that night could see that this guy who wanted to be mayor had forgotten his wallet. (Fortunately you can still register without a license if someone vouches for you.)

Grace, age ten at the time, was writing *Grace's Digest,* an online journal of the campaign. Her entry for that day was called "Gracie's Top Five Tips for What to Do When You Go with Your Parent to File for Office": "5. Make sure your parent has their driver's license with them. (Or at least a photo ID). My father learned that the hard way. 4. Take notice of everything around you. City Hall is a very fascinating place. 3. Wear good clothes. If you happen to be on TV wearing a bad outfit you will never forgive yourself. I myself was wearing my beautiful 'R.T. for Mayor' T-shirt. 2. Greet the reporters and act sophisticated. 1. Wave to the cameras!"

As the campaign began Wagenius, Sether, and I did what most successful campaigns do before they start talking to people: we built the narrative, the elevator speech about who I was. We tried to turn perceived negatives into strengths.

My random-sounding résumé was reworked to describe "a life of leadership in many fields that gave me a unique set of skills to lead":

- Journalism gave me years of listening to people, and years understanding problems without having been mired in the polluted partisanship of politics.

- Business taught me how to put people to work and help the city to grow, and proved this political rookie was a quick study who wouldn't have a long learning curve. I knew what it was like to make a payroll and make tough decisions.

- I had been some form of salesperson most of my life, and the product I believed in more than almost anything was Minneapolis. I came up with the line: "Minneapolis needs to regain its collective swagger." Awkward as it was, people understood that we should have a leader who wouldn't be satisfied with second best.

- We added to this new way of seeing my career a strong narrative that I never strayed from: I may have grown up in southwest Minneapolis, but I was toughened up in an inner-city corner store that taught me our city exists on two levels.

A tougher issue was that our kids went to a private school. No one would have the patience to understand the history of what Breck did for my family when we were in trouble, or the fact that our kids got to ride to school with their grandmother every morning. We knew no matter how we explained this, this was just going to be something a lot of people would hold against me. They had a point: could the mayor of Minneapolis lead a city if he doesn't have his kids in the city's public schools? Not much could be done about it, and we weren't about to yank the kids out of a situation that was working to serve my political ambition. We just had to take the hit.

A remarkably important asset in building our brand was Thom Sandberg, a longtime friend and one of Minneapolis's most successful advertising professionals, who was then working for Fallon.

I asked Thom to help distill our complex narrative. A few days later, after a few hours in his basement workshop, he showed up at my back door carrying a six-foot-high air freshener with a sign that read, "R.T. Rybak: Fresh Air in City Hall."

For a candidate talking about "throwing open the doors of City Hall" this device was brilliant in its simplicity. The air freshener became an icon on all our literature, and we marched with the giant version in every parade.

As we put together our literature, we followed a campaign rule Peter had grown up with while working for his mother, Minnesota state representative Jean Wagenius: measure a great lit piece by whether it has an impact in the time it takes for a person to take it from the front door to the garbage can.

My story was complex and detailed, but Sandberg designed the cover of our first piece of literature to go right to the core idea that a city with as many assets as Minneapolis should be getting more dynamic leadership. Sandberg enlarged a close-up of my face and superimposed over the top a line I felt deeply and that became my campaign slogan: "I was born in a great city and don't want to die in a mediocre one."

The first pieces of Sayles Belton literature, and the pieces coming out of the other campaigns, were intimidating because they were filled with endorsements. We had a few individuals but only two were elected officials: Jane Ranum, Minnesota state senator, and Jean Wagenius. We also had the longtime opponents of airport noise, who had seen my work with ROAR and who were very influential in their south Minneapolis districts—but we needed many more citywide.

We knew almost everyone of note was already committed to Sayles Belton or one of the other candidates. The most popular politician in the state, especially among active Democrats in the city, was Paul Wellstone. He and I had a very good relationship that deepened when we worked together in the Bill Bradley campaign, but it was almost impossible to think he would back me over an incumbent. And why would he take sides in an inner-party fight when he had a close reelection coming up in only a year?

Then we got a big surprise. Bill Lofy, Wellstone's political director, called to say they had been asked to give a quotation for Mayor Sayles Belton's literature. They agreed but said they would offer me one, too. Shocked, but knowing what a big opening this was, we got an agreement to use the following quote from Senator Wellstone: "I have seen R.T. Rybak in action. He is a committed progressive who knows how to get things done."

For reasons I didn't understand then, or now, the Sayles Belton campaign chose not to use their Wellstone quote on their literature. We, of course, put it front and center, and many people who saw both campaigns' pieces assumed Wellstone was supporting me. It had a huge impact. When I was knocking on the doors of people who knew almost nothing about me, I heard over and over versions of "If you're OK with Paul Wellstone, you're OK with me."

WE DIDN'T HAVE A LOT OF LITERATURE, but our pieces were by far the best in the campaign, led by Sandberg and, later, Bruce Bildsten, another Fallon star who volunteered his time. We also had the best way of getting the pieces distributed, primarily by piggybacking on a volunteer network honed over the years by the Wagenius and Ranum campaigns.

We had almost no money. I was not very slick at asking for money for myself. I made it harder by saying I would take no money from people doing business with the city, and we interpreted that broadly to include developers, lawyers, and pretty much everyone else who helped fund city campaigns. Broke and with few prospects for contributions of any size, every few weeks I would have to send back a check with a note that I couldn't accept the contribution because of a potential conflict of interest if I got elected. In the end it didn't seem to matter to almost anyone except me, and to the people who were insulted that I implied they were trying to buy undue influence.

Having no money meant we would be outspent, by a lot, and made it even more important to count on our volunteers. Along with the irreplaceable commitment of time from Laura and Peter to run the effort, we had a highly mobilized network built through our work with ROAR.

My sister, Georgeann, who had recently left her job, put in hundreds of hours, and I had database help from my brother-in-law, Dan Vogel. My mother threw herself into the effort, managing information tables at neighborhood parades and, later, the office. Megan spent day after day with me, and brought along her massive family, especially our young nieces and nephews, who loved putting up posters and passing out literature with their cousins Charlie and Grace.

Megan had just started a new job at the Minnesota Center for Environmental Advocacy, with a long commute to downtown St. Paul. Somehow she kept some semblance of sanity in our personal lives, including bringing us together for a home-cooked meal almost every night.

EACH PRECINCT CONVENTION got us more volunteers, and by the time the endorsing convention came around we thought we possibly had enough people to make a solid showing. I thought we would certainly lose but would at least do well enough to keep alive our chances to win the primary and general election.

When we got to the convention we had far more people than we thought, and quickly got a hand from the other campaigns, who knew we all won if we could stop the Sayles Belton campaign from getting the endorsement.

The mayor's speech was a strong recitation of what she had done in eight years, and it sounded to me like a lot. I went in a very different direction, hitting on the themes of leadership and raising the bar for what we should expect of leadership in a great city.

"The year was 1968 and I was standing in my Boy Scout uniform at the top of the tallest building in Minneapolis: the Foshay Tower," I said. The Foshay, at a whopping thirty-two stories, is now dwarfed in the skyline, but I described my awe looking out across Minneapolis. "I thought I was looking at the greatest city in the world."

I said Minneapolis needed to "regain its rightful place as one of the great cities of our time." The message hit home, and many of the delegates supporting the other two candidates in the race swung to us. When the first ballot ended it was clear this was now a two-person race between Sayles Belton and me.

I worked the room hard, shaking as many hands as I could until the vote totals were announced. When delegates heard what was shocking news, that we were almost tied with a sitting mayor, the room exploded.

We never expected it to be that close—I'm sure the Sayles Belton people didn't either. Gracie, then a little ten-year-old with glasses, caught my eye from clear across the room and ran faster than I've ever seen her run down the center aisle to give me a massive hug that I will never forget.

For most of the next several hours, in ballot after ballot, the lead swung back and forth. All this time stuck in the auditorium seemed downright bizarre to the many new people we had brought into the system—and one of the hardest jobs was for Megan and her sister Bridgid to stand at the door, hand out sandwiches, and beg people not to leave.

We didn't win, but to almost everyone's surprise, we didn't lose either. The convention ended in a draw—a huge win for us that surprised nearly everyone.

THE DAY AFTER THE CONVENTION we were swamped as we marched in the annual MayDay Parade, a Minneapolis institution where pretty much anything goes. There we were, suddenly a major factor in the mayor's race, marching directly behind the Minnesota Naturists (a nudist association whose members were wearing barrels, we noted thankfully).

Later that day Sam and Sylvia Kaplan, the most important fund-raisers in Minneapolis, took a walk with me. They knew everyone in the race, had good relationships on all sides, and were planning to stay on the sidelines and focus on Wellstone's upcoming race. At the end they said they would join us; it was a massive lift for a campaign whose single biggest challenge was money.

We knew we had arrived when perennial candidate Dick Franson put out an attack fax against us: "Who is this R.T. Rybak? This neophyte! This milquetoast!" Charlie and Grace loved learning these new words and still use them to describe me to this day.

WE HAD TO BEGIN to build a citywide campaign and picked an office on Nicollet Avenue South ("Eat Street"), where the restaurants—with every kind of food on the planet—sent a message that we were about a new Minneapolis with people from around the globe. It was the perfect message for the campaign we were running.

My sister, Georgeann, made a major contribution by taking time off work to help Wagenius and Sether set up the office. My super-organized mother took over the front desk, answering the phones to make sure calls didn't get dropped, and helping the volunteers and occasional characters all feel included.

A couple of years earlier my mother's second husband, Chuck Mesken, had died suddenly. After fighting off so many challenges in her life, my mother, for the first time I had ever seen, seemed defeated. She withdrew from almost everything. She says now that the campaign, especially those days in the office, brought her back.

Our improbable early campaign wins were built on raw energy and emotion. We were proud of what we had done, but almost everyone was spent—financially, emotionally, and physically. Our volunteers gave up a lot to get us through the endorsing convention and, rightfully, most were expecting a relatively normal summer with their families.

But to me, this is where the fun began. Instead of focusing on a relatively small group of delegates, making hour after hour of phone calls to delegates each night, our new playground was the whole city and every person. I spent the next few months knocking on every door we could find, going to every neighborhood and every park, and walking up to strangers on the street.

The whole nature of the campaign at this stage had the air of those corny Andy Hardy movies. "My dad has some lumber. Let's go build a playhouse!" It was almost ridiculously grassroots and ragtag. That was also the most fulfilling time I ever had in politics, at least until the Obama campaign came along, and certainly the most affirming to me that elections can really be as simple as two people talking to each other about what they want from the place they live.

I ESPECIALLY LOVED THE PARADES and began to master the art of running full tilt in every one to shake hands with as many people as I could on both sides of the street. In that campaign I never once rode in a car through a parade, nor did I in twelve years as mayor. Where I really think I picked up votes were the rooms and parks with only a couple of people—giving me a chance to talk in places where most other candidates weren't going.

Door knocking didn't go very well at first. I would knock, the person would open the door, and I would launch into a speech about all the wonderful things I was going to do as mayor. I can be pretty overwhelming and, in full sales mode, I was way too much for someone talking to a stranger at the door. Slowly I learned that most people don't like being startled at the front door by a hyperactive graduate of Toastmasters.

When it was becoming clear my door knocking just wasn't having much impact, I remembered I had done a lot of it before. When I was a reporter I spent many nights walking up to doors and asking people questions, sometimes very personal ones. I put aside the campaign pitch in favor of asking people what they wanted their city to be. Once I got their trust I told them what I wanted to do.

After a few months I had hundreds of stories from every part of town about what real people wanted, and what they thought wasn't working. I started to make headway at those front doors, and got voters committed enough to start putting up waves of lawn signs.

When the debates started it was clear that all those one-on-one conversations had given me a very good sense of what was happening in the neighborhoods. It helped that I had ramped down my consulting work dramatically and had a lot more time to spend door knocking than my opponents, especially since one of them was a sitting mayor who also had to be running a city.

Door knocking became an aerobic activity; the more I did it, the more my political endorphins kicked in. I loved it. I met tremendous people and had a series of truly bizarre experiences. One day in a senior apartment building, I knocked on the door and heard a sweet voice from an older woman say "Just a minute." She opened the door: perfect hair and makeup, necklace, no shirt, no bra. "I'm sorry," she said. "I wasn't exactly dressed for company." Actually she was hardly dressed at all.

I encountered a very different tone at a house in northeast Minneapolis. After I introduced myself a woman started talking about property taxes and suddenly broke down. She told me about her husband dying and the escalating housing prices around her. Now she was going to have to sell the house she loved, in the neighborhood she loved, because she couldn't afford the property taxes. I still remember her face and tried to keep her in mind when I sat down to set the tax levy for the coming year.

Our families were invaluable: my mom, Georgeann, her husband, Dan, Megan's brothers, sisters, nieces, and nephews.

There was also a dedicated base of volunteers. One of the best was Naethe Richardson, a south Minneapolis neighborhood activist who gave hundreds of hours.

We, of course, had no money for a poll, but in June one published in the *Star Tribune* showed that only about 20 percent of the people in Minneapolis knew who I was. I don't know how that changed over the summer, but day by day we could feel that more people were getting to know me. My sense was, and still is, that I won the election because I spent the summer at all those front doors and in all those parks.

IN EARLY AUGUST OF THAT YEAR, with no warning, a story broke that Brian Herron, a sitting city council member, had been caught on tape soliciting a bribe. That's a big story in any city but a huge one in a city that prides itself on clean politics.

A few hours after the news broke, there was a debate at the Minnesota State Fair where I joined the mayor and the two other candidates, Lisa McDonald and County Commissioner Mark Stenglein. Right before we went on air the mayor appeared and was immediately savaged by a horde of reporters. She knew very little about the incident at the time, could say even less, and got pummeled. Watching her sweating in the heat, hands tied and seeing her political fortunes collapse, I felt a wave of sympathy. If I ever got elected is this what it would be like? Was I looking at the future?

The mayor's neutral statements about the alleged bribe in that debate, and in the coming few days, were attacked from every side. Suddenly the ground was ripe for a candidate talking about "fresh air at City Hall."

We four candidates continued a series of debates, and it seemed none of us was getting a real advantage. I was getting more confident, sometimes really hitting some crisp sound bites and a few moments of inspiration, but I was also very uneven. It was clear to me, and I assume many of the people listening, that I had a lot to learn.

After a while you get to know pretty much every question but at the end of a debate near the primary, we got hit with one that threw all of us: "Say something nice about the person next to you." Stenglein said something innocuously nice about McDonald, who did the same for Sayles Belton. I said something nice about all three, and then it came time for Sayles Belton to say something nice about me. She froze. For a long uncomfortable time she waited until, finally, she said, "He has nice hair and eyes."

The crowd went silent for a moment, not really knowing how to react, while I thought to myself, "If I said that about her, my career would be over." It was clear that all of us were getting tired.

Overall I kept my cool but there were moments when I lost it. One August day, after a series of fruitless fund-raising calls, I was walking down the street and ran into Jim Smart, who, with his wife, Cindie, was a very visible supporter of Mayor Sayles Belton. Trying to be polite he said, "It looks like your campaign is doing well." Without thinking, I shot back, "No thanks to you"—one of those things you say that you immediately regret. The Smarts continued to support the mayor but in later years became close friends and among my strongest supporters.

RIGHT BEFORE THE PRIMARY Bill Bradley, whom I had worked so hard for when he ran for president, came into town to do a rally for me. This was a great way to excite our base and send a message of legitimacy.

Bradley told the crowd I was "a courageous thinker who respects people." He also talked about my record on the environment, including clean water, which was the topic of the first conversation I had with him when he was campaigning.

My comments focused on affordable housing and a different way of getting things done. "We need every one of us to be involved in affordable housing. I will be a mayor who will have this at the top of the city's agenda, but it can't just be the city; it has to be faith communities, it has to be individuals. Pick up a hammer, write a check, find a homeless family. We all need to be part of the solution."

Al Gore, who had defeated Bradley for the presidential nomination, was campaigning for Sayles Belton a few days earlier and we liked the contrast. One of our supporters, Joe Barisonzi, told Minnesota Public Radio, "Gore was the establishment. Bradley was challenging the establishment with new fresh ideas. Sharon's the establishment, R.T.'s challenging the establishment with fresh new ideas, so I think there's a lot of parallels."

The day was especially important because Bradley got out of town alive, something that wasn't so clear an hour before the event. We were bringing Bradley from a pre-event fund-raiser to the rally and loaded the minivan with him, my family, and the Kaplans, who were active in his campaign and helped convince Bradley to come to town for me. We had no more room in the vehicle, but it felt wrong not to include Peter Wagenius, who also worked hard for Bradley and was helping to run the campaign. The simple solution was to have Peter drive—except, as I would soon learn, his many, many, many talents do not include driving.

We took off from Broders' restaurant in southwest Minneapolis headed to Whittier Elementary School. Peter stepped on the gas, then the brake, then the gas again, and then a car almost hit us. Peter got so nervous it happened all over again. Bradley, a very tall former pro basketball player, was scrunched into the front passenger seat. Now his legs and hands were braced firmly against the dashboard, preparing for the worst. For the rest of the drive, as our hardworking, talented campaign manager lurched the car across town, it got really quiet.

PRIMARY DAY 2001 began with a spectacular sunny morning. We started with early-morning coffee next door at Rodger and Kathy Ringham's, with others from our street who had given us so much support along the way. We all set out to walk to the polling place together, kids in wagons and on bikes. Rarely have I felt so protected and supported. These amazing neigh-bors, most of them not the least bit political, had paid extra attention to the kids, ignored our cacophony of lawn signs, and, more than anything, just had been our friends. After voting we hugged each other and I went off to door-knock in northeast Minneapolis with our super-volunteer Naethe Richardson.

Naethe and I walked into a coffee shop on Johnson Street, and it was stone silent as everyone was watching a TV. "A plane just crashed into the Trade Towers," someone said. A few minutes later we got a call from the campaign office explaining what had happened and that all the campaigns had agreed to stop any politicking that day.

I didn't know what to think, and was only beginning to take in what had happened in New York. Megan and I were horrified and baffled, but we knew we couldn't do anything. We also knew it would do no good to glue ourselves to the blow-by-blow coverage on TV. We got on our bikes and just started to ride.

The airplane noise I had fought so hard against was gone; no one was flying. It was eerily silent everywhere we went, and we said very little.

Voting would continue, a great sign that democracy doesn't stop, but it was clear to us we would now lose. Without the ground game of volun-teers we hoped would level the playing field for us, and knowing in a crisis people usually turn to what they know, we were certain this was the end. The election also seemed pretty much beside the point.

THROUGHOUT THE DAY I was rolling over and over in my mind what I could say that night. How could I even talk about an election without trivializing what had happened? But didn't I need to say something to the remarkable group of supporters who had done so much for us, only to be stopped by something no one could have predicted or controlled? Didn't I need to say something about democracy—how terrorists couldn't keep people from voting, the most basic of American acts?

Our family went to the headquarters around 7:45 to hear the results. I walked in assuming I had lost and two hours later got the news that we won the primary by ten points. We would run in the general election against Sayles Belton, who finished second.

More deer in the headlights than political victor, I came out to speak to the crowd and said, very simply, "Tonight, on the most tragic of nights, our city stands, and our city stands ready for change."

# *Winning*

---

T HE 9/11 TRAGEDY changed the country and certainly the campaign, but no one was sure what it meant. The Sayles Belton campaign seemed to be interpreting that it would lead to people wanting a steady, experienced hand in a crisis. They quickly came out with literature showing the mayor with police and firefighters, a hand over her heart with flag waving.

Next came literature and a radio ad asking, "What do you *really* know about R.T. Rybak?" We were concerned that this line of attack would stick. Plenty of history shows that in times of crisis voters go for stability.

We were especially worried that the police and firefighters unions, still on the sidelines, would endorse the mayor and make things worse for us. We believed we had little chance of getting their support, but I went to the police screening anyway, mostly just to try to stop the union from endorsing Sayles Belton. To our surprise, they endorsed me. In retrospect it wasn't such a long shot to back someone who had just won the primary by ten points, but we saw this as a good hedge against more allegations that I couldn't handle a crisis. We were even happier when the firefighters union followed.

A string of debates between the mayor and me didn't give either of us an advantage, but the good news was that we felt nothing was changing the direction of the campaign, not even the terrorist attacks on September 11.

We spent a lot of time trying to win at least some endorsements, and a month after the primary were able to schedule a press conference with six council members or candidates coming on to endorse us. The head of the Central Labor Union Council stood outside the press conference, threatening each candidate who walked in that if they supported me the union would pull its endorsement. One by one, they ignored him, walked inside, and got on board.

One of those was Paul Ostrow, a council member from northeast Minneapolis who had been an opponent of Mayor Sayles Belton, especially on financial issues. Every Sunday through the election, for hours at a time, he and I jointly door-knocked his entire ward.

One endorsement I really wanted was that of Alice Rainville, the long-time council president from far north Minneapolis and the mother of council member Barb Johnson. I had become very fond of Alice's hard-nosed, commonsense leadership when I was a reporter for the *Star Tribune.* I once told Barb "we were raised by the same mom" because Alice, like my mom, was a strong, "no bull" woman who raised a family mostly on her own and wasn't intimidated in the male-dominated world of those times.

Alice was savvy enough to know she didn't have much to gain by supporting the newcomer, but I kept coming back and coming back to her front door. "Can I put up a lawn sign?" Each time she said no. Finally, the weekend before the election, she said, "OK, now you can put it up," which I took more pride in than almost any other in town.

Saturday night before the election Megan and I were coming back from an event in northeast Minneapolis and crossed the 35W bridge over the Mississippi with its dramatic skyline view. It was such a beautiful night we decided to take a short walk on the Stone Arch Bridge. Up to this point I had studiously refused to think about winning. I am a confident and optimistic person, but I run scared and I just worried it would be bad luck. As we started across the bridge from the downtown end, I said to Megan, "Just this once, let's let ourselves think about what it would be like . . ." We talked about how our lives would be different and this time it was almost all positive. When we got to the other side of the bridge and turned back toward downtown, there was this remarkable image of the city in front of us and the river below us. I choked up with the enormity of the thought that I could actually become mayor of this amazing city. Whenever I'm at that spot—the north side of the Stone Arch Bridge with the river and St. Anthony Falls in front, the skyline rising in the background—I remember that moment, with that view, as the moment I realized I might finally get to do the one thing I had wanted to do most of my life.

The next morning I came downstairs and overheard Grace in the kitchen. "Charlie! There's a poll in the paper that says Dad is winning by twenty points!"

Charlie shot back with the clinical matter-of-factness of a seasoned political pro: "But what's the margin of error?"

Our family had come a long way.

The night before Election Day, the last debate, on WCCO Radio, broke no new ground. It was also clear we were sick of listening to each other and I know at least I was sick of listening to myself. When we finished our final statements it sank in that it was over, and without thinking I walked over and hugged the mayor. She must have thought it was a really odd thing to do to someone you had challenged so hard, and I remember it being awkward. But after going through that long march together, even competing, I felt this strange bond that most other people can't understand. I wanted to win, more than ever, and we disagreed on some fundamental points, more than ever, but I just simply finished with a deeper respect for Sharon Sayles Belton than I had when I started.

I'VE ALWAYS LOVED ELECTION DAY because it's when you no longer have to do much thinking. It's you, the voters, and a lot of adrenaline. I spent that day in constant motion: waving to commuters on the side of the freeway entrances and busy corners, shaking hands in coffee shops, working the downtown lunch crowd and the downtown evening commuter bus stops and finishing, as I always have with any election, by waving to the thousands of commuters who pass on Hennepin and Lyndale Avenues.

We had volunteers all over town. One was our longtime friend Nancy Engh, who was enthusiastically waving a sign on Hennepin Avenue when a car came too close and hit her. She bounced off, unhurt, but continues to remind us she once sacrificed her body to get me elected.

After rush hour we got the kids ready and decided to go out to dinner all by ourselves. We got a tatami room at Fuji Ya Japanese restaurant, the kind where you sit on the floor in your socks. We walled ourselves off for an hour, had some great laughs about the amazing ride we had been on, and tried to convince ourselves we would be fine either way it turned out.

After dinner we drove to the election night party at the Ukrainian Center in northeast Minneapolis. The second we opened the door TV lights turned on and we were surrounded by reporters. It felt like walking into the Academy Awards, only we didn't know what had happened. A big cheer went up and people told us we were leading, but, sadly, just as quickly, we were pulled off to a side room to wait for a concession call from Mayor Sayles Belton. We were told the protocol was to let the person who lost concede before we issued our own statement, so we waited for a couple hours until I got the call from the mayor. Her concession call was quick and matter-of-fact and we made our way to the stage.

I had been wondering for the past few weeks how I could thank campaign workers who included so many grassroots volunteers, but Megan thought up the idea that said it all: "I have a few people I have to thank," I said, and slowly unfurled out across the crowd a thirty-foot scroll filled with the names of all those people who volunteered in the campaign.

I don't remember much else about that night except I'm pretty sure I danced a lot.

# Showtime

A T 5:30 the morning after I got elected, Megan and I woke up blinded by what seemed like klieg lights shining into our bedroom window. We looked outside and found four television trucks parked in front of the house getting ready for live shots on the 6:00 A.M. news. We looked at each other, speechless, for what seemed like a few minutes, wondering what our new life was going to be like. Finally I said, "It's showtime!"

I was even more surprised when I went outside to the interviews because none of the reporters wanted to talk to me about getting elected. The one question they all asked was, "What are you going to do about the Twins?"

A few days earlier news had broken that the president of Major League Baseball and the Minnesota Twins were considering folding the franchise. Attendance had been low and they considered it unlikely they would get help building a stadium to move out of the deadly Metrodome. To me, and a lot of other people at the time, it seemed like a ploy, but it almost didn't matter because immediately there was a huge wave of pressure from the public—and to some degree, the state legislature and governor—for the host city Minneapolis to do something to keep the team.

The Twins situation was more complicated because St. Paul had just elected a new mayor, Randy Kelly, who said he was willing to do whatever it took to build the Twins a new home across the river. A friend at the *Star Tribune* told me one of the reasons I did not get the paper's endorsement was that they believed Kelly when he told them, "If R.T. Rybak gets elected, Minneapolis can kiss the Twins good-bye." Kelly had been a skilled long-time state senator and was already working his former colleagues at the State Capitol to give state support to building a Twins ballpark in downtown St. Paul.

This was not on my agenda, in any way, but now a lifelong Twins fan was confronted with losing one of downtown's most visible assets before I even took office. I couldn't know at the time that there would be one "stadium controversy" or another for the entire twelve years I was in office.

Still sleepy from the night before, I gave the reporters in my front yard that first morning noncommittal answers about the Twins and went off on Day 1 to face the other big issue that hadn't been on my agenda: the city's budget.

MY FIRST MEETING that day was with the city's finance director, Pat Born. I came into office with more business background than most politicians, but I had absolutely no experience in public finance. I understood that the numbers at the bottom of the page should be black instead of red, but otherwise the rookie who had never held public office was starting public budgeting at zero.

Pat Born was a very patient teacher that first day as he walked me through a tutorial on the Minneapolis city budget. I would learn over time that he is a true Minnesotan who stays calm in the clutch, but it was quickly clear that the city's budget was in much worse shape than the public, or I, appreciated.

The budget had come up in the campaign and was the source of great debate. The mayor and other incumbents were arguing that the city was on solid financial ground and that the downgrading of the city's bonds that summer was just an aberration. Among those who disagreed was Wallace "Wally" Swan, the highly respected chair of the city's Board of Estimate and Taxation, who had written an opinion piece in the summer saying the city had dangerously high debt that was made worse by the decision to build a new central library.

It was clear very quickly that Swan was right, and the economic crash after 9/11 was making matters worse by the minute. Born also explained to me that for many years major equipment purchases like computers were charged to an internal service fund with few controls, and that fund now held a multi-million-dollar debt. Worse, the computer systems throughout the city were seriously outdated, and there was no funding source to replace them. Then, slack-jawed, I listened to the details of the city's soaring pension costs. Making all this more complicated, the election had badly split an already divided outgoing city council, and it did not appear council members were going to be able to agree on the budget before they left office.

Walking out of City Hall that first day I was stopped by Kathy O'Brien, a longtime ally of Mayor Sayles Belton and then the city coordinator. She told me City Hall was filled with rumors that I was going to immediately ask all appointed employees to resign. I already knew that would be a big mistake based in large part on my experience running the *Twin Cities Reader*. I had come into that job and immediately tried to save the dying paper by making a series of abrupt changes that ended up destabilizing the operation. It taught me you can't get too many plates spinning at the same time. Months before the election I decided that if I won I would make a very few key surgical changes immediately and wait a year or two to decide if more dramatic personnel changes were needed. That didn't help the rumors that were now the major distraction in City Hall, however, and O'Brien advised me to get to the people I wanted to keep as soon as possible.

By midafternoon that first day—after the predawn press conference in the front yard and the reality therapy at City Hall—it was clear the job was going to be a lot bigger than I thought.

At this point I could have gone back to the office but then something else sank in: I had no office. I also had no staff. The campaign headquarters was being shut down, and the almost all-volunteer staff was focused on getting back to all of the work they had set aside during the election.

Over in St. Paul, Mayor-Elect Kelly had a great situation. The sitting mayor, Norm Coleman, supported Kelly during the election and offered him a transition office adjacent to the mayor's office. He had clean access to city staff and information.

Having run against the incumbent, our situation was very different. We weren't allowed an office in City Hall, and walking into the building was met with real suspicion by a staff that fully expected to be fired.

Catherine Shreves, chair of the Minneapolis Board of Education, agreed to chair the transition, and my friend Dan Boivin helped us set up a transition office in his law firm near downtown. David Fey, a veteran community planner and activist, agreed to be chief of staff. I first met Fey in the Rapson campaign—he shared my love of good city design and had a deep knowledge of affordable housing. Perhaps most important, he had a calm demeanor and a deliberate, linear way of thinking that balanced out my frenetic style.

It seemed like things were collapsing all around us, but Megan and I also knew we were exhausted and needed to get regrounded with the kids. So the four of us drove to a small town in Iowa where we caught a train for a quick trip to Denver. We spent the night in a sleeper car and woke up just before we came into the depot in Denver, and for the next couple of days we walled ourselves off from this huge thing in front of us.

On our way to one of the museums in Denver we passed City Hall and walked in to look around. When we saw the sign for the mayor's office we peeked in the door and the receptionist waved us in. "What brings you to Denver?" When we told her I had just been elected mayor of Minneapolis she excused herself and a minute later this huge man came out the door. It was Wellington Webb, the mayor of Denver, who, coincidently, had raised thousands of dollars for Mayor Sayles Belton's campaign.

He invited the family into his office, gave the kids pencils with the city seal, and, most significant, had a wonderful conversation with us about the importance of keeping close to your family when you were mayor. It was the first of thousands of personal conversations I would have with mayors across the country who, I would come to learn, have a kind of fraternity of support.

When we got back to Minneapolis we found a very welcome invitation. After each election, the John F. Kennedy School of Government invites newly elected big-city mayors to Harvard for a three-day "Mayor School" to hear from veteran mayors and learn about key city issues. This was great news for someone who now fully realized how much he had to learn. The night before classes began I checked into the hotel on the Harvard campus and walked around the same streets in Cambridge that I had gotten to know so well while at Boston College.

After about an hour I walked into the Harvard Book Store and found myself reading books about architecture and city planning. Suddenly it hit me with a powerful sense of déjà vu: I was standing in the same bookstore where I had spent so many hours when I was at college, reading the same types of books about cities, daydreaming about what I could do in Minneapolis. Only now, twenty-two years later, I was actually in a position to do something.

The next day I joined the other newly elected mayors at Harvard: Cleveland's Jane Campbell, Detroit's Kwame Kilpatrick, Chattanooga's Bob Corker, and St. Paul's Randy Kelly. Seattle's Greg Nickels was supposed to come but had to stay away because he was in a recount.

Corker would go on to be a senator from Tennessee, but the rest of those mayors of the class of 2001 would ultimately lose their reelection bids. They were a very talented group, and I believe most lost because the post-9/11 recession required us all to make very politically difficult decisions. Kilpatrick, who ended up in jail, also had a few other issues.

The Kennedy School classes were incredibly helpful, and every hour that went by lowered my anxiety about whether I was up to the task. I got to meet two of my heroes, Boston's mayor Tom Menino and Charleston's Joe Riley, who would go on to become true mentors. Over beers with Baltimore's Martin O'Malley I learned about his CitiStat data management strategy that I would use as a model for Results Minneapolis. I even got to meet the legendary mayor of Providence, Rhode Island, Buddy Cianci, who transformed his city between stops in prison. Flanked by a jackbooted security detail, Cianci told us the key to the rejuvenation of Providence, in an accent straight out of *The Sopranos,* was "the art . . . Use art to make the city you imagine." Who knew?

One of the best discussions I had was with Chattanooga's Bob Corker, who had been Tennessee's budget director and helped me make some sense of the budget problems I was facing. I took full advantage of being able to ask someone who knew what he was talking about some really dumb basic questions.

The other great discussion I had was with Nicolas Retsinas, director of Harvard University's Joint Center for Housing Studies. A brilliant man and patient teacher, he walked me through a series of effective strategies for developing housing for low-income residents. For the first time since election night I was able to imagine ways of clearing budgets and stadiums off the desk and focusing on my goal of developing more affordable housing.

The three days at Harvard were completely rejuvenating, but I got whacked back into reality as I shared a taxi to Logan International Airport with Randy Kelly. He took a call from Pam Wheelock, who led St. Paul's economic development. In what he apparently thought was code but was quite obvious, he sat next to me in the cab talking with Wheelock about how to get the legislature to support moving the Twins to St. Paul.

BACK AT HOME, David Fey began building our staff around my two campaign managers: Peter Wagenius, who would become chief policy aide, and Laura Sether, who became communications director. Most of the department heads were up for reappointment in January, and I told most of them I wanted them to stay. The exception was the head of the city's development agency, where I was planning a major reorganization.

Kathy O'Brien, a very effective city coordinator, said she would not stay but would manage the transition. It was tough finding someone to replace a person who was doing a good job in the top administrative job in the city. A few key candidates were on the other side in the election, which I thought had some appeal as I tried to build bridges, but our top three choices turned us down. I was really in the mood to put the election behind us, but it was becoming clear that running a tough campaign against a sitting incumbent would have consequences.

We were finally able to convince John Moir to take the job. The former finance director, he had publicly quit a year and a half earlier because he didn't think the past administration had the will to solve the growing budget issues. We needed his inside knowledge of how to fix the budget, but the choice of Moir sent a shiver through an already nervous City Hall. The *Star Tribune* criticized the move as an "in your face gesture" to the outgoing administration, but that wasn't the purpose. We needed someone who knew where the bodies were buried and wouldn't be afraid to help us make unpopular decisions.

As we sent signals that we were going to make big changes to the city budget and reorganize the development agency, the labor unions got nervous. They sent a delegation to my transition office to warn me to go slow. They also wanted me to intervene to keep Barrett Lane, an independent and a fiscal hawk, from chairing the city council's budget committee. They gave a hardball message, but I reminded them I had just won the election overwhelmingly, despite their strong objections, and had promised exactly this kind of change. There would be no deal.

IN THE WEEKS that followed the election, the Twins continued to dominate the news and the legislature stepped in. They scheduled a hearing in early December but they didn't want the sitting mayor to come alone. They asked that she and the new mayor present together what the city was willing to do to keep the Twins in town.

This created a major problem: Could the mayor and the mayor-elect agree on what to say? More important, what should I say? This wasn't where I thought a city caught in a growing financial crisis should be spending its money—and I didn't want to spend my first year ensnarled in stadium politics when I needed to be fixing the budget and building affordable housing.

There was also a very different political reality. Did I really want to be seen sitting on the sidelines while Minneapolis lost the Twins? What would the long-term implications be with the legislators if they invited the newly elected mayor and he refused to show up?

In the end I decided that mayors are elected to lead. I needed to go, to let them know I cared and would try in the coming months to find a consensus. I also knew I couldn't commit to any one strategy because the city and I really had no idea how to solve this. There was also the not-so-small issue that I wasn't even mayor yet.

I did tell the people pushing the stadium that I had a condition: I would only go if they stopped pushing a site on the river in the North Loop that would have taken a street of historic buildings near First Street and First Avenue (one of the most exciting parts of Minneapolis today). Instead, I said we should agree on the site where the stadium is today, which required taking no buildings and had most of the necessary infrastructure already in place.

I had that conversation with Jim Pohlad, owner of the Twins, in his office that overlooks where the stadium is today. At that point the Twins were intent on having a stadium be part of a riverfront revival and they didn't think it would fit where it is today. "It's just too small," he insisted as he looked at the parking lot wedged between ramps and freeways. "No, the architects tell us it works," I responded. "It doesn't fit," he insisted. In reality we were both right. The stadium eventually fit into the site, but only because the right field stands were built over the freeway.

I went to the legislature with Mayor Sayles Belton and Council President Jackie Cherryhomes, ignoring the legislators whispering to each other and laughing about the awkward trio in the front row. It was clear the sport they were interested in wasn't baseball; they seemed to be loving watching us squirm. When called on we said the city wanted to keep the Twins and did the best we could to make a noncommittal statement that we would work with the team to try to find a solution.

We got out of the stadium hearing without too much damage, but my appearance there infuriated some of my best and earliest supporters. Those most upset were Senator Jane Ranum and Representative Jean Wagenius—the only two legislators who had supported me and two key people in my campaign; they also were exceptionally strong opponents of public financing for stadiums. Another upset supporter was Wagenius's son Peter, my campaign manager, whom I had just made senior policy aide in my office. Whether or not I felt I was between a rock and a hard place, the stadium issue was ripping apart my fragile coalition before I even took office.

* * *

WITH SO MANY PROBLEMS MOUNTING, the last thing I wanted to worry about was a party, but I was amazed how many people expected me—without any staff in place—to plan a big public inaugural. This was not Megan's idea of where she wanted to spend her time either, but she stepped in, along with the Kaplans and a group of volunteers.

The inaugural itself was a blur but there was one priceless moment. Two years earlier Ginny Kelly, a good friend with a massively outsized personality, found out she had cancer. Trying to cheer her up shortly after she was diagnosed, I said, "Ginny, you and I are going to dance together at my inaugural." It was a nice thing to say to a friend, but she and I both knew she likely only had a year to live, and at that point it was absurdly far-fetched to think I would ever get elected mayor.

On the night I was sworn in, surrounded by a huge room of people, Ginny and I had that dance. She died a year later, but both of us got a lot further than anyone, including us, expected.

# Rookie Mistakes

---

THE DAY I OFFICIALLY BECAME MAYOR of Minneapolis went exactly as planned. For precisely one hour and twenty-five minutes.

Megan and I, Charlie and Grace, all dressed up, walked down the front steps of our home to start a new life. We were met by Medaria Arradondo, one of the best officers in the Minneapolis Police Department, in his crisp white uniform. He opened the door of the big black Crown Victoria that had been Mayor Sayles Belton's car. The kids were really excited about riding in what looked like a limo until I told them, "Don't get used to it. We're trading it in for a Prius Hybrid."

The first stop was Central Lutheran Church for a prayer service that our minister, Mariann Budde, organized with leaders from ten different faiths. It was a moving start to the day, but I couldn't concentrate because there were two big things on my mind. The first was my inaugural speech, which I was still memorizing. It would be the biggest speech I had ever given, and I knew it was important to send a message that helped bring the city back together.

The second thing on my mind was the phone call I had gotten at 10:30 the night before from Paul Ostrow, who, we assumed, was going to be elected city council president that day. We wanted Ostrow to be president because we thought he would be more willing to help pass the tough financial reforms we needed.

But the bombshell Ostrow dropped in his phone call was that he no longer had the votes to be president. Council member-elect Natalie Johnson Lee, who we thought would be a strong supporter, told him she was switching sides.

We were so tied up in the financial mess and all the other dynamics dropping around us that we weren't really aware there were "sides" being formed in the council race. A lot was happening behind the scenes. Council veteran Barb Johnson had started her own campaign for council president. Daughter of a council president, and someone whom I learned never to underestimate when it came to counting votes in City Hall, Johnson outmaneuvered Ostrow and picked up the votes she needed to win.

I had a solid relationship with Johnson, but the dynamic that worried me was that she was getting a strong assist from the union leaders who had tried to threaten me a couple of months earlier. Having her become council president that way could make it harder to get the reforms done, so the Ostrow call the night before the swearing-in was a huge setback.

When we left the church service and got to City Hall I went to find Johnson Lee to try to get her to switch back to Ostrow, but a whole mess of messes got in the way. I couldn't walk two feet without someone unloading a crisis. "No one invited the governor to the swearing-in, and we don't have anyplace for the legislators to sit." "We got into the mayor's office early and everything is gone; no files, no phone numbers, nothing." "The council chamber is still being remodeled, so the council election has to be held in the rotunda as part of the swearing-in."

Most of the problems couldn't be fixed that morning. It was clear that having to deal with all the issues that had arisen since the election had taken our focus off planning a smooth swearing-in and transition. It was also clear that the staff we had was heavy on policy but light on experience in the day-to-day running of a political office. In fact, most of us had never worked in a political office—and from the start, that lack of knowledge had its consequences.

I finally found Johnson Lee just as we were ready to start the procession into the swearing-in. "The people who fought us in the campaign are trying to dictate who runs City Hall," I said. She listened but said nothing. As the new mayor and council walked into the ceremony, almost none of us knew how things were going to end.

We had no seating chart. We wanted this to be a "People's Inaugural" where the inside power brokers didn't have the key seats, and partly out of ignorance, we hadn't appreciated how upset this would make other office-holders and key city leaders. When I later looked at pictures of the event I could see that almost no one you would expect to be at a city swearing-in ceremony was in the picture. Instead, it was a diverse collection of regular people who didn't often get the best seat in City Hall. Partly because we didn't know better, the event made many people unhappy. I'm not proud of that, but I am still very proud that we delivered on the promise to open up the doors of City Hall.

The one exception was Senator Paul Wellstone and his wife, Sheila. They were seated in the prime spot, the front row of the balcony, with a direct line of sight to the podium. When I came to the podium to give my speech, Wellstone jumped up and pumped his arms and made me feel tremendously proud that he had helped me get there. That memory is even more special because eight months later he and Sheila would be gone.

My speech was the first thing in several hours that went right. I was able to deliver most of it from memory, only looking at the paper on the podium a few times.

The idea was to reach out to a divided city on the one point we all agreed on: loving Minneapolis. I started by describing the long campaign. "I just took a walk around the city I love," I said, and described the beauty and the people I had seen during these past few months. The speech was light on specific policy initiatives and more an attempt to inspire people about the potential of the city—to help, as I said during the campaign, "Minneapolis regain its collective swagger." I ended by describing a better Minneapolis: "A city that leads. A city that innovates. A city with big arms that reaches out to everyone. A city as great as its people."

As I finished I remember pausing for a second at the podium to take in the remarkable sight of all those people, from so many different backgrounds, and imagining that we could somehow move in a single direction.

A children's choir sang, and if things had ended there the event would have been seen as a huge success. We weren't that lucky.

Because the council chamber was still being remodeled, and because we had been too preoccupied to come up with a better way of doing it, the swearing-in moved right into the organizational meeting at which the council president and vice president were elected. That meant that the crowd that had come mostly for a ceremonial swearing-in—including the children's choir now seated on the rotunda's hard marble steps—spent the next forty-five minutes watching a hard-edged political drama.

Motions were made for both Ostrow and Johnson to be named president, followed by the council members' speeches on how they were voting. Eventually, the hundreds of people in the rotunda got very quiet as it came time for Johnson Lee to vote.

It was a huge relief to me, and a huge disappointment to a lot of others, when she said "Ostrow." Then the situation got more confusing. When it came time to vote for vice president, Johnson Lee surprised everyone again by not voting for Lisa Goodman, who had been running with Ostrow. Goodman awkwardly stood humiliated in front of the crowd, and you could hear one of the council members, in a whisper picked up by the microphones, say "This is really freaking me out!"

That spoke for a lot of people. By this point I would say most of the several hundred people in the atrium were "freaking out" because this innocent ceremony had turned into a very public demonstration of how this new crowd coming into City Hall—promising to make Minneapolis work better—couldn't seem to make much work at all.

The silver lining was that in sitting through that long debate, I promised myself to never again get involved in the politics of who leads the city council. With a few minor exceptions, I kept that promise for the next twelve years.

IT WAS A TREMENDOUS RELIEF to get into the mayor's office. That office may have been completely empty, and issues were piling up by the minute, but at least we could have a paid staff.

Our almost all-volunteer campaign asked a lot from a lot of people, and the transition asked even more. One of the first victims was Christine Hanson, who, with her husband, John, were among our most committed and selfless volunteers. Right after the election, when we were deluged with requests for meetings, she offered to step in as temporary scheduler. We had no idea how much pressure that would put on her, and shortly after I took office she had to quit. No one blamed her.

We hoped that finally taking office would give us a fresh start, but that wasn't possible because the previous council left a small gift. They hadn't finished the previous year's budget—so the first task was to cut $5 million in the first two weeks.

Five million dollars isn't a lot of money in a billion-dollar budget, but it sure feels like it when you have to cut it in two weeks without any background knowledge on the budget. So in a series of meetings with Pat Born, budget director Tammy Omdahl, her deputy Tara Barenok, and key council members, we went line item by line item through the spreadsheets, getting educated while making choices. We made cuts I never would have made had I really understood the consequences. A civilian review board, which didn't seem to please anyone on any side, got cut—which didn't seem to please anyone, either. The ones I regret the most were deep cuts to the Department of Health.

The cut with the biggest political consequence was eliminating the arts coordinator position, a job former city council member Jim Niland wanted for himself. Niland had been a key part of our campaign, bringing significant savvy to a very green team, and was one of the few people around us who knew the inner workings of City Hall. He was not pleased. *At all.* One more key supporter was now alienated. (Four years later, in the next election, Niland would be a key player in the campaign to unseat me.)

The budget crash course also revealed that one of my campaign promises was now impossible: for more than a decade the city had a Neighborhood Revitalization Program fund to support development by neighborhood organizations. During the campaign I had worked with leaders of the NRP on a strategy to keep this funding in place if they would commit to designating all their funds in Year 1 to building affordable housing.

The situation shifted dramatically when a change in state law in the last session of the legislature cut the legs out from under the program's funding. The NRP organizations would have far less to spend, and now that the economy was in free fall, there was no way the city budget could backfill even part of the money. The NRP couldn't get what it wanted, we couldn't spend anywhere nearly as much on affordable housing, and both of these very important constituencies were angry.

WITH SO MUCH IN FLUX with the budget, a more experienced politician would have focused on solving those problems instead of opening up another front. Instead I pushed us into one of the biggest mistakes in my time as mayor: I tried to change police chiefs, the only department head whose contract wasn't up.

Robert Olson had narrowly won confirmation for another term by a single vote a year earlier and, when campaigning, I thought I heard criticism of him from all parts of the city. True, he wasn't wildly popular, but I would later learn that it's rare when you don't hear some community criticism of a police chief. Rank-and-file cops said they weren't satisfied, but I learned you rarely hear cops in Minneapolis say they love the chief, either. Residents of both high-crime and low-crime areas complained that they didn't see enough police cars, but I later learned it's rare anybody ever says they have too many police officers in their neighborhood. Communities of

color, especially African Americans, complained about inequity in policing, a concern I shared and still believe has a lot of merit, but I learned that
the deep-seated police–community gap in Minneapolis can't fairly be laid
at the feet of a single chief. I would learn all that, and I would later become
pragmatic enough to have known to make the change when his contract
came up in a couple of years. Instead, I decided to do it right away.

I had a plan that I thought could alter the dynamics of Minneapolis
policing, especially in a place where police and communities of color have
had such a rocky history. St. Paul's chief, William Finney, was a far more visible commander in his city than Olson was in Minneapolis, and he seemed
to be able to command respect in both the force and the community. He
also had a rocky relationship with his new boss, Mayor Randy Kelly. I
heard through the grapevine that Kelly might want to make a change as
well, and I saw a big win in bringing to Minneapolis a visible leader who
would be our city's first African American chief.

Quietly, I approached key council members to see if I could get support
to buy out Olson's contract and replace him with Finney. Before I could
get very far, word leaked and it blew up in the media. Within hours it was
a major controversy, which ended any chance I could get council support.
I had to awkwardly withdraw the idea in public before I had even introduced it.

So now I had alienated the police chief I had to work with for the next
two years and given key council members real reason to worry about
crawling out on a limb with me again.

Maybe more than anything, I had exposed to the city that on a lot of
levels its new mayor might not be ready for prime time. Prime time, unfortunately, was where I was spending a lot of time. My inept attempt to fire
the chief got me on pretty much every news show, day and night, for a
run of almost a week. Just when I thought it would never end there was
a major controversy at the University of Minnesota and, thankfully, I got
off the hot seat. Shortly after, I ran into the university's president, Mark
Yudof, and we agreed we had stumbled onto a brilliant strategy: the next
time one of us did something stupid that got splayed all over the news, the
other would wait a couple of days and then do something even more stupid, just to give a pal a break.

It was about this time that I walked into the TV studio on the first floor
of City Hall for *The Mayor's Roundtable,* the public access cable show Mayors Sayles Belton and Fraser had done when they were in office. I put the

mike on my lapel, hopped onto the stool in front of the camera, and the live show began. "Welcome to *The Mayor's Roundtable*," I said, cheerily, then, trying to set a casual tone, began to ad lib. "As you can see there is no roundtable in the studio." Looking around at the only furniture I could find I blurted out, without thinking, "Maybe we should call it *The Mayor's Stool.*"

That was one of many, many things I said, or did, in those first few months that I probably would do differently now.

# Rookie Promise

IN SHORT, I had a very rough start, but the trial by fire was teaching me a lot.

The best example was the budget: making those very difficult cuts in the first two weeks was painful, but it proved to be a valuable crash course. When we finished, we kept right on going, starting to craft the budget for the coming year and, at the same time, a five-year financial direction that we hoped would be a road map for getting the city out of debt.

We knew we couldn't move complex, controversial budget issues unless we had the support of council members. To get them on board we organized a series of meetings that brought department heads and council chairs directly into what had in the past been exclusively the mayor's budget process. This meant we were crafting consensus in March and April that otherwise would have played out as drama on the council floor the following December.

By that May we had unanimously passed the five-year financial direction through the city council and had nearly completed that year's budget—months before it had been done in the past. This gave department heads months more time to plan and helped council members understand they were part owners of the budget when we had to formally pass it in December. More important, the council and I were beginning to believe that even though we were facing huge financial challenges, we could get ourselves out of the mess.

Like a lot of candidates who try to imitate what worked for Franklin Roosevelt, and almost no one else, I had an absurdly ambitious "ninety-day plan" developed in the middle of the election without any help from the people actually running the departments. (Memo to anyone running for office: this is a profoundly bad idea that really impresses no one.) We did the best we could to work our way through the plan, even though most of it was small potatoes compared to what was now on our plate, but it was a relief when it was over and we could settle down to, finally, focus on a realistic agenda.

WE SHED A BUNCH of the smaller ideas that seemed so urgent during the campaign and transition. Instead, we doubled down on one big change: restructuring the city's disjointed development functions into a single stronger, more streamlined entity focused on job creation and affordable housing.

This effort was possible only because Catherine Shreves, who had chaired the transition, helped put together a partnership with the consulting firm McKinsey & Co. When Shreves was chair of the Minneapolis Board of Education, McKinsey performed a pro bono evaluation of the school budgets. Now Shreves helped arrange a pro bono effort to have McKinsey donate what turned out to be the equivalent of about $1 million in consulting help to restructure city development.

We gave the McKinsey team a complex problem: build a model for fusing the city's Planning Department with an independent city development agency, a successful but small jobs function in the Department of Health, and the city's sprawling regulatory functions. A key goal was to cut reliance on public subsidy for individual projects—to tell developers we would cut red tape to make it easier to do business in Minneapolis but not to expect a check. A second goal was to focus less on parts of town that were already moving forward in favor of focusing more on people and parts of town that were being left behind.

We were laying the groundwork for some very big systems changes, but we knew it would be many months before any of our efforts paid off. In the meantime I was struggling with some issues that were hard to solve with a team that was only getting up to speed. It was going to be a rough period, but I knew the one thing I could do to make it better was simply to keep showing up.

# Showing Up

IN THE CRASH COURSE AT HARVARD soon after my election, one of the speakers said very bluntly that it was not the job of a mayor to deliver bad news. Deliver the good news and delegate the tougher stuff to staff. Images on the news should be of the mayor celebrating the good, not mired in bad news.

The second I heard that advice I decided I would reject it 100 percent. I knew from the start I had a lot to learn, and it showed in the first few months, but I also knew people would give you the benefit of the doubt if you were there when the chips were down. From the beginning that meant I tried to be everywhere. Pancake breakfasts, crime scenes, weddings, in front of angry crowds, nights, weekends. If I was asked, the answer was usually yes.

One of the great advantages of this strategy was that even when things were tough in City Hall—and in fact, especially when they were tough—I was reminded that I wasn't in it alone.

People got used to seeing the mayor in every part of everyday life. One of my favorite moments was driving down Broadway Avenue in north Minneapolis and seeing a group of kids picking up trash. I pulled over to tell the kids how great it was they were cleaning up the neighborhood. As I walked up to them, one very suspiciously asked me who I was. I told them it was wonderful that their parents had told them to be suspicious of strangers but, not to worry, I was the mayor. "You're not the mayor," they shot back. "Well, yes, actually I am the mayor." One kid looked over at my puny Prius Hybrid—when they clearly expected to see some kind of mayoral limo—and yelled to his friends, "No mayor would drive something like that! Run!"

* * *

SHOWING UP in tough times isn't something you can schedule, which meant a crucial incident in the city could abruptly throw us off course. That happened in March when we got word that a Somali man had been shot by the police at Chicago and Franklin, the south Minneapolis corner where my parents once had a drugstore.

As we drove to the scene, the police briefed me that Abu Kassim Jeilani, a refugee from Somalia, was walking down Franklin Avenue waving a machete. They said he was threatening bystanders, and when he ignored officers' orders to put the machete down, they shot him.

When I got to the scene I waded into the crowd of Somalis, which included some members of Jeilani's family. I was told many people in the community knew Jeilani had a history of mental illness, but they said he did not need to be shot. There were various reports about how many times the police had shot him, and great concern that his body had been left unprotected for too long.

It was clear it was going to take a few days to fully understand what happened, and we didn't have that kind of time. Tensions were already high between the police and the rapidly growing Somali population. Within the year there had already been several complex incidents, including one in which police ruled that the death of a Somali man was due to natural causes when the medical examiner later ruled it a homicide. A wire service many used to send money to relatives in Somalia was closed by police who alleged it was being used to transfer money to terrorists. There was also increased federal scrutiny of the Somalis in the months after 9/11 because most were of the Islamic faith, and this, too, was creating increased tension with the police.

I knew we had to do something soon, so I invited the crowd to my office the next day. About forty people showed up: members of the victim's family, key community members, and random bystanders.

They asked for more police training for working with people with mental illness and wanted me to fire the police chief, which was ironic because I had just tried to do that. In this case, however, I told them it was unfair to lay what had happened on the chief. In the past two years, after a couple of high-profile incidents between police and victims with mental illness, Chief Olson had set up a critical incident team to respond in such cases. They had been on the scene at the Jeilani incident and reportedly had taken several steps to de-escalate the situation. Mostly I listened and heard that much of their anger was about a broader set of issues. We came out of the meeting calmer and met the media with a message focused especially on long-term approaches to the underlying issues.

"I fully understand that this incident, to many people, is not seen as an isolated incident," I said. "Issues of race, issues of mental health, and issues of policing have become connected for some time. It is important for all of us to recognize that—to the degree to which people connect these issues—we are not safe."

In coming months the police spent a significant amount of time working with Somalis and building trust. We also had a series of meetings with the Friends of Barbara Schneider Foundation, a dedicated group of community members that formed when Schneider, who suffered from mental illness, was killed by police. They worked with the department to develop new protocols and new training, and they deserve credit for saving many lives.

# Mount Weather

**L**ooking out over the Shenandoah Valley as the sun was setting, I remembered where I had heard of Mount Weather before. This secure outpost, where I had been for three days, was where leaders of Congress were evacuated immediately following the 9/11 attacks. In the movies *The Day the Earth Stood Still* and *Seven Days in May* they called it "Mount Thunder."

Only two months into my new job as mayor, I was there with about seventy city employees to drill our emergency preparedness plan. This was not an abstract exercise. In that first year after 9/11, American mayors suddenly had a new responsibility to lead disaster planning. Before the attack it was almost impossible to imagine managing a major terrorism incident in a place like Minneapolis; after the attack you had to assume it could happen at any moment.

I tried to call Megan to tell her what it was like at the Mount Weather Emergency Operations Center, but I couldn't get cell phone reception. It was probably just as well because it was almost impossible to explain.

When I first looked around, everything seemed almost deserted. Then I figured out that most people were working belowground, which is where we spent the three days. We had a few group lectures, but mostly our role was to stay in character as we drilled disaster scenarios: a terrorist attack, a pandemic, a major catastrophe, all happening at once in Minneapolis. I, of course, had to stay in character as "The Mayor" when the federal officials running the drill announced the latest challenge on a mock television network.

I was never in the military and had never been a police officer or firefighter, so I had never worked in a "command and control" structure. My entire career had involved participation in collaborative teams in which you move by consensus. I had never been in situations where I blankly gave or took orders. Instead, I come from the warm-and-fuzzy world of south Minneapolis "servant leadership," where people fight *not* to be seated at the head of the table and kids' first words are "Tell me more about that." The discrepancy was glaringly, painfully obvious to me and, I assumed, to most of those around me. The team at Mount Weather needed decisive leadership as they tried to gain confidence that the rookie mayor could lead in a crisis.

I managed my way through each exercise, gaining more confidence as I went. I learned my first response could not be, "What does everyone think?" Instead, I had to take command and say, "We're going here."

The scenarios had specific incidents meant to expose the weaknesses in our existing plans. We were given a report that traced the contagious illness we had discovered to an office worker in the IDS Center in downtown Minneapolis. Thinking I was protecting all the other workers, I gave the order to evacuate. Later, when federal officials reviewed our actions, they pointed out that my order to evacuate the building meant I unintentionally spread the illness all over town.

The Mount Weather scenarios included an incident on one of the city's bridges, and it became clear we didn't have the equipment to reach it. When we returned to Minnesota we used federal funds to buy that equipment, and it would be deployed in the early minutes following the 35W bridge disaster.

I made it through the Mount Weather event without embarrassing myself, or at least without anyone telling me I was embarrassing myself. But as I packed up and went to the airport, I had an incredibly hollow feeling. Three days of imagining, in great detail, what it would be like for Minneapolis to face every manner of catastrophe took their toll. By this point in my already rocky first term I was accustomed to feeling in over my head, but now I added another emotion: fear.

We were being told in the harshest of terms at Mount Weather and back home, in repeated calls from Washington, that we had to be ready for an attack that could happen any day. I assumed some of this was overreaction and, in some cases, excessively cautious federal officials covering their behinds in case something actually happened. Even so, no matter how well I finally mastered this job that already seemed so big, I would now almost always be expecting the other shoe to drop. I would never be able to relax. Worse, if something happened, Mount Weather taught me I had a long way to go to know how to lead.

The plane ride home from Mount Weather didn't make me feel better. I didn't read or write or sleep or do any of the things I usually did on planes. I just stared out the window and said nothing as I came to terms with the fact that the stakes were now a lot higher than I ever imagined. The stark reality was sinking in that I didn't have the luxury of learning on the job.

# A Safe Place to Call Home

I NEVER WOULD HAVE PREDICTED that some of the most vivid, complex, and emotional issues I faced as mayor involved police and public safety. Nor would I have predicted that I would spend more time working on crime than any other issue—except possibly finances. It's also clear that, like many mayors around the country, I came into office unprepared to oversee an eight-hundred-member force through crime waves in a city with deep-seated community relations challenges.

I might have been unprepared, but I was not unfamiliar.

I almost never saw police in the neighborhood where I grew up, but crime was very much a part of my family's life. Having an inner-city drugstore in the 1960s and 1970s, with narcotics in high demand, meant that my parents were held up or robbed many times.

One of the only vivid memories I have of my father is from a night when I was about seven and he got a call from the police that someone had broken into the store. As he headed out the door to meet the police, I said I wanted to come. I remember my parents arguing about whether I should go, but eventually I did. In retrospect it was a real gift because seeing my father get the details from the police, seeing his frustration and anger at someone trying to steal something from him, gave me one of the only glimpses I ever had of my dad's vulnerability. It also gave me a sense of what a robbery means to someone who works so hard for something only to see someone take it away.

Crime became far more vivid when I got a little older and learned about my mom getting held up at gunpoint, two nights in a row. Putting two and two together I realized at least one of those robberies came very close to making my brother, sister, and me orphans.

After she sold the store she was out of danger, but she started dating, and later married, Chuck Mesken, who owned several apartment buildings in the neighborhood around where the store had been. Over the years the reports we heard from Chuck about Chicago and Franklin were overwhelmingly depressing, especially the drug scene that was making the area increasingly unsafe.

Chuck, whom I came to love deeply and respect even more, died a few years before I ran for mayor. By that time he had become dispirited about the neighborhood where he had spent so much time, believing it was now almost certainly too unsafe ever to return to what it had been. Thankfully, Chuck's pessimistic view of what was happening ended up being wrong, and after years of investment and hard work, by the public, businesses, and hundreds of residents, Chicago and Franklin turned around. He would be astonished and incredibly pleased to go there today, when the area is significantly safer and there are new investments all along the street.

The south side of Minneapolis turned around, but by the time I was running for mayor deep problems persisted in north Minneapolis. One of our best campaign volunteers, Deborah Cridge, lived in the north Minneapolis neighborhood of Jordan, and one day, while marching in a parade, she asked if I would visit her neighbors to talk about crime.

I joined Deborah and her neighbors on their front porch in the Jordan neighborhood, which at that time had the highest crime numbers in the city. On many levels it was just like any other conversation with neighbors on a hot summer night, until it came to talking about crime. They matter-of-factly told chilling stories about what happened at problem properties on their block, about their children witnessing crime, about how often they heard gunshots and, when they did, how accustomed they were to hitting the floor so they wouldn't be struck by a stray bullet.

Replaying the conversation to myself on the drive home I thought about those residents' experiences working with police and about what they did together as neighbors to make the neighborhood safer. Their stories were powerful, but I had to admit to myself I probably would have left by then. I began to understand that so often in high-crime neighborhoods there is a core so toughened, maybe so numb, and definitely so dedicated that they won't be scared away. Over time I found that core group in almost every high-crime neighborhood I worked in and came to understand two very basic things: almost nothing makes a place safer than committed neighbors working together, and almost nothing works without getting them on your side.

During the campaign I also got a real earful from voters about what so many saw as a broken relationship between the police and the city's communities of color, especially African Americans. The LGBT community, which had so many issues with the police when I was a crime reporter, now had officers at every rank, and this had dramatically reshaped relations with the community. It was sadly notable that during the time when so much progress had been made with police relations with one community, so little had been made with African Americans.

This had been a key motivator behind my awkward attempt to replace Chief Olson. After that failed, the chief and I settled into a very uneasy truce, much to his credit. We set aside any differences we had on a hot night that August 2002 when we received a call that one of our officers had been shot. I rushed to the hospital and met the chief, who told me Officer Melissa Schmidt, a highly respected member of the force, had been killed. She had been in a public housing building, escorting a woman with serious mental health issues to the restroom, when the woman pulled a gun out of her shoe and killed Schmidt.

I WALKED THE COUPLE OF BLOCKS back to City Hall to join the chief in announcing Schmidt's death to the media. Only a few lights were on and as we walked down the grand staircase we could only see deep shadows across the rotunda. As we got closer it became clear that in those shadows was a wall of blue.

In the middle of the night a few hundred police officers had come from around the city. They said almost nothing. The officers in that sea of faces had none of the swagger you see on so many cops as they go about their normal days. All I could see was vulnerability. Tough people with a tough job suddenly looked—in a very transparent way—scared. On a normal day cops seem like skydivers, who can only do their job if they don't think about what could go wrong. Tonight, grieving the loss of an almost universally respected friend and coworker, it was clear they saw in very real terms just how things can go very, very wrong.

For years after that night, when I walked down that staircase after a late night at work, I would see shadows across the rotunda and remember the night Melissa Schmidt died. I never forgot the looks on those faces. They reminded me of the moment I really understood the gravity of being the one person ultimately responsible for sending hundreds of people every day into dangerous situations from which they may not come back.

A few days later, when I spoke at Schmidt's funeral in the small Wisconsin town of Bloomer, I tried to capture that moment by talking about an "invisible circle of blue" that surrounds most of us. We go about our day, walking to school, taking the bus to work, going from the parking ramp to our office, completely unaware that we are protected by that invisible circle of blue. As we move freely about our daily lives, the fact that we don't have to think about the police who protect us is a testament to the fact that they are doing their job. Most of us don't realize the privilege we have of knowing our families are safe because other people's loved ones are in constant danger.

Human nature is to run from harm. Who are those people who willingly run *to* the danger? How do they feel when that danger is exposed in the deadliest of ways? What do their families think the next night when they send someone they love off to work for what could be either another routine night or that one time when fate catches up with them?

Officers I've talked to say they rarely talk about the risks of the job with other cops, but they are keenly aware of what can happen. When one of them dies, police from across the nation show up. As I walked down the steps of the church in Bloomer where Officer Schmidt's funeral was held, I saw hundreds, maybe thousands, of officers from all around the country standing at attention along the funeral procession route. They came from everywhere.

I only knew Melissa Schmidt briefly before she died. She had a reputation of being an officer who could speak to both sides of that invisible line between police and community. She had the respect of the officers she worked with every day and the people in neighborhoods she was there to protect. The day after her shooting I door-knocked all three towers of the public housing complex where she was shot with Cora McCorvey, head of the Minneapolis Public Housing Authority. We wanted the residents to know we cared and their building was safe, and to hear what was on their minds. Door after door, floor after floor, we heard one story after the next about small acts Officer Schmidt and other officers had done over the years to keep a building that could have had troubles a safe place to call home. That was the best eulogy you could ever hear.

Not every officer has that gift, to be respected both in the community and on the force. In fact, so often I would learn that being one makes it harder to be the other. It isn't surprising. Almost every image we have of bravery involves protecting against a common enemy—the other football team, the opponent in war, even the competitor in business. For the police and the community, the common enemy is the bad guys who are victimizing people. But sometimes, after years of fighting uphill battles against seemingly unstoppable crime, some cops begin to see the whole community as the bad guy. That's when a random cop on a bad night in a bad neighborhood where he's fought the same criminals for years will make a stupid comment to a victim like "This wouldn't happen if you didn't live here." It's also when you see a random cop do far worse, and the proliferation of videos in recent years has brought to life proof that that are times when some police treat some communities, especially African Americans, with a lack of respect and with force shockingly beyond how anyone would treat people they are supposed to protect and serve.

The circle of protection for a police fraternity then becomes smaller, especially when police begin to believe that the political leaders who control their work don't understand what it's like on the street from day to day. As some of them begin to think they won't get the backing they deserve when they have to make a tough arrest, the circle gets even smaller. "Us" becomes fellow officers, while "them" becomes everyone else, very often including the chief and administration and, almost always, the mayor. That's when trouble really starts.

Trouble can get even worse when the community begins to feel the same way—when the police are seen as an "occupying force" with no regard for the people they are supposed to protect. That isn't surprising either, especially when you consider that generations have passed down stories about unjust treatment where no one was held accountable, incidents that were often not believed until, again, the proliferation of videos shocked much larger audiences with examples of what so many African Americans already knew too well for way too long. It is impossible to see the videos we have seen and pretend public safety is color blind, and as heartbreaking as it was to see in my own city, it was clear to me that many police officers on our force did not have the life experiences, the training, or the cultural understanding to build deep relationships with African Americans. Not most officers, not half of the officers, but, sadly, many have also given up trying.

It's also sad, but true, that generations of bad relations with police make it intensely difficult for many African Americans to arrive at an interaction with a police officer and be able to see that person as someone who will protect and serve. That may not always be fair for an officer to have to deal with generations of pent-up anger and suspicion, but the fact remains that a cop in today's world has to understand that there are legitimate reasons why every interaction with every African American doesn't start on neutral ground.

There were so many times in those early years at scenes of crimes when I could see in the starkest of terms that the gulf between the police and the community was dramatically more complex when you crossed racial lines. It hit home for me personally in one of the least likely settings: the stands at a high school football game. As our sons were on the field, my friend Suzie Robinson and I were talking in the stands. Her son, Brandon, was the star of the team, one of the most talented football players ever to come out of Minnesota and, most significantly, a remarkable young man. I was telling Suzie that our son, Charlie, got his driver's license earlier that year, and she began telling me what it was like to wait up for Brandon to get home at night, especially when he drove through one particular suburb where he almost always got stopped by the police. Suzie, who, I am very sad to say, has since died, was white. Her husband, George, is black. The experience her mixed-race son had simply driving a car was so radically different from my son's. Unlike her, I never had "the talk" with my son about driving—I never worried the police would stop him. Two white parents, same school, same football team, same part of town, but because one of Brandon's parents was black, our two boys faced dramatically different challenges.

Years later I would get an even deeper understanding of the privilege my family and I had as white people when I read Ta-Nehisi Coates's *Between the World and Me*. The book is a letter to his son, telling him what an African American boy should learn from his African American dad. As he tried to explain to his son the life he would lead as a black man, I couldn't help but think about the hundreds of warnings and brutal explanations I never had to give our own kids, and realized how far we have to go.

These issues become more complex when they are compounded by disparities in income, and in places with already high crime rates, as they are in north Minneapolis. I saw that one afternoon when I got word that rumors were swirling in north Minneapolis that a police officer had sodomized a man with a plunger. The police denied it happened, and the account seemed suspect because it was strangely similar to an incident alleged to have happened recently in New York. But what if one of our officers actually had done that? My job was to take the rumor seriously, and within a few hours my job was also to try to find a way to calm a community that was ready to explode with rage. It was going to take a few days to sort through all the facts, but people needed a place to vent their anger immediately.

My first impulse was always to go to the scene, but our team discussed what would happen if we met with the alleged victim, or attended a street corner protest, and all kinds of red flags went up. We needed a more controlled scene, a place where we could try to lower the temperature and get to the facts. So we agreed to do a community meeting.

That night I walked into the steamy gym at Farview Park in north Minneapolis, where a few hundred people, for a couple of hours, lambasted the police department and, specifically, me. One speaker after another demanded the resignation of the officer alleged to have done this. I knew I couldn't act because we had no proof the officer assaulted the man. But I also saw it as my role to let the heat out, to hear the anger as we moved toward the truth. So there I sat in the middle of the room for two hours with people demanding answers I couldn't give. One minister dramatically marched into the room surrounded by an angry entourage and announced he had proof the incident had happened. This got the crowd even madder. He dramatically marched out without giving me a chance to talk.

The meeting ended, the angry crowd just a little bit calmer when they left. As badly beaten up as you get at a neighborhood meeting, I got into the car with Mike Kirchen, the police officer who led my security, and we drove away in silence. We didn't talk for a few minutes. He didn't know what to say, and I didn't have much left. Finally I broke the silence. Defensively, and clearly trying to convince myself, I said, "Even tonight, I still love being mayor of Minneapolis." I'm not sure he believed it. I like to think I did.

Months after that horrible night, it became clear that the officer did not commit the crime. These are the moments when you see the disconnect between the rightful call for immediate justice and the deeply necessary job an official like a mayor has to protect the rights of every person, cop or resident. Facts don't fall neatly into place by the next deadline. Due process doesn't turn on a news cycle. When the community hears about something

like sodomizing a member of the community, there is understandable out-
rage and, rightfully, people demand immediate action. But what if we had
acted against an innocent man?

WHAT I DIDN'T HAVE THE INSIGHT TO PUT TOGETHER in those
early years was that after 9/11 the threat of terrorism was remaking police
departments around the country and, unfortunately, in my own city on my
own watch. Along with protecting their fellow residents of the community,
police were now also expected to be on the lookout for abstract threats
from "elsewhere." Community policing, based on building relationships
with the people they were supposed to "protect and serve," was no longer
the only goal, and departments were suddenly flooded with sophisticated
weapons and equipment that looked very much like what you would see on
a battlefield. "Clinton Cops" grants and other federal resources that helped
pay for more officers on the beat went away, a loss made much worse by
the state's deep cuts to cities. Meanwhile federal funds for anti-terrorism
equipment and critical incident training were seemingly unlimited.

At the time, it seemed we were taking the necessary steps to deal with
this complex and frightening new task. Now it is clear to me that the threat
of terrorism militarized policing around the country and in my own city.
We devalued the importance of individual officers and individual neighbors looking each other in the eye and building the relationships that protect a neighborhood. The focus turned to impersonal weapons of war in
the hands of soldier-cops wearing helmets with darkened glass that made
it impossible to see the eyes of the human being inside. A cop is not a sol-
dier, far from it, but the threat of terrorism and the flood of weapons and
technology coming from the frontlines of Iraq into the country's neighborhoods blurred these lines more and more.

The impact, and my own inadequacy in seeing this earlier, really hit
home very late in my final term as I was sitting onstage during my last
police swearing-in. I watched an impressive class of new recruits march
down the aisle in lockstep as a drill instructor barked out orders. Impressive as they were, honed through tough training into a well-oiled fighting
machine, it became completely clear that we were training them for the
wrong war.

Yes, without a doubt, cops need to be tough, but imagine if we had
marched those recruits down the center aisle, not in unison in a drill line

but, instead, each paired with a member of the community with whom they had built a meaningful relationship. Skip a day or two of the drill training and, instead, send the recruits on foot into a tough neighborhood with an experienced community-oriented police officer and have them simply learn how to gain people's trust. Help them recognize that the neighborhoods they are supposed to protect have, it's true, lots of tough criminals, but the vast majority of people are going to be their best allies. In fact, if they don't understand how to find and nurture these alliances, no amount of weaponry and drilling will keep the peace.

In the year and a half after I left office one incident after the other— Ferguson, Baltimore, and, eventually Minneapolis—exposed the divides we have between police and community. Among the few serious regrets I have about my time as mayor, one of the deepest is that I didn't realize earlier that we were simply training cops for the wrong job.

When I left office and had the space to stand back and think about policing, especially during two years dominated by explosive police issues in Minneapolis and around the country, I spent many hours trying to understand what more could be done. It became even clearer to me that you cannot isolate the issues of police and safety without putting them in the context of a society that has growing issues with economic equity and racism. We can't expect to hire cops to insulate us from the deeper problems we aren't willing to solve ourselves. That was one reason we would eventually stop talking so much about "public safety," which sends a message that protection is the only goal, and spend more time talking about "building a safe place to call home," which says more about mixing enforcement with deeper systemic changes in housing, employment, and community building.

Demilitarizing and diversifying police forces can help bridge these divisions. Even more important would be to have a much more public conversation about the type, and level, of force we are willing to tolerate to be safe. Those choices are made every day by the police professionals, but what if that discussion became far more public so that citizens were informed about the options police have in a crisis and police gained a much deeper understanding of how far people are willing to go.

We had such a conversation in a less public way later in my time in office when we saw several tapes of officers using a series of kicks to subdue someone resisting arrest. We asked Chief Tim Dolan whether this was necessary; he reviewed the policy and decided it was not. He clarified the training and procedure, and we arrived at a balance of safety and values by making it clear that officers should not kick to subdue.

So often when someone is shot members of the public will rightfully ask why an officer did not simply shoot at the person's leg to injure him or her, like you see in so many cop shows. Police I have asked about this will often say this tactic works on television but that in real life a shot at the leg of a person who is running away has a very low percentage of success and, when dealing with someone who may be heavily armed, missing that shot could mean the lives of everyone in the area are at risk. If members of the public are in clear danger, do they support a police officer using deadly force?

These are horrendous choices, but they are, in fact, the choices that have to be made in a split second by an officer. Right now those decisions are being made primarily within police departments. Opening that topic to uncomfortable public discussions would at least mean that when a horrible incident occurs, the conversation can be about whether the officer followed the agreed procedure, instead of the much more explosive issue of values in the middle of a crisis.

WHEN YOU HEAR ABOUT A CRIME on the news it appears far more clear cut, but I was seeing over and over as mayor that the reality is rarely that straightforward. I saw a reality that had far fewer good guys/bad guys—white hats/black hats. The "truth" doesn't always come as easily as it should.

The most complex example of that reality that I encountered involved an officer named Duy Ngo. I first heard his name during a middle-of-the-night call from Chief Olson telling me that one of our officers, who had been working undercover, had been shot by other officers. I got to the hospital quickly and met his parents, a quiet couple who had immigrated from southeast Asia. It was so moving hearing about a family coming halfway around the world and being so proud that their son was a police officer. His parents, brother, and wife were rightfully horrified that he was in grave condition. Later, my wife joined us to sit with them until morning as they waited for him to get out of surgery.

I braced myself for the worst, for another officer killed like Melissa Schmidt. But there also were reports that the situation was more complex,

and the details were very confusing about why the officer had gone undercover without authorization the night before taking military leave.

Ngo survived, but for months the rightful sympathy people had for an
officer hurt in the line of duty was met with suspicion that something more
had happened. It was hard to get the truth but years later, based on the
facts and the complexity of the case, the city council and I awarded a badly
injured Ngo $4.5 million.

DURING THOSE DIFFICULT TIMES when we confronted so many issues
of public safety, I had the extreme good fortune to work with V. J. Smith, a
former drug dealer who turned his life around and now leads the Minneapolis chapter of the nonprofit organization MAD DADS (Men Against
Destruction, Defending Against Drugs and Social Disorder). This group
of men—who once led lives filled with crime and drugs—show up within
minutes of any critical incident in the city with their trademark green van
and green T-shirts. V. J. gets on his mobile mike, tries to calm the crowd,
and tries to bring the attention back to the victims and their families' suffering. I saw V. J. at so many horrible incidents, murder scene after murder scene, surrounded almost always by people in deep grief and usually
rightful anger, and never once saw him lose his cool. I would watch him
fearlessly wade into one explosive situation after another, usually diffuse
it, and always react with nothing but compassion.

Two other people I came to deeply respect from their work at those
tough moments at crime scenes were Don and Sondra Samuels, two
remarkable community activists from the Jordan neighborhood. They dedicated themselves to keeping more middle-class homeowners from leaving
the high-crime neighborhood where they lived.

The Samuelses were outraged about how differently people saw crime
in different parts of the city—an incident in a low-crime neighborhood
was covered in the media for weeks, but the same sort of incident in their
neighborhood could go virtually unnoticed. Every life lost, they said,
needed to stand for something, so they began holding their own vigils
for victims. No matter who died, or how the person died, the Samuelses
would go to the scene and pay their respects. Eventually they developed a
following of people from all around the metropolitan area, especially from
churches in more affluent areas, who came into the highest-crime areas
after the worst acts of violence to stand on a corner and mark the loss of

a life. Don continued this work when he was elected to the Minneapolis City Council and, later, to the Minneapolis School Board. Sondra attacks the root causes of crime in her leadership of the Northside Achievement Zone, Minneapolis's version of the Harlem Children's Zone, which builds cradle-to-career supports for children in the same neighborhoods where we so often stood at vigils for those murder victims.

DURING MY YEARS IN OFFICE, with so many things on my plate, it became clear that the mayor who wanted to spend time working on everything but crime—like the reporter years ago at the *Star Tribune* who wanted to write about everything but crime—was finding himself consumed by police issues.

I had a lot to learn and the more I learned the more I realized I didn't know. I made many mistakes, but I kept showing up. I knew my job wasn't to be the police chief. I didn't have to direct the force. But the force, and far more important, the victims' families and people in high-crime areas, needed to see I cared.

So when something happened I went to the scene. Over and over and over again.

# Officer Mike

---

A S PUBLIC SAFETY ISSUES gobbled up more and more of my time, and as I struggled to understand the complex world of police culture, I was spending more and more time with cops. In particular, I was spending hours each day with Mike Kirchen, the police officer assigned to me for security.

When I got elected I was strongly against the idea of having security. I value my freedom to walk down any street, and after winning a grassroots campaign by being accessible, I hated the idea of approaching people with an entourage announcing that "the mayor is here." Megan and the kids also worried about having a police officer around all the time. We wanted to protect our privacy, and we simply didn't want to have to worry about another person. Family dinner was an important part of our lives and we couldn't even imagine what it would be like to try to act normal when a cop was at the table. Would he bring his gun into the house? Would he run background checks on the kids' friends? It seemed completely bizarre, and not at all like us.

I was finally convinced to try it for a few weeks, largely because we were getting so many messages about safety in those first months after 9/11. The department picked three officers to try out and on the night of the inaugural party, Kirchen gave us a ride to the party.

When it got late he offered to take our kids home. I'm not 100 percent sure what happened on the ride home—I think it had something to do with a siren—but by the morning, I no longer had any choice about whether to have security.

The next morning Charlie and Grace launched a major lobbying campaign. "You have to pick Officer Mike!" "Officer Mike is so cool!"

Almost immediately "Officer Mike" became a part of the family. Sometimes more so than was necessary. He would show up unannounced at the house and head straight for the the refrigerator, usually with a few negative comments about the kind of food we kept in the house. He would drop me off at dinnertime, ask Megan what we were having, and, if the menu had anything to do with nutrition, he would head out the door saying, "I think I'll go to McDonald's."

He would ask Grace nosey questions about some boy. He gave Charlie and his long-haired friends no end of grief, calling them "Hair Club for Men" and trying to get them to shave their heads like he did.

To Mike's dismay I decided I was not going to use the formal-looking black Crown Victoria assigned to the previous mayor and, instead, made him drive me in a Prius Hybrid from the car pool. This fit my image but not Mike's, and other cops would pull up next to us at a stop sign and say, wryly, "Nice ride." Or when we passed by they would yell out a Flintstonesesque "Yabba Dabba Doo!"

The car became a standing joke but I soon learned it was a safe zone where I didn't have to worry about what I said. "Car 10," the police code for the mayor's car, was where I knew my phone calls were confidential. As I began to develop trust with Mike, I realized he was someone who could give me an honest opinion from the perspective of a beat cop, and this became more and more valuable as I struggled to find the right mix of ways to lead a police department.

It was a plus that Mike has an amazing sense of humor, which helped take the edge off the crisis of the day. Leaving the scene of a horrible crime, or coming out of a rough political meeting, I got some space by cracking a joke with Mike or blaring the official Car 10 song: "Theme from Shaft." It became almost a bad version of *Starsky & Hutch.* (Mike's cop buddies told him it was more like *Driving Miss Daisy.*)

PEOPLE WHO WERE WATCHING my first few months wondered how I could take the seemingly never-ending onslaught of bad news and occasional missteps. What they didn't see was that in between all the tough stuff, Officer Mike was helping to keep me sane.

A few times we overdid it. One day early on we heard that the Krispy Kreme doughnut chain was coming to a Minneapolis suburb. The news received an absurd amount of hype, and sensing an opportunity to promote independent Minneapolis corner bakeries, we came up with the idea of a doughnut contest judged by cops. We were really excited when the idea got tons of publicity, and even more pleased when *The Jay Leno Show* asked me to come on with some cops. Not everyone thought it was so funny, including the police union, which held a press conference denouncing the contest as demeaning to police.

Another time I was backstage about to give remarks to the Human Rights Campaign Fund. I told Officer Mike I was going to say how proud I was that two of the five police precincts had GLBT leaders.

"No, there are three," Mike said.

"No," I said. "There are two. Rob Allen and Sharon Lubinski."

"Nope," he insisted. "Allen, Lubinski, and Tim Dolan."

"I could swear Tim Dolan is married."

"Nope," Mike insisted. "He's gay."

As I was about to walk out in front of five hundred people and proudly declare that we had three GLBT commanders, Mike finally admitted, "Actually, Tim Dolan's not gay."

Food played a large role in everything involving Mike. It was like working with a goat; he ate *anything*.

At 6:30 one rainy and dank spring morning, we drove to Lake Harriet to meet a group of schoolkids who were on a fishing field trip. I had left the house without having time for breakfast, so I grabbed a PowerBar, took a quick bite, and then set it on the dashboard before going out to the dock to freeze with the kids and the fish none of them were catching. It was a miserable hour, and, as I was hungry and shivering on the dock, I was counting the minutes until I could get back into a warm car and finish my energy bar. When I finally got back to the car, the half-eaten bar was nowhere. Mike said nothing as we drove down the road, with me frantically looking for my food—on the floor of the car, in the glove compartment, in the backseat. After about ten minutes a lightbulb went off in my head and I turned to Mike.

"Did you *actually* eat my half-eaten PowerBar?"

His lame defense: "It wasn't secured."

POLICE SPENT A LOT OF TIME trying to get Mike to lobby me about some issue, and a fair number of them also complained to him about me. One thing never failed to get cops complaining to Mike: one of my pet peeves was cops standing around talking to each other. With all the pressure we faced trying to fund enough cops on the street, it burned me up to see a cluster of them talking to each other instead of walking around talking to members of the public. Usually I would make a comment to a supervisor, but from time to time I would just go up to the cops and say, "Don't you think you should spread out?" Whether Mike was with me or not, his phone would go off immediately with some disgruntled cop asking, "Who the hell does the mayor think he is?" Whenever we would walk by a group of cops standing together, Mike would not so subtly try to stand in front of me to block me from seeing them.

Mike also did an exceptional job keeping me safe, especially considering how many events I was doing, how many crime scenes I went to, and how aggressively I would jump into crowds at parades.

One of the most precarious was at an Aquatennial parade one year. Running from one side of the street to the other, plunging six rows deep into the crowd, I suddenly felt my hand grabbed harder than ever before in my life. A large disheveled man looked me intensely in the eyes and said, "I'm gonna get you, Rybak!" Luckily my high school wresting training taught me the best way to break a grip is to tear toward the thumb. I got free but the man jumped up and came toward me. Mike got between me and the man and slickly diffused the situation until I was a block away. Then, when the crowd was no longer paying attention, he took the man down in what we used to call a "cow catcher" move and handcuffed him.

Occasionally Mike was required to provide protection not only for me but also for others who were with me. That was the case the week before the 2004 election when I joined Josh Hartnett and Sharon Stone at a Get Out the Vote rally on the plaza in front of Northrup Auditorium on the University of Minnesota campus. Sharon Stone, who is exceptionally knowledgeable about politics, gave a tremendous speech, and I thought I did all right, but the crowd that day was really only interested in Josh Hartnett. After we all talked a group of young women swarmed around him, then more came, and more, and pretty soon as we tried to move him down the main mall on campus it got so out of hand that we worried we couldn't get him out. Mike began to lead Hartnett away, but the crowd followed and pretty soon Mike and Hartnett broke into a full sprint followed by a gaggle of running admirers. (If you are old enough to remember the Beatles' movie *A Hard Day's Night* you get the idea.) They finally escaped and Mike snuck him down a back staircase, where he called a car to take Hartnett to safety.

Every once in a while Mike would take a day off, and was usually replaced by another great officer named Mark Klukow. Ironically, the times Mike had Mark work for him were the times when something weird would happen. That was the case the night Mark was supposed to meet me and my family at the funeral of a homeless man that was being held under a bridge downtown.

There were complicated logistics getting to the funeral: I needed to drive across town, meet my family at a designated intersection in south Minneapolis, and then meet Mark downtown. As I pulled up behind my family's car I was preoccupied with a call I had gotten about some complex deal points in the Sears building redevelopment. I finally hung up, got into the car with my family, and drove to the funeral expecting all to be well.

When we got there, Mark looked as if he had seen a ghost and asked if I was OK. He had just heard the announcement on the police radio: "Car 10 in transit. Mayor's whereabouts unknown."

Apparently I was so preoccupied when I pulled up to meet my family at the intersection that I didn't turn off the car. Those early Prius models were like golf carts; they stopped when you took your foot off the gas but rolled on an incline. After I drove off with my family in their car, the Prius apparently slowly rolled across the street and into a snowbank. When the police realized it was my car, and I was not in it, there was panic.

THERE WERE VERY FEW TIMES when I was in danger—which was surprising considering how many times I was at crime scenes and how much I was putting myself on the line. There were also times when I went too far.

One night there was a holdup at a south Minneapolis convenience store, and a couple of hours later Mike and I walked around the neighborhood to make sure people were calm. The store was open again, the neighborhood was quiet, and everything seemed fine. Just as we were about to leave we heard a lot of noise coming from a nearby beauty salon. Looking closer we couldn't see inside the windows because it appeared the place was filled with smoke. We walked over, opened the door, and were overwhelmed by so much smoke you would have thought Bob Marley's whole family was inside inhaling blunts. In the salon were about six beauticians, seemingly busy with customers at their stations in the middle of the night.

One of them recognized me and through the haze she yelled, "Rybak, get in here. I wanna cut you!" Maybe she was threatening me, or maybe she was offering to give me a late-night hairstyle, but we thought it best not to stick around and find out.

Another very hot summer night we were in north Minneapolis when we heard a report that water pressure was dropping precariously low because people were opening up fire hydrants all over the neighborhood. We pulled up to an intersection where water was gushing out into a flooded street filled with kids getting soaked. About five police cars were pulled up, with the cops staying inside. In a move of pure idiocy, I got out of the car, let the kids get me wet with their squirt guns, and then walked into the crowd. I started talking to a group of teenage girls: "This looks like a ton of fun, but if it goes on for another hour there probably won't be any way for anyone in this neighborhood to shower tomorrow morning."

"We can't shower?!?" they said to each other.

"And none of your neighbors can either."

The realization that they, and their neighbors, were going to really stink in the morning was apparently enough to get the girls to help convince the crowd to let us close the hydrants.

My gamble worked that time, but as I thought about it I realized my showy move also created great risks for Mike and all the other cops who would have paid the consequence if something had happened to me. Over the years I learned to pick my shots.

BY 2005–6, when the city was at the peak of youth violence, Mike and I spent a lot of time talking about crime. He was never officially listed as a member of the Youth Violence Prevention Task Force that eventually got a lot of credit for developing a community safety plan, but he made huge contributions behind the scenes. About a year after we launched the plan, Minneapolis schools agreed to have a select group of officers become school liaisons. Their job was not to arrest kids but to build bridges. This sounded very familiar to Mike, because it was the kind of police work he and I talked about for years in Car 10.

One day he came into my office to tell me he wanted to leave the mayor's office to work in the schools. I hated to lose Officer Mike, who played a much bigger role for me and my family than many saw. But it made me very proud to see him become a role model for kids in a couple of the toughest schools in Minneapolis. He and Mark Klukow also started a nonprofit called Bike Cops for Kids, which funded them to spend summers riding bikes through the streets of north Minneapolis. Mike would go on to become a full-time bike cop, spending the day building the kinds of community relationships that are too rare.

Every once in a while he stops by my office. Not surprisingly, he usually comes right before lunch. And I make sure I haven't left any half-eaten PowerBars "unsecured."

# Jesse Ventura and Two Drunk Firefighters

THE 9/11 TRAGEDY hung over much of my first year in office, and on its first anniversary there were moving tributes on the Government Center Plaza and at the Lake Harriet Band Shell.

There was also one tribute that didn't go quite as planned.

To mark the anniversary, New York City flew firefighters around the country to Minneapolis and other cities that had sent police and fire teams to help in those days after the tragedy. New York firefighters had now acquired rock star status, and we wanted to do things right when we learned we would host two of them. We planned a major media event at a fire station and a presentation before a Timberwolves basketball game. Governor Jesse Ventura's staff arranged for him to sit with me and the firefighters during the game.

We sent two of our most upstanding firefighters, Roger Champagne and Stan Murzyn, to meet them at the airport, and I went to the fire station to get ready. Cameras from all the stations showed up, and the Minneapolis firefighters were really charged up to meet the heroes. There was tremendous excitement as their car pulled up.

The car door opened and in about five seconds I recognized a problem we hadn't anticipated. When New York firefighters were on a flight, in uniform, in those days, what was the one thing everyone on board wanted to do? Buy them a drink! Or two. Or, by the smell of these firefighters, several.

We managed our way through the press conference; I gave some lofty statement about honoring those in the line of danger, and the firefighters said a quick and sincere (if slightly garbled) thanks. My daughter, Grace, who was eleven at the time and always observant, asked why they were hugging people so much, but aside from that we seemed to have dodged a bullet. Now all we had to do was go to a basketball game.

After a quick stop at my house to change, I went to the arena and met the firefighters, who had also made a stop. When New York firefighters are in a bar, in uniform, in those days, what was the one thing everyone wanted to do? Buy them a drink! Or two. Or . . . you get the picture.

Then I remembered we had to make a pregame presentation on the floor. Fortunately, it's very easy to get to the center of a basketball court: you just follow the straight line that leads right to the middle. I did that. The firefighters did not, weaving their way back and forth across the line until they ended up somewhere in the general proximity of where we were supposed to be. I took the microphone, issued another lofty statement about honoring those in the line of duty, and one of the firefighters grabbed the mike and muttered, "Thank you."

We careened our way back to our seats in the lower bowl and there was Governor Ventura. He gave them a nice greeting and we all sat down: the governor, me, and the two firefighters to my right. The four of us started making small talk, but it was quickly clear that the firefighters had no interest in me and only a passing interest in Ventura. They had fixed on two women to their right, who seemed equally as drunk as the firefighters, if not more so.

As the game started the governor and I were talking but then he, too, got distracted. All those years in pro wrestling apparently taught him something about fan behavior because he launched into a massive taunting of the ref, complete with a series of f-enheimers. He has a very loud voice.

In those days there were probably no better known people in the country than New York firefighters and Jesse Ventura, so, as you can imagine, a lot of people were looking at us. We were right in the center of the bowl where everyone in the building could see the scene of two drunk firefighters hitting on two drunk women, the governor of the state cussing out the ref, and, in the middle of it all, the mayor of Minneapolis.

I thought back to a few hours earlier when I was walking out of the office. Peter Wagenius handed me the talking points about the state's local government aid I was supposed to raise with the governor. I laughed at him. "Peter, there's no way on God's green earth Jesse Ventura wants to talk about local government aid at a basketball game!"

Then, right after launching another f-bomb at the ref, Ventura turned to me and asked, "What do you think of that new local government aid formula?"

# The Ripples of 9/11 and Paul Wellstone

---

**M**Y PLATE WAS SO FULL the first year I didn't have much time to pay attention to the rest of the world, but it was impossible to ignore that the country was changing. The 9/11 tragedy had turned from something to mourn into something that was being used to justify a lot of actions that I felt had nothing to do with what happened in New York and to the Pentagon that day. Most significant, a massive wave of anti-immigrant fervor had overtaken the country, and it was having a highly negative impact on the many immigrants in our increasingly diverse city.

Much of the fire was being fanned by the Bush administration in Washington. One day I saw an Internet news item that several U.S. cities were on a terrorism watch list, including, to my surprise, Minneapolis. I didn't know what it meant to have our city on a "watch list," but in those days, in a very nervous country made jumpier by near-daily changes in terrorism alerts, this seemed like a very big deal. It seemed even stranger that, after checking around various departments, no one had mentioned this to the mayor of that city.

After finally tracking down the U.S. Justice Department official in charge of the report, I asked the simple question: why? "It's because you have so many Muslims." My simple follow-up was, "Have you seen any evidence that the Muslim community in Minneapolis is connected to terrorism?" He said no but that I had to understand how dangerous Muslims were; they represented a very real and present danger. "All Muslims?" "Wherever there is a Muslim community," he said, "we see a great potential for terrorism."

I came back with: "Our city is doing a lot to prepare to fight terrorism, but I don't think every Muslim is responsible for 9/11 any more than every Christian was responsible for Hitler." Then things got hot and he told me the Justice Department would keep a very tight watch on my city, but he still gave me no information about what the problem was or what we should be doing about it.

The more we talked the more concerned I got that a country built on the values inscribed on the Statue of Liberty was being led by a government that was using the tragedy to dramatically overreach on limiting civil liberties.

A couple of nights later Megan and I were at a dinner at the Kaplans and I pulled Paul Wellstone aside. I told him about the exchange and how I was worried about what kind of intelligence work was happening in Minneapolis that I didn't know about. I was also very worried that the exchange I had had with the Justice Department official would jeopardize the millions of dollars in federal grants in play for our police and fire departments.

Wellstone understood from the start what I was talking about. We both knew that, like it or not, we were facing real threats and needed to do some things that made us uncomfortable. But he also gave me some chilling examples of what else was going on in Washington at the time. He promised to help and was going to assign a staff person to work directly with me. He was running in a very tight reelection in a period when terrorism was a big issue, but he didn't flinch for a second about taking this on.

I never had a chance to fight this battle with Paul Wellstone because a month later, he was gone.

I FOUND OUT about the plane crash while I was standing outside the council chamber and heard Council President Ostrow announce, "We have just learned that Senator Wellstone's plane has crashed."

Stunned and horrified, I thought about all the great things he had done for me. I also thought about what it meant to lose the progressive fighter we needed in a state, and a country, that I saw pulling dangerously to the right after 9/11. We got back to my office, turned on the TV, and just as I said, "Thank God Sheila is still here," we learned that Sheila Wellstone had died, too. As had their daughter, Marcia Wellstone Markuson, a beloved Democratic activist and teacher with whom I had campaigned the week before. Also gone were Professor Mary McEvoy, staff member Tom Lapic, and pilots Richard Conry and Michael Guess.

The eighth victim was Will McLaughlin, an energetic young aide I got to know and like at a series of campaign events earlier that year. That summer, while campaigning with the senator in Minneapolis, Will was driving the Wellstones in the front car and we were following in another car. Realizing we were headed to the wrong address, I got out at the stop sign to explain, but as I approached their car, the light changed, drivers began honking, and Will yelled, "Get in!"

Without thinking I jumped in as if we were in a chase scene in a movie. Will took off with me halfway out the door and halfway on Sheila Wellstone's lap. We laughed about it for half an hour and you could tell Will was loving the experience of being around the theatrics of the Wellstones and the campaign. Thinking about losing an innocent young person like that at the very beginning of what would have been a great life was almost more than I could take.

Devastated as so many others were by the loss of those fine people, I closed myself off in my office for several hours until Megan finally came and helped me paste myself back together.

The next morning, waking up after a vigil on the steps of the Capitol and nonstop news coverage, I went downstairs full of grief. Then I got an idea, hopped straight in the car, and drove to the home of Alan Page, the former NFL star and, from 1993 to 2015, a Minnesota Supreme Court justice. I rang the bell, his wife, Diane, answered, and without any introduction I blurted out, "Alan should run for Paul's Senate seat."

Shocked by the idea, and full of grief like I was, Diane opened the door and called Alan downstairs. I had long believed Alan was one of the best candidates we had in the state and a few years earlier had unsuccessfully tried to talk him into running for the Senate. A deep thinker but definitely not a political schmoozer, Alan quickly rejected the idea back then, but we all agreed that the loss of Wellstone had changed everything. It would be a campaign of only several days and we needed a person with high visibility whom people trusted. We also knew there was a very real danger that we could lose the seat to Norm Coleman just as the Iraq war and so many other issues were in the balance. After several hours Alan and Diane had definitely warmed up to the idea, and I left saying I would start making some calls to float the idea.

What we didn't know was that at the same time the Wellstone brothers were calling on former vice president Walter Mondale, asking him to run.

Once I heard Mondale's name I knew he was the right choice, but I have often wondered what might have happened if Alan Page had been the candidate.

In the next few days I became involved in hosting some of the dignitaries coming to Minneapolis for the memorial. I was as depressed as I could be, but so was everyone around me and I did my best to hold it together. I went to the airport to pick up Bill Bradley, whose presidential campaign I had been working on when I really got to know Wellstone. As he got off the plane, I looked in his eyes and for some reason this was the moment, standing on the tarmac at the charter terminal, that all my grief came pouring out. You don't get to choose when you lose control, but Bradley was remarkably supportive.

Megan and I sat at the memorial between Bradley and another of my political heroes, former U.S. senator Bob Kerrey of Nebraska. Just down the aisle was Congressman Jim Ramstad, a Republican who had been close to Wellstone because they worked together on mental health legislation.

There were some touching and inspirational speeches that day, but the one that was most remembered was by Wellstone's campaign treasurer and friend Rick Kahn. Kahn, clearly hurting badly, talked about the passion Paul brought to his work. Kahn's remarks then took on a more political tone. To those of us who had been part of the Wellstone rallies, it first sounded almost like a balm, as if somehow we could keep rallying around that kind of passion in politics even when the Wellstones were gone.

Immediately Bradley and Kerrey saw it differently, saying to each other early on that the speech had crossed the line into the inappropriately political. It got more uncomfortable when Kahn called on Ramstad to honor Wellstone by switching sides in the next election and voting for Mondale.

Kahn was deeply committed to Wellstone and he was speaking as a wounded friend opening his heart. The impact, though, was immense and created a serious problem in the election.

THE MORNING AFTER THE MEMORIAL SERVICE, sitting at my desk, I couldn't concentrate on anything. Staring out the window, my mind on nothing but the incredible loss, I saw across the plaza that, strangely, the famous Wellstone green bus was parked next to the Hennepin County Government Center. I ran down and standing outside was Dick Miller, the volunteer driver of the bus in both campaigns. He was delivering all the flowers from the memorial to domestic abuse centers as a tribute to Sheila Wellstone's commitment to the issue.

Miller was lost trying to find all the shelters, so I just left work, hopped on the bus, called Megan, and we spent the next few hours sharing a bit of the Wellstones with the people who were carrying on the work. That afternoon spent delivering flowers regrounded me in the comforting fact there were many, many people who could and would keep up the Wellstones' many fights.

But there was a more immediate concern. The next day at the Democratic campaign office Bill Harper, who was managing Roger Moe's campaign for governor, showed me a poll. Moe, Mondale, and every Democratic candidate in the state were now behind, and falling, in what was being attributed to a backlash over politicizing the memorial. None of us had any great ideas about how to turn things around.

I campaigned as hard as I could over the next few days, and so did many others. The night before the election, I crammed into a union hall in south Minneapolis with a few hundred other activists for our final Midnight Madness literature drop.

We picked up our packets, filed outside into the parking lot where a stage was set up, and a few of us gave speeches to rally the crowd. After we finished Mondale stepped up. I still vividly remember the image of this man who had seen so much, his breath visible in the cold night air, trying to comfort the mostly young crowd of activists who were physically exhausted and emotionally played out from days of grief. Public service is a noble cause, he said, and you should never give in to cynicism. Learn to accept the defeats that make the victories better.

He told us exactly what we needed to hear, just as he would twenty-four hours later when it was clear he had lost the election. I went home deeply depressed but knowing I had just witnessed a great man remind us why what we did mattered.

# Balance

B Y THE END OF THE FIRST YEAR I felt like I was working all the time. I saw almost none of my friends. My social life revolved around work and a never-ending diet of "events" interrupted by "galas" that usually still felt a lot like "work."

Megan was now handling almost everything to do with the house, our deteriorating finances, and a lot of scheduling. She had quit a job she loved because it was almost impossible to balance work and run the family, and now there was so much more on her that it was almost impossible for her to take on any freelance projects. If a project did come her way she often had to turn it down because it was a conflict with my work.

People would ask, "How do you do it all, R.T.?" The simple answer was, "Megan." She was also the reason we still kept a remarkably balanced family life. The key was family dinner. I would leave early, work all day, go to an event almost every night and most weekends. The four of us, though, had dinner together four to six nights a week. My schedulers, and at least most of the community, understood that I was likely to show up to almost anything—*but not between 6:00 and 7:00 P.M.* Remarkably Megan cooked a great dinner almost every night.

After dinner I would go to evening events, but I would be back home by 8:30 to say good night to the kids. Since Charlie and Grace were both early risers, I usually was able to see them for breakfast.

When we were telling the kids about my running for mayor I very directly told Charlie it meant I wouldn't be coaching his baseball team. As things turned out, this is one thing I didn't let go. My co-coaches, Dave Drake and Paul Fling, did more of the work, but after some wrenching days I would make my way to the park. I think Charlie liked my being there, but on a lot of levels that very rare oasis was even better for me.

I remember one night after a particularly bad day, I was coaching first base; my mind wandered and suddenly I realized our kid had been picked off base. That was the coach's fault and, more important, what I was doing wasn't fair to the kids. I had to find a better way to focus, not only when I was on the baseball field but also in everything I was doing. I'm naturally very distractible and with so much on my plate it was getting out of hand.

I started doing something simple that really worked. If I found my mind wandering I would repeat to myself, "Be here. Be here. Be here." Somehow that helped me find the blinders I needed to ignore what had just happened or what I worried was coming next. The only way to make it work was to be extremely present in that place at that moment. It meant those around me, who did the policy work and, more importantly, scheduled the meetings, had to take on much more. Like a trapeze artist who lets go of one swing because he knows the next one is coming, you have to trust your team.

We went through several schedulers in the first couple of years, and because it was a tough job, few stayed long. Eventually Janna Hottinger took the job, teaching me that sometimes the best people who work with you are very different from you. Janna is a true unflappable Minnesotan who doesn't waste a lot of time on chitchat. She doesn't answer the phone by talking about the weather or asking about your aunt Sally's bunion. You call and she says, "Hello." Period. A few days after she started I went into her office and asked what was wrong; every time I called she seemed mad. "That's just the way I am," she said matter-of-factly, and she went on to be the incredibly efficient ballast that let me focus on being in the moment.

You learn a lot about yourself when you are repeatedly pushed to the edge of your comfort zone. All that budget work with all those spreadsheets started to remind me that one of the reasons I did so poorly in school was that I had a lot of trouble internalizing information on paper. About eight years earlier, when I was vice president of Internet Broadcasting, the founders of the company did everything on white board. For me it was a breakthrough. Something about seeing information on the boards made it easier for me to quickly understand complex issues and especially easy to connect seemingly disconnected issues. As I learned this about myself, people got used to my jumping up to translate what they were trying to tell me onto the board with multicolored markers. And as I figured out how to explain these issues to myself, I developed the simplified shorthand to explain it to constituents whose tax dollars were involved. Complex issues about debt and pension obligations were distilled into analogies about the family's credit card. Decisions about debt paydown versus infrastructure investment were put in terms of a corner restaurant choosing to bank the night's profits for a cushion in slow months or spend them on remodeling to increase business.

We took this show on the road for a series of neighborhood meetings and faced a lot of skepticism that residents would give up a night to sit in a community center to hear a dry presentation of the city's budget. This sold people in Minneapolis short: our community budget meetings were packed. Those meetings had some of what you would expect—people rightfully mad about property taxes yelling at the new mayor. Mostly, they were really helpful sessions for residents. It was good that my own limited understanding of city finances early on in my term had taught me to translate a complex billion-dollar budget into understandable English. (If you have to educate yourself you may as well educate the people whose money you are using at the same time.) It also helped that Wagenius, who led the budget work and, like me, came into office knowing almost nothing about city finances, is a remarkably quick study. Hour after hour he turned himself into an expert. He and the budget staff created a tool called "Budget Math" that simplified the key choices we had into a worksheet that gave the crowds a way to help us set priorities. We weren't patronizing people by asking them for their opinions about what we already planned to do. We were figuring things out as we went along, and it was really useful to have honest feedback on where residents wanted us to cut and invest. Unfortunately we were usually teeing up choices for residents that let them pick their poison: do you want fewer cops or less annual street maintenance? But those meetings were truly beneficial.

WITHOUT REALIZING IT AT THE TIME, we were fundamentally changing the way we solved problems. In the early months, with so much blowing up in our faces and with some of our best campaign supporters now alienated, we had developed a "bunker mentality": we closed the doors of the office, worked with a small group, and tried to find ways to protect ourselves from everyone and everything.

Those public meetings helped us change course. Instead of shutting ourselves off, we took the toughest, most complex financial problems directly to our constituents. Doing so gave us the confidence that using the brainpower of a whole city—a city filled with active people who generally wanted us to succeed—was a whole lot better than depending on just the few people around us.

Applying this approach to snowplowing convinced me to break a campaign promise. During the campaign I talked a lot about improving the way we got snow off the streets. In Minnesota this is one of the most visible city services, and there was no reason it should take three days. I promised we would take a hard look at having the entire city plowed within twenty-four hours.

We set up community meetings to talk about this exciting new plan— and a lot of people didn't see it that way. One speaker after another at those meetings taught me that a city with so many dense neighborhoods without garages needed those three days to sequence the streets where people should move their cars: move cars off the side of the street with odd-numbered buildings, and once that side is cleared, move them back so that the plows can do the even-numbered side. My brilliant idea for twenty-four-hour snowplowing was a perfect plan for a mass towing of cars. The people who would suffer the most would be renters, students, immigrants, and the poorest people in town—the people without garages or with language issues—who would be hurt the most by paying the towing fine.

The city staff had told me about some of those challenges, but they soft-pedaled the problems in what I now see was an effort to please the new mayor. Hearing the drawbacks so clearly from both residents and the snowplow drivers who came to those community meetings convinced me my campaign promise was a bad idea.

Community meetings on the budget and snowplowing may seem like the driest possible part of running a city, but they regrounded me in a simple fact: when you get in trouble you should open the office doors, not close them. In retrospect I realized that my most successful times as mayor were when I got that right, and my least successful were when I got it wrong.

This felt so much closer to how I wanted to run the city, and who I was. I had first gotten onto people's radar through community activism and online forums. I won a grassroots campaign, with virtually no support from the usual power players, because I listened to people door to door. I had just come out of the Internet business environment, where open source coding and Napster were showing the world the value of putting what you had out in public and building something bigger together. Opening doors simply opened more doors.

It was an important midcourse adjustment, but in retrospect, it may have given me too much confidence that developing a strong bond between the people in office and the people I represented was all I needed.

Between those in office and the voters who put them there are a whole lot of people who can ultimately make it easier to get things done. The people who work in government, the partners in other governments, the people who do business in the city, the people who run community and nonprofit organizations: none of them were strong partners coming into office and, to date, I had done little to get them on board. It would take me awhile to realize that, and longer to figure out what to do about it.

I SAW CHANGES in the way I was doing the work, and changes in myself. It was clear that for at least the next few years I would be taking a lot out of myself, both physically and emotionally. Part of that was OK because being around people usually charged me. The answer to any problem remained: show up. The more I was out in public the more energized I became. My staff quickly realized I got double-charged when I was around kids, so they starting looking for ways I could spend more time in schools and parks.

At the end of the most grueling days, which sometimes had been filled with up to fourteen different events, I would come home practically bouncing off the walls. "And then this happened, and this happened, and they said this, and I should really do that . . ." Megan's unenviable nightly task was to wade through the many faces of this overcaffeinated version of the person she married, and somehow try to find the one she could live with.

I was also getting unexpected support from an unexpected place. A few years earlier my sister, Georgeann, had started going to back to our childhood church, St. John the Baptist Episcopal in Linden Hills. I had fine memories from when I was a kid, and they left me with a spiritual core that has stayed with me all these years, but I didn't see that church being part of what I needed at the time. If I spent any time committed to a church, I thought, I wanted something more activist, more connected to the life I was leading. Georgeann kept talking about St. John's and after a while Grace said she wanted to go there with her cousin Tori. Then Megan joined them. Finally I went along and realized it was a very special place, especially because of the minister, Mariann Budde.

Even before I was elected, Mariann's sermons built a bridge between the public life I was living and the spiritual life I recognized I needed. Once I got elected, and as I struggled with finding any more energy after a depleting week, her words became even more powerful. After listening to her sermon and taking communion I would close my eyes and visualize my completely empty vessel filling up to go back at it. This was all very new for me. I have always had a pretty deep spiritual sense, but church was never a place I had gone for this kind of support. I really needed it then.

Mariann's sermons also helped frame what I was saying to the community in some of the toughest moments. One Sunday I was really down, thinking I had to go to a funeral of a baby who had been shaken to death by a parent. What in the world could I possibly say that could be helpful? Sadly I can't remember all the words in Mariann's sermon that day, and I can't do it justice, but she talked about how having faith doesn't mean you expect God to be a puppet master who pulls the strings for every move. Faith gives you the power to reach inside yourself to find the part of you that can rise to what needs to be done. A few days later, with that idea in mind, I told the congregation at the child's funeral, "The hand of God did not strike a child. The hand of God holds all of us so we can bear this kind of pain." When I delivered that line to the tense funeral at Shiloh Temple, the crowd immediately responded, and I knew it was Mariann who really made them feel at least a little better.

To the great credit of the people at St. John's, they almost always let me be R.T. and not The Mayor. Once, half a minute after the closing song, someone came up to me in the sanctuary with a zoning complaint, but that was exceedingly rare. St. John's became the place where I could let down my guard and be myself as part of a spiritual community filled with people trying to connect what happened on Sunday morning with the rest of their lives.

During some of the hardest moments I had faced, or would face in the future, church was where I felt the most supported. That was certainly true the week Paul Wellstone died, when, after spending so much time being the strong one helping many other people who felt such a deep loss, I let myself go. In the middle of an exceptionally powerful sermon from Mariann about Wellstone, I finally felt comfortable breaking down and crying as hard as I wanted. In a roomful of people on their own journeys, I didn't feel judged and I didn't have to act like The Mayor. I just felt surrounded by support.

# New Year, New Governor

I N THE FIRST FEW DAYS of my second year in office, Minnesota changed governors.

When Jesse Ventura was elected four years earlier, in 1998, he said he "shocked the world"—and that really wasn't much of an overstatement. People around the world were truly amazed that Minnesota had elected a boa-wearing ex–Navy Seal pro wrestler.

There were times when Governor Ventura lived up to this cartoon version of himself, including the *Playboy* interview in which he said he wanted to come back as an extra-large woman's bra. There were also times when it amazed many, including me, that this guy who once made his living body-slamming people could be so remarkably thin skinned with the media.

There was also another side to the governor. He was far more intelligent and perceptive than the cartoon version painted of him and, sometimes, painted *by* him. I saw that the night at the basketball game when he shocked me by starting a detailed conversation about local government aid policy.

Governor Ventura's greatest strength was that he surrounded himself with really talented people. That started with his top appointment, Steven Bosacker, who built a strong, tightly meshed team of mostly nonpartisan professionals dedicated to making government work.

Steven was also a friend. I didn't overplay the friendship, but when I really needed something from the state or the governor it sure helped that I could call the guy at the top, or at least next to the top.

When I first got elected I tried very hard to recruit Steven to come to Minneapolis. I tried again when Ventura left office, but Steven wanted to work in Europe. (In a few years I would try again and, in a move that would be the key to much of my later success, Steven finally said yes.)

The political fiasco surrounding the Wellstone death also helped tip the governor's race to Republican Tim Pawlenty. The House also went to Republicans. That was immediately an enormous problem for Minneapolis and for me.

ON ELECTION NIGHT in November 2002, standing at the Democratic election party, Hennepin County commissioners Peter McLaughlin and Mike Opat and I heard the results, turned to each other, and said in unison, "We're screwed!" Actually I remember using a stronger word.

By the beginning of the year, as those Republicans were about to take office, it was clear that things might be even worse than we thought. I had been campaigning a lot for Democratic House candidates around the state and had seen a lot of anti-Minneapolis literature, usually Republicans from Greater Minnesota saying the city was getting more than its fair share from the state. Now that they had won and were ready to take office, those claims were becoming more and more extreme.

Right before the session was to begin in January, our lobbyists took the city council and me to the Capitol to meet with some of the Republican leaders. Representative Mary Liz Holberg from Lakeville, a southern suburban community, addressed the group with a clear message that things were simply going to get a lot worse for Minneapolis. The city had too much waste, was too liberal in its social policies, and was going to have a far tougher time getting support for anything, including its local government aid.

As I met with other legislators I got an earful about what they thought were past wrongs committed against their part of the state, and against them, by what they said were arrogant Minneapolis legislators who controlled committees when Democrats were in the majority. A lot of their stories were from years ago and often involved legislators no longer in office. I reminded the Republicans that much of what they were mentioning happened when I was in Boy Scouts, but that didn't seem to matter.

The governor was worse, and he usually mixed his message about ending the perceived free ride for Minneapolis with a healthy dose of misinformation about how badly the city was managed.

The session started and proved to be the nightmare we were expecting. The governor's budget proposed a major cut in local government aid to

Minneapolis, and he cleverly wrapped it in a lot of rhetoric about the good citizens of Minnesota no longer "bailing out" the dysfunctional city of Minneapolis. It was time for the city to stand on its own two feet, he said.

Actually the opposite was true: Minneapolis was sending more than twice to the state than it was getting back in return.

St. Paul's mayor Randy Kelly didn't help much. He made some of the same public statements I did about the need to maintain a partnership between the state and its largest cities, but in public and in private he was making it clear that St. Paul was the city that functioned well and Minneapolis was the problem. I had no legislative experience and he had been there for much of his career. He worked the system well, including getting the legislature to pass a mostly symbolic but damaging resolution to move the Twins to St. Paul. He also worked his contacts to try to exempt St. Paul from some of the cuts and target more to Minneapolis.

Our logical allies weren't helping—which made it even more moving to get help from those who had nothing to gain. At the peak of the attacks, with very little support coming from anywhere, I was standing in the hall getting questioned by a group of reporters before I was about to testify. Karen Anderson, the Republican mayor of Minnetonka—a city that got no local government aid—joined the group and made one of the most compelling cases anyone could for our city. She said that as Minneapolis rises and falls, so does the region, and she reminded people that Detroit had some great suburbs that were being dragged down because of their failing central city. At a fairly dark moment, Mayor Anderson made a selfless defense of the common good that went beyond her own self-interest, and, for at least a rare moment in those days, we got out a bit of our message.

Another rare ally was Congressman Martin Sabo, an exceptionally strong political veteran who mastered the art of bringing dollars back home to help his district. In February of that year I got a matter-of-fact email from Sabo's office listing the truly amazing appropriations he had secured for the city. With so much crashing down around us I felt truly blessed to know that someone with this kind of skill was on our side.

I really wanted to thank Sabo and it happened to be Valentine's Day, so we had a tray of red and white cookies on the conference room table. I put a bunch of the cookies on a nice plate, grabbed a beautiful bouquet of flowers someone had put on the table, and walked them over to Sabo's office with a note: "I love Megan tonight but I really love Martin Sabo today." This is strange enough but more so to those who know the exceptionally

low-key Sabo and wonder what this no-affect Norwegian thought when he
got a Valentine from the mayor. It got stranger when I got back to the office
and David Fey asked what happened to that beautiful bouquet of flowers
his partner Michael delivered for Valentine's Day.

GOVERNOR PAWLENTY KEPT UP THE ATTACKS on the city but
never to my face. He would drop a nasty aside in a press conference when
we couldn't defend ourselves, and in the rare moments when we were
together, be as nice as he could be. During one media interview, when I
had had enough, I unloaded on him, telling the reporter that Pawlenty had
been on the city council of suburban Eagan when that city erected a lavish
city hall, so I thought he was in no position to be lecturing us on public
spending. He built his career at a law firm in downtown Minneapolis, so
I thought he was in no position to be questioning the spending of a city
whose well-maintained streets he used and whose police department protected the streets where he could walk safely.

It sure felt good to let out all my frustration, and the governor didn't say
anything. Council member Barb Johnson definitely did. She unloaded on
me as hard as I had unloaded on Pawlenty, reminding me of the difference
between speaking for myself and representing the city at a critical time
when millions of dollars were at stake. She was right, and it was really the
start of many years of Barb playing the role of leveling both me and council members in a city that needed to work harder to build partnerships.

Minneapolis got crushed in the final bill. All that effort getting the city's
financial house in order was suddenly thrown up in the air. Back at City
Hall, we had to create a new budget for the current year and a new version
of our five-year financial framework. For those of you scoring at home
that means in the first eighteen months in office we cut five million dollars
to balance the previous administration's budget; created a budget for the
coming year; created a five-year financial framework to make up the substantial debt we inherited; and re-created the current budget and framework to react to the massive state cuts—all while creating a new budget
for the coming year.

The state cuts were worse because they were retroactive, so cutting a
year of revenue in midyear meant cuts had to be twice as deep. If you had
already paid half of a person's annual salary, you would then have to leave
empty a vacant twelve-month position.

In the budget-cutting work we had done up to this point we shaved line items here and there, then went back for deeper cuts. The health and regulatory departments, and the economic development staff, suffered—critical but low-profile administrative areas like finance suffered more. We had mainly stayed away from the core areas of public safety and public works. Now we had no choice but to look everywhere.

The budget choices we made to react to the midyear and ongoing state cuts fell, again, on those departments we had already cut deeply the first time around. And this time, they also fell hard on the public safety and public works departments.

Public works actually got the deepest cuts, as we very reluctantly took an ax to the budget for street maintenance. But the biggest public pushback came from our cuts to public safety. The firefighters were the most vocal, organizing protests in the community and confronting me at City Hall.

City budgets are about a lot of things, but more than anything, they are about people—so you can't make much of a dent in a shortfall without an impact on payroll. The only two ways to cut payroll are to limit salary increases and cut positions. We thought it was better to save jobs and services, so we imposed a 2 percent salary cap on all employees. The employees were not happy, but they grudgingly acknowledged that if everyone gave something we could save jobs. We also eliminated many vacant positions, so, like a game of musical chairs in which the person who doesn't move fast enough loses out, the departments that didn't respond quickly by completing a hire were out of luck long term.

IN THE END we were able to make significant cuts with remarkably few people actually losing their jobs. The consequence was that employees did more work and got less money so that coworkers lower on the seniority list could keep their jobs.

It was easy to feel, and act, like the Minneapolis city government was the victim, but it was also clear something deeper was going on. That was illustrated at a meeting after the session with the Youth Coordinating Board, which brings together the leaders of the city government, park board, school board, county government, and some nonprofits working with youth. We went around the table and, one by one, laid out what the state cuts meant for each of us. When we finished we paused for a second as the magnitude of what was happening sunk in. It was clear the people who would be hit the hardest by the state cuts wouldn't be people in the city government—cuts would have the greatest impact on the children in the city, especially those living in poverty.

Near the end of that meeting, someone made it clear that things were even worse because the slowing economy meant it would be the worst year. for summer jobs in decades.

When I got back to my office, I told my staff I needed to get on the phone and find a way to line up some summer jobs for kids. That's how we started STEP-UP, the summer jobs program that would become the most meaningful project I ever worked on as mayor.

With the help of Achieve Minneapolis and U.S. Bank CEO Richard Davis, by the time I left office STEP-UP had become one of the country's most successful youth employment programs. To date twenty-two thousand young people have worked in almost every major business in Minneapolis. Eighty-six percent of them are kids of color and more than thirty percent are from immigrant families. Together they represent a "farm team" for a global community that not only has an exceptionally diverse population but, now, a global workforce.

Living in a city ideal for bikes always gave me a leg up.

Muscle Beach at Lake Harriet in Minneapolis. My childhood was blessed with lakes and parks because early Minneapolis visionaries saved the city's best spots for everyone, not just for a few rich homeowners.

If I had met Megan earlier, I wouldn't have had to do shameless stunts to get dates, like participating in the 1983 book *Where the Good Men Are: A Look at the Most Interesting Single Men of the Twin Cities.* Photograph copyright Sandy May.

On the construction site of the Norwest Building during my time as director of development for the Downtown Council, where I got hands-on experience in commercial real estate. Photograph by Regene Radniecki.

My seven years as a reporter for the *Star Tribune* helped teach me how Minneapolis works—even when we were on strike. Here I am with fellow reporter Roberta Walburn and photographer Art Hager. Photograph by Earl Seubert.

Campaigning around the University of Minnesota was always fun. Photograph by Jerry Holt.

Our campaign had almost no political experience and almost no money, but I believe we won the first mayor's race because of hundreds of one-on-one conversations on front steps, like this one with Gene Olson in northeast Minneapolis. Photograph by Tom Sweeney.

Campaigning for me was an aerobic activity, and no one enjoyed sprinting through a parade more than Representative Keith Ellison. Photograph by Joey McLeister.

Our parade routines became more elaborate over the years, including this well-intentioned dance move we tried at Gay Pride. Photograph copyright Renee Rhodman.

Usually not one to keep my mouth shut, I learned in the first mayor's race to let the other candidates attack each other, as in this TV debate with Mayor Sharon Sayles Belton, council member Lisa McDonald, and Hennepin County Commissioner Mark Stenglein. Photograph by Judy Griesedieck.

The first campaign over, the family intact, we played a game of football in the front yard a few days after the election, just as I was getting hit with the reality of the challenge ahead. Photograph by Marlin Levison.

Walking through Minneapolis neighborhoods was a regular activity during my years as mayor. Photograph by Glen Stubbe.

As we began to get the budget and crime under control, I played a larger role in schools and with kids, including this effort in 2007 to connect summer programs with transportation. Photograph by Richard Tsong-Taatarii.

This Youth Farm Market with Emmanuel Roberts would become part of the Homegrown Minneapolis project that Megan inspired, which brought together gardens, school lunches, small-batch food manufacturing, farmers' markets, beekeeping, and a range of efforts to reframe the local food system. Photograph by Anthony Souffle.

In summer 2002, the morning after Officer Melissa Schmidt was killed in Horn Towers, I door-knocked the three-building complex to reassure residents like Ruthie Carter *(right)* and Hester Wilson. Photograph by Kyndell Harkness.

I met so many people experiencing real trauma, like this man watching everything he owned burn in an East Lake Street fire. My goal at these times was simple: show up, listen, and let people know the rest of the city cared. Photograph by David Joles.

There were no words to describe the surreal and tragic scene in those early days after the 35W bridge collapse. Photograph by Kevin Rofidal, Edina Police Department.

# City Builder Starts
# Building City

I DIDN'T GROW UP dreaming about becoming mayor so that I could devote almost all my time to finances, emergency preparedness, crime and police, which is how I was spending most of my first two years. I wanted to be a city builder who helped turn Minneapolis into one of the world's great cities.

It sounds like a grandiose idea, but it makes more sense when you know that when I about twelve years old I started faithfully reading every column by Barbara Flanagan in the *Minneapolis Star*. In an era when Americans had fallen in love with suburbs, Flanagan was an unapologetic city booster. Her columns about all the great things happening in Minneapolis would probably sound too chirpy in today's world of journalism, but to an impressionable kid who loved where he lived, she laid out every week a road map for a better Minneapolis: big ideas like recapturing a riverfront that was then walled off by train tracks, and hundreds of smaller ideas like having sidewalk cafés and painting buildings so that they added color to drab winters. I gobbled it all up, believed even more in Minneapolis after each column, and began to convince myself someday I could make some of this happen.

I didn't come into office prepared to run a complex police department or a 1.4-billion-dollar operation in a financial crisis. I did come into office with significant background in how to build a city.

For years before becoming mayor I was learning how to make a city grow—in my time as a reporter covering city development, in helping to attract new businesses when I was at the Downtown Council, and in crafting downtown development projects when I got my real estate license and worked in commercial real estate. I wanted to be the kind of city-building mayor who transforms neighborhoods, builds thousands of affordable housing units, attracts businesses, creates big transportation visions.

After a couple of years in office those goals seemed further and further away, and it didn't look as if it was going to get any better. Our financial mess with the budget cuts meant we would have far less money to get things done than in the past—and with one crisis after the next, it was looking as if there would never be a good time to make a physical mark on the city. Worse, the economy was slowed by 9/11, so not only was the city in no position to spur growth, but the private sector wasn't doing much either.

There was so much I wanted to do: build more transit and affordable housing, redevelop more of the riverfront and north Minneapolis, redo an aging Nicollet Mall, renovate the Farmers Market, and so much more. It seemed unlikely that I would get to any of those projects.

If the city couldn't directly have much of an impact on economic development we could, at least, make it easier for the private sector to invest. The one thing I knew we could accomplish right away was deliver on a campaign promise to restructure city government's convoluted development and planning functions.

Almost immediately after I was elected, I was working with McKinsey & Co. on a plan to merge all these scattered functions into a single department. McKinsey came back several months later with a brilliant, if depressing, first look at how economic development worked in the city. More accurately, they showed how things didn't work: boundaries overlapped, one person's responsibilities contradicted another's.

The consultants illustrated a laughable number of lines of authority swirling around each other like a bowl of spaghetti. The so-called Spaghetti Chart they produced was tied to a series of recommendations to make it easier to do business with the city.

A subtle, but hugely important, part of the work is that it was not written from the perspective of city government. McKinsey wrote its report from the perspective of the scores of people they interviewed who were trying to help Minneapolis grow: An entrepreneur trying to open a restaurant ran out of cash before opening because it took so long to get a permit. A developer building space for a company moving to town almost lost the tenant because he was getting conflicting directions from the Planning Department, the Heritage Preservation Commission, and the independent development agency.

The other key to the report is that the end result wasn't to build buildings. The end result was to create jobs. This meant that getting a permit for an existing company to expand was often even more important than building a new office tower. It also meant rethinking staffing; the entire operation was built on transactions—a permit, a building, or even a subsidy—but there were very few people within the system who could simply be that resourceful city employee who could let a growing business know someone in City Hall was on its side.

The overarching theme was that we wanted to give far less to individual developers with individual projects and invest more in the common ground that helps everyone succeed—transportation, public space, public buildings. This meant alignment needed to move beyond traditional economic development to include public works and business regulation.

My chief of staff, David Fey, led a working team to put McKinsey's recommendations into action with two very unlikely partners: council members Gary Schiff and Lisa Goodman. Schiff and Goodman were usually my harshest critics on the council, but they also both knew development and I would need them to get something big done.

Working with the volunteer McKinsey team over the next few months we developed a sweeping redesign. We would merge the city Planning Department and the independent Community Development Agency. This would change the absurd situation that had two city departments giving often-conflicting recommendations that usually played out in drama on the council floor. A very effective small-jobs program would be moved from the Health Department into this new department, and the Regulatory Services Department would be re-formed to cut red tape that made it harder to build in the city. All this together would form a new, single department called Community Planning and Economic Development (CPED).

The idea sounded straightforward enough, but it had huge, controversial implications for the already skeptical unions and a workforce that generally saw the McKinsey report as an indictment of their performance. A series of community meetings showed that residents loved the Spaghetti Chart and its promise of making better use of their tax dollars. But in one contentious meeting in north Minneapolis, McKinsey's lead, Tim Welsh, was shouted off the stage when he took the brunt of years of frustration with city development efforts that the crowd said had left some parts of Minneapolis behind. In response, Welsh and his team, now aware that presenting plans at community meetings was different from presenting in a corporate boardroom, rewrote parts of the plan to build in more intentional measures to close disparity gaps.

THIS NEW SUPER-DEPARTMENT also needed a director with enough strength and savvy to lead this big change without the city's job growth engine shutting down.

We found the right person to make that happen. Lee Sheehy had held leadership positions with Vice President Mondale and the Metropolitan Council, as well as had a long history in business and law. Almost as important, he had more key contacts in the first three letters of his Rolodex (we still used those back then) than most of our team had established in our whole careers. Convincing him to lead this new economic team brought the political skill we had been missing, and he helped even more when he added Mike Christenson to his team, who was as much of an experienced insider as Sheehy.

The political coalition we built with Goodman and Schiff, as well as council member Scott Benson, helped us move the first phase of the reorganization through the city council. It would take a long time to implement the whole plan—the last piece was in my budget eleven years later—and the workforce was slow to accept some of the changes. But by focusing on both the strategy and the necessary politics, moving a few boxes on an organizational chart had created a significantly more powerful, focused, economic development department.

WITH OUR ORGANIZATIONAL CHANGE came a new philosophy that was in stark contrast with the oversubsidized projects of the past. By saying to developers that the city's job was to make it easier to do business in the city, to take care of the common ground and set the table for private investment, we were also saying, "We want you here but you have to stand up on your own two feet."

During the campaign I explained this in shorthand by saying the mayor needed to "put down the checkbook and pick up the phone." This meant we must communicate clearly which businesses the city wanted to help grow and work hard to make it happen. The mayor would need to be a salesperson: cutting through red tape and investing in transportation and other pieces of infrastructure that would help everyone succeed. Further, we should try to use public subsidy only when it was absolutely necessary and, when we did, negotiate hard on the public's behalf so that people stopped thinking the city was a chump.

We then focused this new leadership, department, and philosophy on a massive eyesore: the former Sears building in south Minneapolis. The area around the building had made major progress before I took office, in large part because a partnership of the city and private companies spent years investing in economic development, housing, and crime fighting. The Sears building was another story. The second-largest building in the state, it was empty and had few prospects, an unavoidable sign of weakness in a fragile part of town that could go either way.

Ryan Companies won the competition to develop the project, and we all quickly agreed the most likely candidate to be a major tenant was Allina Health System, parent company of the nearby Abbott Northwestern Hospital. Sheehy and Christenson, the latter of whom used to lead the Allina Foundation, laid out a series of contacts with each of the company's board members. This set the stage for me to make the pitch to the new CEO, Dick Pettingill, to move Allina headquarters in from the suburbs.

None of us knew much about Pettingill because he had just moved from California, but a few minutes after we sat down for breakfast at the Minneapolis Club I knew I was in serious trouble. Pettingill wasn't much for small talk, so after a few awkward minutes and some dead air, I launched right into my peppy sales pitch. He listened, stone-faced, and every few minutes leaned into the table and, emotionless, asked a question: "What is the condition of the building?"

Knowing it had been vacant for several years, and was filled with bat dung, I said it "had great bones."

Silence. I nervously added, "They just don't make buildings like this anymore!"

"What about crime?"

Knowing that violence in this neighborhood had helped earn that part of Minneapolis the title "Murderapolis" just a few years earlier, I said, "It's really a lot safer."

"Can you make it easier to get there by building a freeway interchange at Lake Street?"

Knowing that interchange had been one of the most controversial and complex debates in south Minneapolis for many years, I admitted that getting it in place would be very hard but added, "I'll try."

This went on for about an hour: the enthusiastic salesperson with his metaphorical checkered sport coat trying to find some way to break through to a poker-faced executive who had absolutely no connection or debt to the city. The good news is that my nose didn't grow, but I left utterly convinced that there was absolutely no chance.

Pettingill turned out to be far more complex than I knew, however, and over the coming months he slowly convinced his board to make one of the boldest, most transformational decisions ever made in Minneapolis. They moved their 1,400 employees into the refurbished Sears building, now called the Midtown Exchange. Showing the kind of leader he is, Pettingill's "CEO suite" was a main-floor cubicle. Because we were able to attract Allina, Midtown Exchange also revitalized a dying corner with a hotel, and both affordable and market-rate housing.

On the ground floor we developed the Midtown Global Market. The market came about after the developers proposed leasing the prime retail space to a giant Latino grocery. This would have been an attraction to the growing Latino population nearby, but it would have also put out of business many of the Latino entrepreneurs on Lake Street. Instead, we worked with the highly effective Neighborhood Development Center and created the market as a center for food-oriented businesses owned and operated primarily by immigrants. Today, this active marketplace—where you can get food from around the world—is one of Minneapolis's top tourist destinations and has incubated some of the city's best restaurants.

This massive undertaking showed the importance of our development reorganization. In fact, pulling together all these pieces to meet Allina's timeline may have been impossible if we had to cross all the old, overlapping boundaries.

An added side benefit of the Allina deal was that the city's business community started to see we could get things done. One of those alliances we began to develop during that time was with Jim Campbell, who then led Wells Fargo's banking operations in Minnesota and was a key Allina board member who had helped sell the plan inside the company. He had been a Sayles Belton supporter in the last election and was highly skeptical of me when I first got elected. Our partnership deepened when we landed Allina and got even better when I helped him raise the private funds needed to help make Midtown Global Market sustainable.

WHILE WE WERE PUTTING TOGETHER Midtown Exchange, we received terrible news: Target had decided to close its store on Broadway

Avenue in north Minneapolis. The store was the most visible business on the challenged main street of the most distressed part of the city. When one of the country's top retailers, a hometown company, makes one of its very rare store closings, the rest of the retail community takes notice . . . and runs the other way. We didn't think any retailer in America would lease the building now, which essentially said that Target was wrong in its hometown. Even if we could get one of those liquidator stores it would send a horrible message that the already-troubled street was going down even further.

We decided to focus on a different kind of retail and address the neighborhood's food desert by going after a grocery store. A market study showed there was a lot more spending power in the neighborhood than expected of a place with such marginal retail. People from the area were going other places to shop, in part because they thought north Minneapolis stores weren't as good as those in the suburbs. This is a common problem in low-income inner-city neighborhoods, where residents with the greatest needs often pay more and get less. That was even true of Target, which had made few improvements and kept a smaller product mix than at suburban stores. Why shop at an inferior Target if there was a better one a short drive away?

Armed with the market study—and a partnership with north Minneapolis council members Barbara Johnson, Natalie Johnson Lee, and Don Samuels—we made the pitch to Cub Foods that they could succeed. The key, we said, was that they had to develop a first-rate store that convinced people in the neighborhood to keep their surprisingly strong buying power close to home. They agreed, and the new Cub store quickly became a community hub and a source of pride.

ONE OTHER BIG EARLY VICTORY in community development came from our environmental work. For many years the largest source of air pollution in Minneapolis was the Riverside Generating Station, a coal-fired power plant whose plumes wafted over a wide band of neighborhoods that had, by far, the city's highest childhood asthma rates.

Shortly after getting elected I partnered with a group of community activists who had been fighting the plant for years. They were led by the feisty Fran Guminga. Her brother was the priest at St. Hedwig Catholic Church in northeast Minneapolis, and the plant had been such a prominent part of the community that it's depicted in a stained-glass window in the sanctuary. It may have been where many members of the congregation worked, but Guminga thought the plant was also making a lot of people sick. She and her neighbors reminded me a lot of the people I had worked so closely with fighting the seemingly unwinnable airport noise battle years before. Like good community activists, they said they were happy I was on board, but kept pushing me to do more.

Council member Paul Ostrow, who represented the area, and I went to Xcel management. We said we wanted the plant converted to cleaner natural gas and that they could partner with us as we brought the issue before the Public Utilities Commission. If they didn't want to play ball, they could fight us—but they should know we were prepared to fight hard.

The Xcel team agreed to partner. They said the biggest challenge would be that they would have to seek a higher rate to pay for the conversion and that the business community would resist. I said the city had bigger utility bills than most of those businesses, and I would testify that we supported the increase—even in our rough financial position—if it meant that more kids could grow up without asthma attacks.

It was during this period that I deepened my partnership with state representative Keith Ellison. His district was on the other side of the Mississippi from the plant, and we had both seen the maps we believed showed that the plumes moving across the river were causing health issues for his constituents, especially children. While we were partnering with neighbors in northeast and negotiating with Xcel, Keith was holding powerful community meetings that illustrated this was a classic case of environmental injustice where those most in need were hurt the most.

It was a strong coalition and after a series of meetings with the Public Utilities Commission, we won the rate increase to convert the plant. There was an added bonus: the commission also approved a plan to clean up two other coal plants, one in St. Paul and the other in Stillwater.

I CAME TO REALLY ENJOY working with Keith. We were from different parts of town, with a different base of constituents, but he had a fire and independence I admired, and we had a similar grassroots approach. We were the two political leaders who first began working with the emerging Somali population. He was also one of the only other elected officials who would run a parade route with me, and we would compete with each other to see who could crisscross the street faster to shake another hand. (You will notice in the picture section of this book that he and I are running together but I am ahead. I rejected the picture that had him in the lead. He can use that in his own book.)

Keith and I were also two of the only high-profile political leaders protesting the Iraq War. I had enough on my hands without worrying about a country on the other side of the globe, but I was outraged by the attacks on Iraq. Before the invasion, when Dick Cheney and company started what turned out to be a misinformation campaign about "weapons of mass destruction," I looked for ways to lend my name to protests. At one of them, standing on the Government Center Plaza in front of City Hall, Keith and I looked around at the crowd and realized we were the only elected officials there. We were mystified and angry and wondered, "Where was everyone?"

This wasn't an isolated event. In the first couple of years after 9/11, it was hard to find many places where progressive voices were being heard. Unlike later years, when Democrats dominated state government and Barack Obama was in the White House, I was a rare high-profile progressive— and knew I needed to find ways to broaden my voice.

One great opportunity grew out of a conversation with Mayor Greg Nickels of Seattle. We were both ashamed that our country was standing in the way of signing the Kyoto Protocol to create a global framework for fighting climate change. We agreed this wasn't our job, but we also knew the people of Seattle and Minneapolis wanted action. Nickels drafted the U.S. Conference of Mayors Climate Protection Agreement of 2005, and I was one of the original signers who committed to having my city try to meet the standards of Kyoto. The Riverside conversion, coupled with many of the transportation and energy actions we took later, would move us a long way in that direction. The Mayors Agreement went on to have several thousand signees from around the country, and is sometimes cited as one of the few signals the United States sent at that time to the rest of the world community that many of us, unlike the Bush administration, wanted the United States to partner in the global climate battle.

ONE CHANCE TO RAISE my progressive voice that I didn't take came in the middle of 2004 when Mayor Gavin Newsom started performing same-sex weddings in San Francisco City Hall. As soon as I heard I walked into my chief of staff's office to talk about whether I should do that too. David Fey and I agreed that we would follow the lead of organizations like OutFront Minnesota that had been fighting these battles for years. The groups we asked came back with the strong stand that I should not do any-thing because at that time their battle was to try to keep same-sex marriage off the ballot, where they were sure they would lose. Performing weddings in Minneapolis City Hall could fuel the efforts of groups trying to get an anti-same-sex-marriage amendment on the ballot, and if we lost that vote it could take years to overturn it.

So we did nothing and, sure enough, over the next couple of days it all played out like we hoped: Republican legislators were saying at the Capitol that they had to put an anti-same-sex-marriage amendment on the ballot "so R.T. Rybak doesn't start performing marriages in Minneapolis City Hall." When reporters called I told them I had no plans to follow the lead of Mayor Newsom. The issue died.

Until then I really didn't get the full importance of all the inequity chal-lenges the GLBT community faced: Shouldn't we be fighting more for issues that had a more direct impact on people's lives, such as employment justice, housing discrimination, police bias, AIDS, and other health con-cerns? Weren't civil unions enough?

Fey, who was in a longtime relationship with his partner, Michael, taught me that marriage isn't just a compact of love but also a legal compact tied to more than five hundred pieces of Minnesota law and fourteen hun-dred pieces of federal law. By being unable to marry, he and Michael were denied many basic protections concerning issues that very directly affected them, such as property and hospital visitation rights. He didn't have to add the inequity it created in the office. Every night I went home after a rough day, Megan heard my complaints, helped paste me back together for another day, and, in return, the citizens of Minneapolis extended my benefits to her. David went home to Michael every night to get support for dealing with exactly the same set of issues, but they didn't get the same rights that went to Megan and me.

I didn't get to start performing weddings then. But I got the education I needed to help make it happen later.

# McManus

CITY BUILDING may have been my passion, but I could never get too far away from crime and police.

After my awkward attempt to replace Chief Olson had blown up in my face, I was determined not to repeat the fiasco. We settled into a peaceful coexistence. He deserves a lot of credit for graciously and professionally working with the guy who tried publicly to fire him.

As Olson's contract approached its expiration date we got ready to hire a chief the right way. Too much of my time was already being eaten up with public safety, and we wanted a leader who could aggressively and visibly command the department. Too much of my time was also being eaten up trying to bridge the divide between the police and parts of our community, so we wanted a leader who would be out in neighborhoods building partnerships.

I didn't expect the chief to take crime and police off my plate totally. The chief has to lead the force, but the city's residents need the mayor's engaged oversight. The top–down command-and-control structure of the police department implements safety strategies, but the mayor represents the people and ensures that each of the department's actions reflect community values. It would be a huge mistake simply to hire a chief and step back. I wanted to stay closely involved, but I needed a far more activist chief who would lead.

I also wanted the next chief to be African American. It wasn't quite that simple, but in a way it was. I knew from my days as a police reporter, and my time campaigning and now as mayor, that there continued to be deep-seated issues between the Minneapolis police and African American residents. That is true to some degree in all cities, but more so in

Minneapolis—much deeper, in fact, than even across the river in St. Paul, which, to this day, I can't fully explain.

Simply putting an African American in the position of police chief would send a positive message. More important, I saw few things harder than being an African American working your way up through a police department, which was why it was such great training to bridge all the divides in our city. To get to be a top cop as an African American you had to explain to other African Americans why you wanted to be a police officer. You had to explain to mostly white colleagues why African American parents worried about their kids getting stopped for DWB ("driving while black"). You had to see the black kid you are arresting as yourself at that age and find a way to win him back.

One of the great joys of working with so many police officers over the years is that I learned many, many of them can bridge racial divides regardless of who they are. Crossing the boundary between two worlds every day as a person of color, especially an African American in a profession where that isn't easy, just makes it much more powerful. I wanted a person with that direct experience at the very top because we needed those values at every level of the department.

I told our search firm I wanted a diverse pool—not one person of color, but many. They gave me what I wanted, and I flew to the national police chiefs convention and interviewed some very good candidates of color from around the country.

When Bill McManus, the last candidate, came in, I have to admit the first thing I thought was, "Too bad he's white." We talked for about half an hour and when we finished I realized it had been, by far, the best conversation about race and the police I'd had. He wasn't a slick talker but instead just very insightful about the issues communities of color face with police. He also clearly saw those issues in very personal terms, connecting them back to his experiences growing up in a mixed-race neighborhood in inner-city Philadelphia.

On the plane ride home, I reread all the bios and went back over my notes. McManus was clearly at the top of the list. Was it really right for me to look at all those candidates of color and pick the white guy?

When I was narrowing the list to three with the internal team, the names leaked to the media. One of them was McManus. The other two were African Americans, including Charles Moose.

Moose became well known nationally a few years earlier when he was chief of police in Montgomery County, Maryland, at the time the Beltway Sniper was at large. Moose's articulate, calm press appearances during that crisis launched him into a national career as an author and speaker. He was qualified, but I was worried Minneapolis would be just a quick stop on a fast-track career, so I asked him the question everyone else had: "Why do you want this job?" He said his life had taken him too far away from the police work he loved. He was famous and doing well, but his experience was to walk into one auditorium, give a speech, walk out, go to the next town and do it all over again. He wanted to get closer to the street. It was a real reminder that fame isn't the end in itself so many people make it out to be. Ultimately, however, I was too worried that Moose had so many opportunities in front of him he wouldn't be around long.

Then I got a call from William Finney, the St. Paul chief I had tried to lure away during the Olson mess. "It looks like you have an interesting issue on your hands," he said.

"I sure do!"

"I think you should pick McManus," he said.

I was somewhat stunned, especially because I had talked with Chief Finney at length about the need to make a dramatic breakthrough in order to improve police relations with African Americans.

He said he had talked to Chuck Ramsey, a highly respected chief who led the department in Washington, D.C., when McManus was starting his career. He gave Finney a glowing recommendation and said McManus had especially strong abilities to build partnerships with African Americans. Finney said he thought this was a breakthrough moment for race relations with the Minneapolis police.

The Minneapolis City Council was not as excited. Some wanted other candidates, and some were supporting the Police Federation, which was pushing for a local candidate. On the day I announced I was nominating McManus, seven of the thirteen council members announced that they were opposed. Unless I changed one of those votes, McManus's nomination would go down. That would be bad for the city, bad for the police department, and very bad for the green mayor who would now have his second strikeout with the police department in one term.

That night I couldn't sleep, going over in my head how I could get the votes, the consequences of having the Olson fiasco followed by being unable to get my nomination for chief approved. I realized that if we lost this we would lose the chance to move the department where it needed to go. It would also be all too clear that I was not a very effective mayor and make it even tougher to get reelected. The stakes were high and we were already losing.

Around 4:30 in the morning I got up, went into the office, and started writing on a white board all the people in the community whose support we would need to get McManus approved. By about 7:30 other members of the staff came in and by 9:00 we had about a hundred names in small writing on the white board, each assigned to a staff member to contact. Chief Finney gave us a huge boost by meeting with a group of significant African American residents and getting their strong support.

We dropped pretty much everything else in the following days, and the office turned into a campaign-style war room with team members and volunteers working the phones. When we got another person on board we went back to that giant white board, circled the name, and in a couple of days had a broad and significant coalition.

We continued to try to get one of the seven opposed council members to switch sides. Finally Barb Johnson agreed that McManus would not have been her choice but that the mayor needed a chief he could trust. She changed sides, McManus was confirmed, and the vote was seen as a major victory for those who wanted change in police community relations.

The confirmation was a high point, and it demonstrated that we could be effective, but almost immediately McManus ran into trouble. Two weeks after taking office he suspended three members of his top team, saying they could have been involved in a complex story about destroying a confidential memo. The most senior of them was Deputy Chief Lucy Gerold, a twenty-seven-year-veteran who was highly respected in the community and by me. (I tried to get her to consider being my first chief of staff and talked to her about being interim chief when I was trying to remove Olson.) It didn't help that she had also been a candidate for chief when McManus was picked. Gerold strongly denied the charge about the memo. The attorney she hired was David Lillehaug, a friend of mine and now a Minnesota Supreme Court justice, who brilliantly worked the media and who quickly elevated the controversy into a major media event.

The momentum we had gained from the confirmation seemed to vanish almost immediately as the community tried to understand this complicated "he said, she said" internal squabble. Gerold returned to the force and clearly came out better than McManus in public opinion. The chief we worked so hard to get on board had been badly damaged in the public eye.

McManus would go on to make some important moves to open internal investigations and bring more African Americans into higher ranks in the department. He was, however, unable to promote more people of color, especially African Americans, into the officer ranks.

At the time of his appointment there was great excitement that this would finally be the moment when the police department would build stronger bridges with communities of color. To the great disappointment of many, including me, the appointment never lived up to that promise, and when McManus's contract expired he left for San Antonio.

# Making the Save, Giving Up the Rebound

---

G ROWING UP watching a lot of Minnesota high school hockey—the best in the country—I learned there are two ways to judge the performance of a goalie. The first and most obvious way is to see how many goals the player gives up. The second, less obvious but very telling way is to see where the puck goes *after* the save. The best goalies not only make the save but also find a way to control the puck or direct it back to their teams. The less effective goalie can make the save—even a spectacular one—but if the rebounds consistently set up the other team for another shot, eventually that goalie is going to give up a lot of goals.

I wish I had learned earlier that there is a very similar dynamic in politics. The most obvious way to judge politicians is to observe how they handle a crisis. The other, less obvious but very telling way is to see whether the way they solved the problem left another problem unsolved.

Without knowing it, I had turned into the wrong kind of politician: I was tackling some really big issues, and generally having a lot more success than even I had anticipated, but in the process I was making enemies a lot faster than I was building new partnerships.

Some of this is just inevitable, especially considering some of the no-win choices I was facing. But I also knew that too many natural allies were being forgotten on the sidelines. Too many alliances that could have been easier to build went unrealized. If you added it all up there was now a critical mass of people who now thought it was not in their best interests to have me succeed.

Unfortunately I was not the only one who noticed this, and a lot of other people saw it more clearly than I did at the time. With about a year and a half left on my term I started hearing that other people were going to run against me in the next election.

We also heard that the unions representing police, fire, and some city employees had commissioned a poll that they were telling people showed I was vulnerable. We didn't know if that was true because we didn't use any polls in the first race or once I got into office. People who talked to the unions about that poll said it showed that the two issues most important to city voters were safety and education. Any political rookie can tell you safety and education are key issues in almost every city election, but this political rookie's sprawling agenda was so broad, so seemingly unfocused, that it was clear to us that an opponent running a campaign centered on cops and schools could do well.

The most obvious candidate within City Hall was council member Gary Schiff, who was consistently on the other side from me on almost every issue. When a crime or fire occurred he told the media I was underfunding the police and fire departments. When we made tough budget decisions to spend less on housing so that we didn't have to make such deep cuts in the police and fire departments, he held a press conference to say I was breaking my promises on affordable housing.

Even the times when we tried to work together were complex. Early Mother's Day afternoon, 2004, I was making dinner for Megan and the family. Just as I was filling the cavity of the chicken with lemon and onion, Gary called. Bad timing, I thought, but really great he was trying to work together. He told me he wanted to lead a smoking ban in the city and asked for my help; I said thanks for the heads-up, and for a minute felt good that Gary was trying to bring me in early. Two minutes later the phone rang again and it was a reporter from the *Star Tribune* who said he had been working with Schiff for several days on this issue and wanted my immediate comment on the plan. So much for working together.

Schiff and others who were considering running for mayor quickly stepped back when one of the strongest possible candidates stepped forward. Peter McLaughlin had represented Minneapolis for twenty years, first in the state legislature and then on the Hennepin County Board of Commissioners. He was very well known and very well respected, especially within many of the groups most upset with me. He had also been very close to Mayor Sayles Belton and was generally assumed to be her heir apparent when she was done.

We saw McLaughlin as a serious contender. The only other candidate who I thought would be tougher would be Lucy Gerold, who had just come through the controversy with McManus. Gerold had a strong base of support around the city, and her attorney, Lillehaug, is one of the craftiest political minds in the state. She never showed any public interest in running.

The dynamic between McLaughlin and me got complex very quickly because the commissioner and the mayor were in many meetings together. One of us would talk, eyes around the room would shoot to the other, people would whisper to each other about what something one of us had just said *really* meant. It was a lot like high school, when everybody knows which two guys want to date the same girl, and a lot gets read into every move in the lunch room, only in this case both of us wanted to take the whole city to the prom.

One by one we heard about the impressive list of people and groups supporting McLaughlin: the police and fire unions, the American Federation of State, County and Municipal Employees (AFSCME), a majority of the most active downtown business leaders, and a lot of the DFL establishment who hadn't supported me the first time. There were also some pretty significant people who had supported *me* the first time.

We were also really surprised by some who stayed with me, including two of McLaughlin's colleagues on the board of commissioners: Gail Dorfman and Mike Opat. A number of key legislators, such as Keith Ellison, Margaret Anderson Kelliher, Frank Hornstein, and Scott Dibble, also supported me. Council member Lisa Goodman, who had opposed me on many issues, supported me for reelection, as did council member Barb Johnson.

McLaughlin had a strong campaign announcement, focused as we knew on safety and schools, and almost immediately the police and fire unions went on the attack against me. They soon hit close to home, holding a press conference in front of the corner store in my neighborhood where there had been a robbery.

In the early calls, as I tried to line up support, I spent a lot of time listing my accomplishments, including straightening out the budget, restructuring economic development, and redeveloping the Sears building. Almost always the conversation quickly devolved into the caller raising an individual issue that had not been resolved.

It was also clear that unlike the first race—when having no record allowed me to focus on vision and sweeping initiatives—this time I was going to spend a lot of time making a detailed case for the past four years. Some of my best work, I thought, especially fixing the budget and reorganizing the development arms of the city, wasn't usually obvious to the average voter, especially right away. It was clear this kind of obscurity wasn't going to give me much help in getting votes and I was going to be spending the reelection fighting about issues I wouldn't have chosen. Politicians, like sports teams, usually do better on their home field, and this was definitely going to be an away game.

After a few weeks I had to come to terms with the fact that I was in a difficult race that I could very well lose. I could tell that after so many nights of tough calls with unhappy delegates, my confidence was shaken. Hearing people repeatedly say, or at least imply, that they thought I was not up to the job started to take a toll.

When the first debate came, with all these doubts going through my head, I thought the most important thing for me to prove was my competence, so I intentionally dressed for the debate in a conservative suit and muted tie. Just as I was about to walk down the stairs Megan said "Try this" and handed me a tie—the flashiest tie in my closet, one with big blue and red color blocks that you can see from fifty yards away.

Megan doesn't usually dress me, and if anything, is the one telling me to tone it down, but in this case she was right. That little touch, and the message that came with it, helped send me out onto the stage in Washburn High School's cavernous auditorium knowing I had to take control and not let anyone else define the substantive work I had done as a failure. From start to finish I took the offensive, defended every inch of my record, and, most important, spent much of the time painting a vision for the future that had gotten me elected in the first place.

Near the end of that debate I ad-libbed a line I would repeat many times up to the end of the campaign. The line confounded McLaughlin because it was true: "People in Minneapolis like Mayor Rybak and they like Commissioner McLaughlin, and they want us both to keep our jobs."

The simple fact was that if McLaughlin won, I would no longer be working for the people of Minneapolis. If I won, we both would. So really, I didn't have to make the case that he was bad for the city—just that we were both good for Minneapolis.

THE FIRST PART OF THE CAMPAIGN was the toughest, and the single worst day was the endorsing convention. For most of the convention I felt like a punching bag, much as I remember Mayor Sayles Belton had been four years earlier. Many years later I can finally admit there was a certain poetic justice in seeing a guy who used a convention to unify the many factions with gripes against an incumbent mayor, now having the tables turned on him.

It was definitely not my room.

The convention started with an organizing snafu that delayed balloting for several hours as the entire room was reseated. We had recruited scores of first-time delegates to the convention, but as hours went by without any balloting, those political newcomers were increasingly baffled and disillusioned. With no real start in sight many of them left before the convention had even officially begun. In the meantime, serious attack pieces against me were going out, especially from the police and fire unions, as well as AFSCME. As good as my convention speech had been four years before, this one was mediocre at best. Balloting finally started; it was tight, and the lead switched back and forth.

Near the end of that very long day I was standing with one particularly hostile delegate who was in my face about—at that point—who knows what. I stood with my hands clasped behind my back as I tried to keep calm in the face of a tirade that was going on and on and on. Just as I was ready to lose my cool, I felt a small hand slip between my own clasped hands. Megan, having seen what was happening, came up to my side and simply held my hand. She didn't have to say anything; I knew at that point I may have been feeling alone, but, thankfully, I wasn't.

After many hours McLaughlin had a slight lead but not enough for endorsement. We adjourned with no winner but a big moral victory for McLaughlin.

At a postmortem the next day, Sam and Sylvia Kaplan gave me the same advice they had been giving me for four years. This time I finally listened: I ran as an outsider but that didn't mean I should try so hard to keep experienced political people away. I needed to reach beyond my team and include more smart, savvy civic leaders.

The Kaplans and I pulled together a few people who fit that description and had a series of meetings with this "kitchen cabinet." We agreed I had to focus both my message and my agenda. In addition, I shuffled the staff and brought on a new communications director, Jeremy Hanson, who had deep political experience.

I also changed campaign managers but for other reasons. Bill Hyers was an intern in my first campaign; eager, humble, and an incredibly hard worker, he did whatever it took. He then went on to Don Samuels's successful campaign for city council and, in the next two years, ran nonstop campaigns around the country. He had just run an exhausting coordinated campaign in Alaska when I talked him into managing my reelection. But now he needed a rest and we hired John Blackshaw, who had strong Minnesota political connections. (Much later, Hyers would go on to run Bill de Blasio's surprising win in the 2014 New York mayoral race and is now considered one of the country's better political operatives.)

WITH A NEW FOCUS in my office and the campaign, and a broader coalition of advisers, everything seemed to finally work. It helped that the campaign map moved from the inside game of caucuses and conventions in the spring to the grass roots, outside game of summer events, picnics, and parades. This was always my turf.

Hanson had the toughest job, coming into the mayor's office as a self-described "minister of focus" who would keep the message, and the agenda, squarely on the basics. In this first week, when there were two homicides, it was clear that the focus had to be public safety.

I agreed we needed focus but that was never my strong suit, especially when I was out in the community. On Hanson's first weekend in the job, he went with me to the Gay Pride Parade, which is, by far, the largest parade in the city and, in those days, by far the most flamboyant.

I love parades and this one in particular is usually three or four hours long. My pattern had been to march as the mayor early in the parade and then join a series of groups as they were marching, until I had been through three or four times. Usually I ran most of the way, so I typically carried three or four shirts to discreetly change into throughout the day.

On my fourth time through, Hanson momentarily lost track of me. When he found me again, it was in the middle of the street, where I had joined a group of women with a float that I can delicately say was a giant female body part on wheels. (It made a little more sense in context, but maybe you had to be there.) Hanson almost had a stroke and pulled me away. I was going to end the parade there but then saw the Twin Cities Gay Men's Chorus come by, waving me to jump onto their float. I leapt up and joined them in some song—but as I jumped down from the moving float to the street, I felt something rip in my knee. I had torn my meniscus, which would become a serious problem as the campaign went on.

For the rest of the parade, and for the next few months, Hanson and the team did a remarkable job keeping a very distractible mayor and candidate focused. Hanson, especially, did an exceptional job introducing message discipline into our office's communications without stifling my quirkier instincts, which people seemed to appreciate.

AS HARD AS THE FIRST PART of the campaign had been, the second actually started to be fun, with only a couple of problems. First, the meniscus I tore jumping off the float got worse fast—so that for much of the rest of the campaign, I was icing my knee several times a day. I didn't stop door knocking in high-rises or running in parades, but I sure felt the discomfort. Second, the better I started to do in the campaign the harder the attacks came, especially the pieces of mail and at the debates.

As I walked into one very important debate that summer, the room was filled with firefighters wearing yellow McLaughlin shirts; they were cheering him and booing me. It didn't really hit me too hard until I looked out into the audience to see a firefighter named Roger Champagne, whom I had met during my first campaign. A veteran on the force, he had campaigned with me the first time and had given me a lot of insight into how to understand the everyday challenges of firefighters. My heart really sank that I had lost his support, too.

I took a pretty good pounding that night, but after the debate decided to suck it up and go into the bar downstairs to shake hands with the firefighters. If people were going to take shots, let them do it to my face. I walked in, got a bunch of dirty looks, and a few firefighters walked out. Champagne started to, then turned around and said, "At least let me buy you a beer." Moments like that help you not take it personally.

The campaign stayed rough through the end of the last debate, where I finally turned to McLaughlin and said, "Over these last few months we've heard you say a lot about what I've done wrong. How about telling people just one thing, over these past four years, that you think I have done right?" Silence. "Just one thing?" I asked. Again he couldn't answer and I finished with: "That's just sad, because I can say lots of great things you've done. People in this city like Mayor Rybak, they like Commissioner McLaughlin, and they want us both to keep our jobs."

It was clear the McLaughlin team knew the right issues to attack me on, but they got the approach wrong. The ongoing attack wasn't working because I believed people generally liked me. I believed the majority of people in Minneapolis also wanted me to succeed; they just wanted me to do better.

To most people in town it was playing out more like a family feud between two political camps without any big ideological differences. That didn't end up being a compelling case to change—and a race that we seemed likely to lose turned into a comfortable win.

Election night was a huge relief, but it also felt a little hollow. Of course, I was happy I won, but it had been the kind of election that didn't bring a lot of light to issues. It didn't feel fresh or even exciting. I just wanted to take a long shower and get back to work.

I took a few days off to get my knee repaired, and shortly after I was back at work I ran into McLaughlin on the street. He had had the same kind of operation on his knee awhile before and ended up giving me a great exercise tip that helped speed my recovery. Both of us seemed very ready to get back to normal and pretty soon we were, once again, in those many meetings together. This time the others in those rooms didn't have to wonder what political subtext was behind each comment.

I now had run against two people, both Democrats and both of whom shared almost all my core political views. Unlike Mayor Sayles Belton, who was far less active after our election, McLaughlin and I had work that constantly overlapped for many years to come. McLaughlin led efforts to build two light rail lines, create a regional transit authority, help build the Twins ballpark, and much more. During the time I was in office he was, by far, the one political leader outside City Hall who delivered the most to Minneapolis. He is almost certainly one of the most consequential political leaders in Minneapolis history.

Over the coming years, sometimes in partnership, sometimes in a sort of adult political version of "parallel play," he and I amassed an impressive collective body of work. It didn't always feel like it at the time, but two people who fought a hard race against each other ended up being a good team.

In the end the people of Minneapolis got what I believe they wanted all along: Mayor Rybak and Commissioner McLaughlin both got to keep their jobs.

# The Thin Line between
# Love and Respect

EXHAUSTED BUT SATISFIED, and after a quick surgery to repair my knee, I spent the weeks after what had been a bruising reelection coming to the realization that I now had a fundamentally different view of my job.

In the simplest of terms, I had gone from desperately needing to be liked to needing to be respected. More important, I now understood the enormous difference between those two needs—and that it is a lot better to have a mayor who needs the second more than the first.

At some point in my first term, almost every constituency that had supported me the first time, and seemingly every person who was part of that original coalition, was angry about or at least disappointed by at least one decision I made. Now I had faced them in a second election and learned something that to my naive viewpoint was a true revelation: many of those disappointed people voted for me anyway. They may have been in my face at the time of some tough call, but a surprising number of the people who fought me hard on an issue that mattered deeply to them were willing to look at the larger body of my work. They may not have agreed with me on one issue, but they respected how I got there.

Driving by the home of a first-term critic and seeing my lawn sign in the yard, or having someone who laid into me at the beginning of the campaign show up at a fund-raiser near Election Day—moments like those helped me build something that had been missing in the way I approached the job. Slowly I comprehended that there was a thin line between love and respect and now knew that, in politics at least, the second lasted a lot longer than the first.

* * *

TRYING TO GET DISTANCE from my own self as I looked toward the beginning of my second term and what I hoped we could accomplish, I stepped back and saw a former political newbie deepening the relationship with the people he represents. The compact was now different: my mandate was not to do everything everyone wanted but instead to do what I thought was right. It struck me that if people really wanted elected leaders to do every single thing they wanted we could install robots in office and have them take directions from the latest poll.

I knew there was also a tremendous danger in over-reading this point. I believed I was initially elected, and now reelected, because of the significant efforts I was making to connect with as many people as possible: door knocking the whole city, showing up virtually everywhere, trying my best to actively listen and visibly change direction if someone convinced me I was wrong. I couldn't lose that edge and had to make sure staying connected to the people I represented was a hedge against being arbitrary or arrogant. I just knew now that I could solve a problem by opening a door— getting as much input as I could—and then closing the door and making the tough call myself. I was reelected because of my ears but also my gut.

I also had become self-aware enough to understand that I didn't get sent back to City Hall for another four years because people loved every single thing about me. I saw that voters made a decision that, while I was seen as flawed, on the whole they respected where I was going.

THE ONLY ANALOGY that seemed to fit was that feeling you get on about your fifth or sixth wedding anniversary, when you stop trying to change everything about your partner and instead make that pragmatic calculation that the things that bug you are nowhere nearly as important as the reason you fell in love in the first place.

I did, however, learn a lot from the people who didn't vote for me, especially those first-time supporters who were now so alienated I probably wouldn't ever get them back. In some cases it said something about them. In most cases I found I had lost early supporters for reasons that were totally avoidable. It was deeply depressing to find how many relationships had been severed because either I was sloppy about reaching out to someone at a critical time, or I didn't get the person the results he or she deserved.

The rookie mayor who came in with a team proudly new to City Hall and "above" politics ultimately needed a team that knew more about the way things work. Knowing this, I hired two people who would become an exceptional political team.

The first was Steven Bosacker. After a few years of effort, I finally convinced him to come to the city. During the election year we hired him on a contract to start developing a 311 phone system and a results management system. After the election I nominated him to implement that work as well as lead all administrative functions as city coordinator.

The other person was Tina Smith, a longtime behind-the-scenes player in Minnesota politics who became my chief of staff. I first worked with Smith on the Bill Bradley campaign, and she was a key member of the kitchen cabinet the Kaplans set up that helped turn around my second campaign.

Bosacker and Smith—running the city, and running my office—formed a tight bond. They put my best ideas into action, stopped most of my dumb ones, and most important, reached out well beyond City Hall to build the partnerships we needed to get results.

After a very rough first term, we came into the second feeling that we finally had the job and the city under control.

And then we didn't.

# *When Kids Kill Kids*

---

I NEVER HAD THE PRIVILEGE of meeting Tyesha Edwards, but she had an impact on me from the moment I heard her name in the emergency room at Hennepin County Medical Center on November 22, 2002.

I had gone to the hospital fifteen minutes earlier when I got word that an eleven-year-old girl had been sitting at her dining room table doing her homework when a stray bullet from a gang dispute broke through the walls and stuck her. Tyesha's mother, Linda, and Linda's husband, Leonard, met me at the hospital, and almost immediately a doctor told us their daughter was dead.

I was now in a very small room with people I had never met as they dealt with the crushing news that their daughter was dead. They were joined by Tyesha's father, Jimmy, and other family members, including Linda's mother, Cora.

What could I say to give them any kind of comfort at a horrendous time like this? I tried to imagine what I would feel, and what would help, if my own twelve-year-old daughter, Grace, was the one who had been shot. The thought was almost beyond comprehension, but I did everything I could to feel that kind of pain and find anything to say that could matter. I had been around death before, and the last thing I wanted was to say one of those well-meaning but clueless things people said when my dad died.

I was in this room almost by accident and wondered what a "mayor" was supposed to say. I realized I had to put the public official thing aside and just be another parent who also loved his twelve-year-old daughter and understood there was nothing magic to say that would ever make it better. I can't remember anything about that conversation; I just remember looks on faces that I won't ever forget.

After about an hour, reality sank in for Tyesha's family, and they began to think about what needed to happen next. A hospital social worker came in and helped them pick a place to have the memorial service. They asked me to come with them.

Two days later at the funeral home, as they made the arrangements, Tyesha's eight-year-old sister took me around a corner and asked me to come with her to see the casket. It was a private moment that is hers to tell, but it was very difficult. Linda and Leonard had a lot left to do in the office, but I knew it was best to have their young daughter somewhere else. The funeral home happened to be near my mom's house, where I was supposed to go to watch the Vikings' game. So I asked Linda and Leonard if I could take their daughter with me while they finished the funeral plans.

Watching the game gave the little girl a break from the horrendous reality of losing her sister in such a terrible way. About an hour later, when Linda and Leonard came to pick her up, we invited them in to see the rest of the game. That started a wonderful friendship between our two families.

I can't remember if the Vikings won, but the game was a great common ground for two groups of strangers trying to help each other through a horrible moment.

At Tyesha's funeral we learned much more about her success in school, and how loved she was by her teachers and the youth workers at her church. The sanctuary was filled with mourners, some sobbing and most clearly crushed by the reality of such a senseless loss.

I wanted so badly to give remarks that honored who Tyesha was and who I had come to understand her family to be. A few lines into my speech I looked at Linda's face in the front row, thought about the ordeal she was going through, and my mind went completely blank. For the only time in my career I was totally frozen in front of a group of people. I'm not sure how long I stood there, but after what seemed like a very long time, I heard a voice from the congregation: "Take your time, Mayor. Take your time, Mayor." I looked up and saw that it was Steve Belton, Mayor Sayles Belton's husband. A few years back we were on opposite sides of a very tough election. Now he walked me back and helped me finish the eulogy.

We stayed near Tyesha's family through the funeral and the burial. When it was over we all said we wanted to see them again and impulsively we invited them to Thanksgiving dinner later that week.

Up to this point, the dynamic was our family helping theirs, but at that Thanksgiving gathering, the relationship shifted. Our family had been really down because we weren't going to be together for the holiday, but suddenly Tyesha's family filled the house. We had a Big Fat Thanksgiving Dinner filled with great stories and laughs and all of us seemed to put a wall around very complicated times to simply enjoy being with each other. Just as we finished eating and clearing the plates, the phone rang. It was Delilah, the sister of Tyesha's father, Jimmy. She and a carful of other relatives were in town and, again impulsively, we invited them over. Out came a whole new set of dishes, and I went into the kitchen to carve more meat off the worked-over turkey carcass. For a few more hours, well into the night, we had an entire second Thanksgiving dinner with the next wave of Tyesha's family telling us hilarious stories about growing up in the rural South.

Delilah finished the long, wild night by telling us that every morning she woke up and said, "Jesus, let me be a blessing in someone's life today!" That night, and on a few holidays after that, Tyesha's family—in the middle of their horrific grief—was a real blessing to us.

SADLY, Tyesha Edwards was not the only young person whose family I met after their child died. Hardly.

In June 2006, a few months after I started my second term, Brian Cole was killed in north Minneapolis. It was shocking enough to lose a popular young man simply because he was in the wrong place when gangs were fighting. It was worse because it was not an isolated incident. In recent months there had been a series of shootings, some deadly, that primarily involved very young people, many of whom were in gangs.

Don Samuels, my public safety policy aide, Sherman Patterson, and I got ready to visit Brian's parents. I asked myself the same questions I asked when I first met Tyesha's family: What could I say that would mean anything to them or be of any help? Do I talk to them as "The Mayor" or as a parent?

The stories in the media about Brian's death told about his love of sports, and hearing about his friendships with teammates rang so familiar to me as I thought about our own son, Charlie, and his pals. I thought about Charlie going out for just another night and simply never coming home again. What would it be like to get that call? Before visiting Brian Cole's parents I visualized what it would be like if this were my child. What if Charlie were shot?

Brian's parents were wonderful people in obvious deep pain. It was even harder for them because they saw their son doing everything right, navigating around all the conflicts and affiliations around him. He was making it and on his way. Now this.

We talked parent-to-parent, and I left their house so impressed with their strength. I also understood there were ways to make it through a conversation, or a few days, but the pain would never really go away.

Thinking about all that as I got into the car, I felt the most massive wave of grief. I thought about Megan's and my trying to come to terms with Charlie being gone and the thought was unimaginable. I wondered how many people would see something about the shooting on the news and not see Brian as someone's beloved child but, instead, write it off as another statistic in a part of town where we collectively have come to accept that children were just going to be murdered. The grief deepened when I came to terms with the fact that Brian Cole, like Tyesha Edwards, died on my watch and I honestly didn't know how to stop it.

AS THE YOUTH CRIME WAVE SURGED there were tragically more Tyesha Edwardses and Brian Coles. By late summer I began to lose track of how many funerals I had been to, how many times I had stood at street corner murder scenes with horrified family members, how many times I had been in the emergency room to hear the bad news with people I had never met.

Most of the deaths were happening in north Minneapolis, the part of the city with the highest rates of crime, and I felt it was especially important that the mayor was present to let families know their lives, and the lives of their children, mattered.

Each time before I talked to a victim's family, I visualized this happening to my own family. This helped me bring a level of sincerity when it was very important, but it was starting to have a significant consequence. One afternoon in late summer, after going to several funerals in two weeks, I turned to Don Samuels and admitted that the way I was approaching things was taking a real toll. "Don," I admitted, "in my mind I have killed my kids six times in the past two months."

More important than admitting my feelings to my colleague and friend, I could not understand how Don and his wife, Sondra, were handling it. The crime wave was taking a huge toll on me, but Don and Sondra Samuels were putting far more of themselves on the line. So was my aide Sherman Patterson, who monitored police radios and had the rough task of calling me when someone was shot. When I heard the phone ring in the middle of the night, my heart would sink because it was usually Sherman. He didn't need to say much, just the address. I learned how to dress and get out the door without turning on a light, and then drive through dark streets until the flashing lights and crowd of police on the corner led me to the murder scene.

DON, SONDRA, AND SHERMAN were then and are today heroes to me— able to turn over huge parts of their lives to let people know they weren't suffering a loss on their own. An even more astonishing commitment was made by Mary Johnson. In 1993 her son was killed by another young man. Still filled with grief twelve years later, she went to Stillwater Prison to confront the killer. Somehow Mary found the compassion to forgive the boy, and they continued to talk. Mary eventually adopted the boy who killed her son. She formed the group From Death to Life so that she and other mothers of victims could be there for families when their own loved ones die as the result of violence.

The Samuelses and Sherman, Mary Johnson and V. J. Smith got to know each other well, in the worst of circumstances when I knew part of my job was to do what I could to reach out to those in pain. Being mayor meant I also had another responsibility: I was in charge of the Police Department, and, more than anyone else, I had to find a way to stop the killing.

That was more complicated because Police Chief Bill McManus had left for San Antonio. I replaced him with Tim Dolan, who, as McManus's deputy, had already been overseeing much of the day-to-day operations. A native of north Minneapolis who had also run the precinct there, Dolan knew the problem and the troubled area very well.

While McManus was the ultimate outsider, Dolan was hands-on and understood how to get a better performance out of a department he had worked in his whole career. He was controlled in public—not a person who wears his heart on his sleeve. I learned quickly not to interpret his stoicism for not caring. It was clear to me that Dolan was a deep man with a strong sense of moral justice who took the violence as personally as I did. He was from the neighborhoods that were becoming so unsafe, had worked there for many years, and, unlike a lot of those numbed by all the violence, he had not given up on making the area safe again. Without fanfare, he built strong relationships in the community over the years, and those who worked closest to him usually had the most respect for him. He seemed to be especially effective with the younger officers who worked for him—-those who too often got sucked into cynicism or became resigned that the streets would never get safer. As Dolan began to give the department a sharper response to the murders, I began to finally sense I had an engaged, skilled partner willing to get his hands dirty to take on something that seemed almost overwhelming.

DRIVING HOME ONE DAY, I was thinking about the long meeting I just left with Dolan and others about how we should respond when I got a call from Ellen Luger of the General Mills Foundation. She said she, too, was deeply worried about the violence.

I had a lot of respect for Luger, whom I had tried to recruit to be my first chief of staff, so I admitted to her something I was only beginning to admit to myself: "Kids are dying on my watch and I honestly can't say I know what else to do."

She reminded me that she had been part of an effort a decade earlier in south Minneapolis called "Minnesota Heals," which built a public–private partnership when the crack epidemic made south Minneapolis so violent it acquired the nickname "Murderapolis." The partnership was effective in connecting safety efforts by police, community, and business, and crime eventually decreased dramatically.

We agreed we needed to get smarter about the true drivers of the violence, and Luger offered General Mills Foundation funds to have the Police Executive Research Forum from Washington, D.C., take a harder look at our crime trends. Their raw assessment was that the violence was being driven by increasingly younger kids who were more unpredictable because they were usually operating outside traditional gangs with unchecked access to guns. The researchers also said Minneapolis was experiencing a national trend, so we quickly put together a meeting of U.S. mayors and police chiefs to see what we could learn from each other.

For the first four hours of that meeting in Washington we had a realization that was both comforting and deeply unsettling: we weren't alone. Mayors and chiefs, representing every part of the country, would tell exactly the same story about crime going up, perpetrated by very young kids who acted unpredictably, had more guns, and were very willing to pull the trigger. The second half of the meeting we talked about what we could do about it, and it was clear there was no one simple answer.

Back home Dolan took what we learned and rethought our response.

A few years earlier, when we had to make deep cuts to public safety to react to Governor Pawlenty's big cuts to local government aid, we decided to put as many officers as possible on the street. This made sense at the time: shift as many people as possible out of specialized units and get them on patrol.

As the crime wave grew, Chief Dolan and I recognized the city's response to the cuts had gone too far. One of the units that had been dismantled was the Juvenile Division, and now a couple of years later it was clear we had lost our focus on early intervention with kids.

Dolan reinstated the Juvenile Division and made a series of other tactical moves, but at first nothing seemed to change.

Rethinking our enforcement efforts was part of the solution, but we came out of the meeting in Washington with an appreciation that the answer was going to take more than tough policing. We heard a lot about upstream actions to prevent juvenile crime. This "public health" approach was already being explored by our Health Department and by the Minneapolis Foundation. I combined these efforts and got Luger and Karen Kelley-Ariwoola from the Minneapolis Foundation to lead a youth violence prevention community committee.

I had high hopes for this diverse group but was very worried when we started our first meeting. We brought in Deborah Prothrow-Stith, a Harvard professor who I was told was the leading expert in youth violence prevention. She began by talking about the early days of the nation when Alexander Hamilton, Aaron Burr, and other respected leaders tried to solve big issues with duels. I looked around the table at our grassroots committee, several of them very skeptical that this presentation could come to anything, and cringed at what they would be saying about the clueless mayor trying to solve murders by bringing in a Harvard professor who talked about duels.

But as Prothrow-Stith talked what she said began to make a lot of sense. There was a time when the community norm was to settle disputes with guns. Somehow we collectively changed that value and now we needed to do the same for the kids who were killing kids. It was abstract, to be sure, and I was sure as hell not going to tell a hostile community gathering that our big answer to making north Minneapolis safe was to have Harvard professors tell us about duels in the 1800s. But the point was clear: we had to change community values, and how the rest of the community looked at people and places with the crime, and that couldn't be done just by putting more cops on the street.

MURDERS KEPT HAPPENING and crime kept rising. I went to more and more crime scenes and funerals, but we stayed at it. We tried to understand everything that was being done in Minneapolis and around the country. The more we saw, the more we realized a lot was already working, especially small, community-based efforts. The challenge was that they were usually totally disconnected from each other: what we were learning from one effort about one kid wasn't being connected to that child's family or school. This was not only about kids learning to work together, but, probably even more important, we had to get the adults working together.

On a big white board we listed the most promising solutions, the ones we believed did the most to keep kids from violent behavior. For several days—between all the other meetings about all the other things I was working on—I kept staring at those random items and eventually they fell into four "buckets" or goals:

- Connect every young person with a trusted adult.
- Intervene at the first sign of at-risk behavior.
- Rejuvenate *every* kid; give up on no one.
- Attack the culture of violence.

We redrew the white board to separate all the actions into these four categories and showed it to Gretchen Musicant, our health commissioner, who, unlike me, had years of training in public health. As she looked the board over it became clear to her that the first three of these buckets fell pretty closely into what public health professionals would call primary, secondary, and tertiary intervention. I told her I definitely did not want to tell a mother whose child had been shot that we were going to respond with "tertiary intervention," but it was comforting to know the path we were on was grounded in proven public health practices.

We began filling in each of the four sections of the plan with the work that was already being done in the community, and noted what was missing. We also had deeply moving conversations with the kids on the front lines.

A few days after a really heinous shooting in the middle of the day in a north Minneapolis restaurant, I went to two classrooms in nearby Patrick Henry High School. The kids told me the very stark reality of how they navigated day-to-day existence knowing their lives could end at any minute; the practical decisions about what route to take home from school; the moral dilemmas of associating with a group of people they didn't like or trust because they believed this was the best way to get at least some protection.

One group we put together included a young man who got in my face and said, "My friend was in school all day with a gun in his locker. What are you gonna do about that?"

That was a pretty heavy thing to lay on me, but he was right. I thought for a minute and said, "I understand that but what are you gonna do about the fact that all day long someone had a gun in school that could have killed your friend, and you didn't tell a single person?"

He came back: "I'm not stupid. I know the law lets him know who reported him and when his friends find out, I'm dead."

Out of that honest conversation we started working on ways for kids to confidentially report the information we needed to keep them safe.

The strongest parts of the plan were in the second area, about intervening at the first sign of at-risk behavior. My commitment to this idea had grown from being at so many crime scenes when so often someone—a neighbor, a friend, a teacher, a social worker—would say some version of "We knew this would happen."

This infuriated me, and I usually thought, but rarely asked, "Why the hell didn't you do something when you could?"

It became clear that collectively we as a community almost always have early warning signs that a child is moving in the wrong direction, but almost never is the community coordinated enough to collectively catch that child before he or she falls. This awareness made me challenge people—and systems like schools and county social services—over and over, to specify how they defined the first sign of at-risk behavior and what they would to do intervene.

For the police it was clear: the first signs of at-risk behavior are truancy and breaking curfew. A kid missing school or out too late is showing the first signs of behavior that can get much worse. Working with Hennepin County, we set up a new intervention center in City Hall where we actively sought out kids who were missing school or out too late. The goal wasn't to build arrest records; it was to step in early so that we didn't have to step in later at the tragic end of a life. The center had caseworkers who tried to get at the root cause of what was going on, and connect the kids to services that could help. Within a year more than 70 percent of the kids who came to the center never came back—a huge victory.

We realized the hardest part of our plan was the third goal, about never giving up on a kid. That is a simple philosophy, but it is much harder to implement when you are asking a community to welcome back a child who was wreaking havoc in the neighborhood or, worse, had killed another child. Who can we really ask to do what Mary Johnson did and find a place of love in your heart for someone who broke that heart by murdering someone you love? Making it harder, the city does not control any part of probation, the justice system, or any supportive human services. But as the plan took hold, the county and the city's broad network of nonprofit providers shifted more of their efforts to winning kids back instead of locking them away.

We connected our efforts to key indicators, and slowly at first we saw progress. By the time I left office the indicators showed a dramatic improvement:

- Juveniles involved in violent crime dropped from 2,652 in 2006 to 1,071 in 2013.

- Juvenile gunshot victims dropped from 810 in 2006 to 431 in 2013.

- Simple assaults of juvenile victims dropped from 1,217 in 2006 to 588 in 2013.

- Juvenile homicides dropped from 25 in 2006 to 13 in 2013. (It hit a low of 3 in 2009).

Many parts of the plan have been tweaked, or changed completely, as we learned more but those four buckets held up over time. The Minneapolis youth violence prevention plan is often cited as one of the better efforts around the country, and every few months someone from another city calls to find out how they can launch a plan like it.

I DON'T THINK I have ever felt as hopeless as I did in those days when I realized kids were dying on my watch and I honestly didn't know what to do about it. A few years later we had at least some answers.

For all those years in office—and to this day—I keep a picture of Tyesha Edwards and her grave in my office. I never met her, but she had a huge impact on me, and on the city where she never got to grow up.

# Results

IN EARLY MARCH 2006, I walked into the meeting room at the Minneapolis Depot with the new city council and the new city coordinator, Steven Bosacker. Five hours later we came out with seven big things we had agreed to get done in the next four years.

We wanted to build "One Minneapolis": "A Safe Place to Call Home" with a "Cleaner, Greener Downtown," "Connected Communities" with "Lifelong Learning" opportunities, and "An Enriched Environment" that was a "Premier Destination."

It was surprising how easily a group of fourteen elected officials could agree on what kind of a city we wanted to build. It was also important that we had just come through an election in a grassroots town, where day after day of door knocking and community forums had given us a fresh, direct, intense take on public opinion. That meant we were pretty sure the city we wanted to build was close to what the rest of the city wanted, too.

Developing a strategic plan is a conventional process in most organizations and businesses, but it has been very rare in government. Even rarer, four years after that March meeting at the Minneapolis Depot we were able to stand up and say something you don't often get to say in politics: we had done what we said we would. And we had the measurements to prove it.

It happened in part because in spite of some of the usual political drama, we had found a way for people who didn't always agree to work together. Most of the credit has to go to Bosacker, probably the best person I ever hired for anything. Steven is also a couple of other things: a workaholic and a bit obsessive. (I used to torture him by reaching across the table and mixing up the blue, red, and black pens he always had in perfect alignment in front of him.) The best part of both those qualities came out in the next couple of months as Steven turned our instructions into a strategic plan that operationalized our vision into every part of the organization. That road map laid out everything of consequence we did over the next four years.

Steven and his team developed thirty-one specific strategic directions from those goals. Each of those directions had its own working documents, including the lead in the organization and partners outside City Hall. None of our goals was isolated to a single department; if we were going to make this happen we would need people to work across traditionally defined domains.

While the goals sounded straightforward, they forced reinvention. "Connected Communities" included green space and transit, which meant the Public Works Department would collaborate with the independent Park and Recreation Board. A "Premier Destination" meant Economic Development would work with Meet Minneapolis, the city's independent convention and visitors bureau. "Lifelong Learning" required the city to state for the record that it had a role in education, even though the city had no role in the schools—and it also meant reaching out to the very independent University of Minnesota and other institutions of higher education, and taking some steps to connect with the growing base of senior residents.

Each strategic direction was also tied to a series of specific indicators in Results Minneapolis, the data-based accountability system Steven had been building over the previous year. Each series of indicators, in turn, was tied to the performance management system we built to assess every department manager.

What all this meant was that each Wednesday, when we reviewed data on a different department in the Results meeting, we weren't as concerned with measuring just the department's performance as we were about whether we were meeting the goals of, say, a "Cleaner, Greener Downtown" or "Connected Communities." When the head of that department had a job review, his or her work was measured against those key goals. And because our job reviews included 360-degree feedback from partners outside City Hall, we weren't the only ones determining whether we were meeting these goals; our partners and the rest of the community had a say as well.

Each of the departments built its business plans around these goals. When I met with the department heads as I was building the annual budget, I had information about who wanted how much, but I let them know I was making my decisions based on how they met the goals.

Steven had the goals put into a large wall-sized graphic hung up in different places around City Hall, and converted into wallet-size foldout cards we carried with us. When someone came up to me and demanded to know "What the hell's going on in City Hall," I would pull out the card and say, "Glad you asked."

WHILE ALL THIS WAS HAPPENING, we also launched a 311 phone system. This accomplished several things. First, it helped address the incredibly frustrating problem of getting a straight answer out of City Hall. There would be no more getting bounced by one person who couldn't solve your problem, being put on hold, transferred to another person, and another, until finally you gave up. Now you could talk to an operator who had been selected because he or she was good with the public, trained to know how to find answers, and armed with a script that answered key questions.

The second thing 311 did was fix broken parts of the system. To develop those scripts we had to answer the question, who is in charge? This is not an easy thing in government. When we asked who was in charge of graffiti—the single largest complaint that comes in by phone—five people in the organization raised a hand. Wrong answer. So for graffiti, and each of the other areas where scripts were developed, we also redesigned how we delivered the service . . . and made clear who was in charge.

The third benefit of 311 may have been the most important: it made it easier to have two-way government. Pre-311, the city sent a team around the city to find potholes and then sent out crews to fix them. Meanwhile, if you found a pothole, you would call someone at City Hall, maybe one of those six people in charge, maybe get bounced around a lot, and maybe, if both you and the city were lucky, your complaint would get to the people deciding which roads to repair. Now, with 311, we still sent those crews out, but your call became part of accumulating more data; the operator would ask where the pothole was, how big, what side of the street, and that information went directly into a GIS map. The process meant we had every citizen on the lookout for where to direct the crews. Government became you.

One of the side benefits of all this was that it transformed the way our outside partners looked at City Hall. Minneapolis, to many people, especially in the private sector, was "unmanageable" and "out of control." It got harder and harder to say that when City Hall had a transparent plan and was clearly executing against its goals. This, along with the significant financial reforms we were making, transformed people's view of our work.

The most obvious change was in the attitude of the downtown business community, which during my first few years was openly dismissive of my leadership and then grudgingly moved to just this side of tolerant. As business leaders saw all these reforms now working, much more was possible, including a long-planned innovation that made downtown much more livable.

For years, since I was at the Downtown Council in the 1980s, there had been a plan to create a Downtown Improvement District partnering public and private dollars to give the central business district the kind of coordinated management you find in suburban malls. Talks always broke down because of suspicions that City Hall wouldn't be able to deliver on its side of the bargain.

With City Hall now working so well, the business leaders changed their minds and, after a year of talks, they agreed to assessments of about $5 million a year on top of their property taxes to pay for safety ambassadors, enhanced plantings, more complete snowplowing, power-washing the sidewalks, and a series of other quality-of-life improvements that absolutely never could have happened without our reforms.

The reforms also made it easier to attack disparities, most notably in our area of biggest need: north Minneapolis. Every department had north Minneapolis at the top of its agenda. The Police Department knew it had the highest crime; the Health Department knew it had the worst health outcomes; the economic team knew it had the fewest jobs; and the housing team knew it had the greatest housing needs. It was number one on every list. But before, almost every one of those departments had acted in isolation. This new method of working made it dramatically easier to cross boundaries, so we launched the North Force Initiative, which had these departments weave together their business plans on a broad quality-of-life push for the part of the city that needed it the most.

After all these efforts had run for a few years, Steven went out to determine how our partners outside City Hall thought things were working. In his typical obsessive style, he interviewed stakeholders around the city. That wasn't always a pleasant task, but this time it was. The overall feedback was simple, but it meant a lot to hear something most politicians don't hear: "You did what you said you would."

# Not So Isolated after All

WHEN I FIRST GOT ELECTED, Minneapolis and St. Paul had mayors who could almost not be more different. St. Paul's mayor, Randy Kelly, was far more experienced in government, especially politics at the State Capitol; I was far more visible and more of a community activist. Mr. Inside and Mr. Outside. We worked together on some issues but competed on a lot more, most notably the Allina headquarters, which he wanted on a site at I-94 and Snelling Avenue.

The toughest part of the relationship with Mayor Kelly was that he had a partnership with Governor Tim Pawlenty, who repeatedly positioned Randy as "the good mayor" in contrast to the flake over in Minneapolis. An example occurred when refugees from Hurricane Katrina were suddenly coming to Minnesota: Pawlenty and Kelly had a press conference talking about resettlement and "forgot" to invite the mayor of the city where most of the refugees would be coming. I showed up anyway.

The path between Kelly and me diverged sharply when he announced he was supporting George Bush for reelection in 2004. This did not go over well in his heavily Democratic city, and many believe it was a key reason he lost reelection to Chris Coleman. Shortly before the election, Democrats on St. Paul's East Side were having a rally and their leader announced, "We have a surprise! The mayor is here!" Outraged activists began to boo loudly, thinking it was their mayor, who was helping Bush. They laughed when I walked out instead.

Kelly and I eventually ended up on good terms, but I admit I wasn't exactly broken up when he lost to Chris Coleman. Coleman and I, while friendly, didn't know each other well before the election, but I was almost as happy about his victory as I was about my own race. I saw the change as a great opportunity for the two cities to finally find a way to work together and, possibly even more important, have the mayors of the two largest cities in Minnesota form a united front against what I saw as Governor Pawlenty's attempt to shift his problems onto cities.

A few days after the election Coleman and I had lunch. The plan was to have a low-key meeting at DeGidio's Restaurant in St. Paul, but it turned into a media circus. A friendly meeting between the leaders of two cities that have competed for more than a century was big news, and cameras and microphones were coming from every direction. Coleman, who always has great lines, said something to the effect of "This was the most newsworthy meal since the Last Supper." We really didn't have much of a chance to eat, which was OK. We were hungry, but people were hungrier for the two mayors, and the two cities, to finally work together.

We followed that with a joint appearance before the Minneapolis and St. Paul Chambers of Commerce—and quickly both of our offices were flooded with requests to speak together. The *Star Tribune* headline about the two mayors suddenly working together was "Brokeback Mayors." The morning that article came out Coleman was meeting with some officials of the Catholic Church. When one asked him how he was he said, "Well, I just picked up the paper and found out I'm having a homosexual relationship with the mayor of Minneapolis." They didn't quite know where to go with that.

Even our wives got into the act. Megan and Connie Coleman met for a simple lunch and left two and a half hours later as fast friends.

In the early days we put a lot on the table about how we could work together. Were there departments the two cities could merge? Could some services be shared? Unfortunately, those ideas fell by the wayside pretty quickly, but Coleman and I did help form a united front on most issues, especially at the state level.

While Coleman and I were forming a partnership, other alliances with other mayors were also developing. A few years earlier I had worked with Mayor Karen Anderson of Minnetonka and Mayor Elizabeth Kautz of Burnsville to start the Regional Council of Mayors, a monthly forum for leaders of cities around the region. By the middle of my second term they were both playing major roles in issues such as transportation and siting affordable housing.

I was also on the founding board of another group that built new alliances. The Itasca Group, started with the McKnight Foundation and McKinsey Group in 2004, was a coalition of the region's top CEOs, the president of the University of Minnesota, and the mayors of Minneapolis and St. Paul. I started with very few connections with business leaders, but by 2007 Itasca was bringing me into close partnership with many of them on issues regarding higher education, income disparities, and the achievement gap. They would eventually launch the regional economic growth organization Greater MSP and, again, I was on the founding board.

Itasca and the Regional Mayors both helped build the bipartisan coalition that ultimately got the votes to override Governor Pawlenty's veto of a significant transportation bill, making it possible to have the region's first major investment in transit infrastructure in many years.

Mayors and business leaders were finding better ways to work together. So were faith leaders of the large downtown congregations, including the Basilica of St. Mary's Father Michael O'Connell, St. Mark's Episcopal Cathedral's Spenser Simrill, Temple Israel's Marcia Zimmerman, Westminster Presbyterian's Tim Hart-Andersen, and Central Lutheran Church's Craig Lewis. There may never have been a more powerful group of leaders representing thousands of the most connected people in the community. When they talked together, people listened, and we partnered on a series of social justice issues, including immigration and affordable housing.

Without my realizing it at first, these partnerships were broadening my view of the job. My direct responsibility was to run Minneapolis city government, but now I had multiple forums, and multiple partners, to have an impact on issues that had been well beyond my reach. I did that formally by starting public–private partnerships to attack a wide range of issues from youth violence to homelessness to exports. I did it informally by picking up the phone and finding ways to partner with a much wider, much more powerful, and more diverse coalition of allies.

These new partnerships were also showing me I could help lead a civic agenda by building civic coalitions. I was learning how to lead in City Hall, but I was also learning how to lead in the city. Unlike the early years, when the job seemed so big it was defining me, now I was starting to redefine the job.

UP TO NOW, I saw the term "collaborative leadership" as something politicians hid behind when they didn't want to stand up and make tough choices. Now I was seeing that if I spent the time to build coalitions, and parked my ego enough that I didn't have to have my name at the top of every news story, my role as mayor within a partnership had the potential to influence broader issues such as regional economic development, transportation, youth, and education.

All these efforts were far more effective because Tina Smith, my new chief of staff, was especially good at the people side of politics. She helped reach out to people I hadn't brought in before or who hadn't been willing to partner before.

The collaboration outside City Hall was also helping me learn how to be more effective inside City Hall.

Minneapolis city government has one of the most complex charters in the country: the mayor controls the budget, the police, and the Civil Rights Department, but many other departments report to an executive committee with council members and the mayor, except those departments that report to the city coordinator, who is appointed by the mayor but needs the council's approval . . . I could go on. People sometimes call it a "weak mayor" system, but it really is a "weak mayor–weak council–weak coordinator–highly random" system that scatters authority widely and has very vague lines of authority.

I was asked once if I thought Minneapolis had a long-term drug problem. "Absolutely," I answered quickly. "Read the charter and you know the city founders were clearly smoking something."

The image you have of a powerful mayor—a single person barking orders at a cowering, compliant bureaucracy—wouldn't work in this system. Increasingly I also believed it shouldn't work. I learned in the first term that we could move complex, controversial budget reforms forward if we brought the council in early and gave them part ownership. Now we were applying that approach to almost everything in City Hall.

It was becoming clear to me that the cartoon of cowboy governance where the mayor rides roughshod through the corridors of power masked the fact that true change rarely comes in such a clean package or, even more important, from a single person. Maybe I couldn't get everything I wanted, but I could get almost everything I really needed if I didn't try to do it all myself. We realized that if the council president, the city coordinator, my chief of staff, and I agreed on what needed to be done, we could get almost anything we really wanted through this complex bureaucracy. And the simple other fact was, four heads were better than one.

In these first months of my second term, I was getting a deeper understanding of who I was as a leader. I wasn't trying to be a strongman; I was trying to get things done. Both inside and outside City Hall, I was giving up power in the short term to have more in the long term.

# Bridge Collapse

THERE WAS A FLAWLESS SUNRISE on August 1, 2007, as I sat on the edge of the dock trying to make what I thought would my most important decision of the day.

This was the last day of a much-needed week at Megan's family's cabin in Nisswa, Minnesota. About the last thing I wanted to do that night was leave the cabin and drive to a political meeting an hour and a half south, but it was clear that I really should. The Obama campaign volunteers we had been recruiting in St. Cloud were having their first meeting, and they wanted me to give the welcome. Late that afternoon I grudgingly headed off to the event, planning to drive back later that night.

I didn't get to the event, and I didn't go back to the cabin, because just as I was pulling into St. Cloud my phone and Blackberry went off in unison. I picked up the phone to hear our son, Charlie, trying to stay calm, say "The 35W bridge collapsed."

"Which part?"

"The whole thing."

Struggling to even understand what that meant, I picked up the Blackberry to hear the emergency operator give me the details. Minneapolis was an hour away—but had I not made that decision to go to St. Cloud I would have been two and a half hours away in Nisswa. I stepped on the gas, working both the phone and my Blackberry, getting the surreal details of the collapse and reports from the emergency response center being set up in the basement of City Hall. Few people noticed that night that there was a massive rainstorm that mercifully stayed just north of the bridge site, but I drove through that and got to City Hall in forty minutes.

I was shocked, and the details were more shocking, but I knew just what to do because of the response planning we had done many years earlier at Mount Weather.

Our daughter, Grace, met me at City Hall with a change of clothes, and I joined the group in the response center. No one was panicked, decisions were made, and much of that credit goes to Rocco Forte, then the city's fire chief and director of emergency response. Forte had years of experience commanding teams at fires, extensive response training since 9/11, and the take-charge style that you really need in a crisis. With all that pressure the only time I saw him lose his cool was when someone from one of the remote sites being set up called asking where they could find pencils.

We could see the site on a television monitor because, fortunately, we had just set up WiFi cameras on the bridge. Department heads surrounded the table. Public Works director Steve Kotke was directing equipment and street closures. Others had long-term roles, like Finance Director Pat Born, who tracked each dollar spent during the response to make sure we had records to qualify for federal reimbursement. Much of this we wouldn't have known to do if we hadn't trained at Mount Weather.

It was a well-oiled machine, and each of us was calling on our preparedness training. I flashed back to the big mistake I had made during the Mount Weather training when I gave the order to evacuate the IDS Center, inadvertently spreading infection throughout the city. Then I remembered there was a Twins game going on, so we contacted the team, which announced the collapse on the PA and asked people to stay in place.

A couple of hours after the collapse, Governor Pawlenty and a group of Hennepin County officials arrived. We briefed them and the details at that time were grim. We knew there were deaths, but had very little idea how many people could be in the water. It could be more than a hundred and many could be buried beneath the wreckage. Crews were in the water, but it conceivably could take days to find everyone.

The recovery was playing itself out live on broadcast and the Internet so the public knew most of what we did, but we held a press conference to say that the response was extensive and well organized. Panic would only complicate the response

I tried to give people a reason to stay calm, but I had to be honest that this would almost certainly be the worst tragedy in the city's history. (Thankfully, that ended up not being true.)

Then the governor and I went up in his helicopter to view the site. On any other night the skyline would have been stunning as we circled downtown and headed upriver, but in front of us was a scene that literally took my breath away. Massive twisted girders and enormous concrete blocks were crumpled in the water.

As we flew over the remains of the bridge, cars, a truck, and a school bus looked frozen in place, precariously pointing down the sloping bridge to the water. Having spent all those years reporting on crime scenes had trained me to see the people behind the tragedy, so as I looked at those cars I wondered whose brother was in the vehicle submerged in the water, whose mother was near that girder when it twisted and fell, whose son and fiancé were under that concrete block in the water.

When the helicopter landed, unable to say much of anything, I headed to the makeshift family center in a nearby hotel. Minnesotans, being who we are, always bring food when a family is in crisis and, sure enough, one entire wall was already lined with hot dogs, sandwiches, snacks, and soft drinks.

The first family I met were the Engebretsens. Sherry, their mother and wife, worked at Thrivent downtown and shortly before the collapse called to say she was leaving the office. The family put dinner on the table and waited for her to take her drive, which was always across the 35W bridge. They feared the worst.

At the next table was the brother of Pat Holmes. Pat never showed up for their meeting, which wasn't like him. His brother was alone and clearly deeply traumatized, so I turned to the Engebretsens and asked them to keep an eye on him. Even in their deepest trauma, they reached out, started a conversation, and helped, at least temporarily, to muffle the pain.

I met Christina Sacorafas's family. She was supposed to be at St. Mary's Greek Orthodox Church on Lake Calhoun to teach Greek folk dance. It wasn't like her not to show up and they were also fearing the worst. We talked for a few minutes and as I was walking away her cousin pulled me aside: "Christina cared a lot about her appearance and she never left the house without makeup. I can't imagine the last picture of her being her dead body being pulled from the river. Please don't let that happen."

I hadn't thought this through until then, but, because of this request, I told our team to do everything possible to protect the dignity of victims as they were removed from the river. I am so grateful, to our team and the media, that there was not a single picture published of a dead body coming out of the water.

* * *

LEAVING THE FAMILY CENTER I realized our work would need to have two tracks: One was the physical response involving equipment and first responders. The other was the personal and emotional response for those at the family center, and all around town, who were just coming to terms with loss.

I had been closely following the controversy surrounding the 9/11 memorial in New York where families were complaining about being left out of the loop. We didn't know what would be coming, but an hour after the collapse I asked our Constituent Services director Erica Prosser to track the families who lost loved ones and make sure we ran as much as possible by them for approval. Starting that night—and continuing through the opening of the memorial almost two years later—Prosser was a critical link with the families and helped us do what we could to follow their wishes.

Because the response team was working so well at City Hall, I was able to focus that first night on people. I spent about an hour visiting hospitals, especially Hennepin County Medical Center, which was swamped with injured victims. Then I went to the site to thank police and firefighters, who were doing heroic work in terrible conditions.

Our first responders deserved every bit of the credit they got for the remarkable response, but few will know that many also saw deeply disturbing sights of bodies in the water. They went to great lengths to hide these from the public, out of respect, but I have talked to some who still live with those images to this day.

After stopping into the response center back at City Hall, I went home for a couple of hours' sleep.

At 5:30 A.M. I got an overnight briefing from Forte and then went to the north side of the bridge to brief reporters. I had never seen anything like the media scrum there that morning. One by one by one, they had their positions in a seemingly never-ending line along University Avenue, the collapsed bridge in the background. One by one by one I did on-camera interviews, giving them details of the response but still unable to say how many lives were lost.

That aspect became clearer throughout the day as we looked at pictures of the bridge just before the collapse, counted the cars, and did the math. Maybe there weren't hundreds of people in the water after all, but it was clear there were still going to be many people dead.

I spent a lot of time with family members during this time, and as the hours passed it became clear who was lost. It was also clear how much worse it could have been, and everywhere I went people told me near-miss stories about themselves or their loved ones. The most compelling was the kids on that bus, which teetered on the edge of the bridge but never went over. The schoolkids onboard from Waite House in south Minneapolis were traumatized, but counselors on the bus led them to safety.

In briefings throughout the day the media began to focus their questions on Minneapolis being a city that works; many of them spent years going from one tragedy to another, but rarely had seen a team so well organized with such a clear plan. This was a horrible tragedy, but under Forte's leadership, the response was going as well as it could.

It was also clear that there were hundreds of stories of personal heroism—not only by our team of first responders but also by regular citizens, whose first reaction to a tragedy was not to run away but run to help.

Calls came from all over—from almost all members of Minnesota's legislative delegation and from Barack Obama. One of the very first was from Congressman Jim Oberstar, whose years of work on transportation led him to be rightfully outraged that a bridge would collapse during rush hour.

THE FOLLOWING MORNING I was at the airport with Governor Pawlenty and his wife to meet President George Bush. Standing on the tarmac watching Air Force One land, I thought how surreal it was to meet a president for the first time, under these conditions. The president walked down the stairs, greeted the Pawlentys, then came up to me and said:

"Yereysarered."

I couldn't understand so he repeated:

"Yereysarered."

Finally, a third time, slower, he said, "Your eyes are red. You have to get some sleep."

"Thank you, Mr. President, I understand that but we kind of have a lot on our hands with . . ."

"Sleep is really important!"

This wasn't exactly what I expected to be talking with the president about at this moment but it was nice, and he continued to be exceptionally kind as we got into his helicopter with Senators Norm Coleman and Amy Klobuchar, as well as members of the congressional delegation.

We got to the bridge and, as we walked, the stories of all the families I had met washed over me. As we turned to see the site, and just beyond the horrible sight of all the destruction, we saw a giant American flag someone had draped over the neighboring Tenth Avenue bridge.

Deeply moved, I turned around with the president and an entourage and began walking away when I noticed a man in a Twins cap yucking it up a few yards away. I thought, "What kind of a jackass would be cracking jokes in a Twins cap at a time like this?" As I got closer the man reached out his hand and warmly introduced himself: "Hi, Karl Rove."

Before the president left, he and I went into the nearby Red Cross building to meet a couple of the families of victims. I was struck by how warmly and sincerely he connected on a very personal level with those families. I was also struck that I was standing with the political leader I disagreed with on almost every issue and how much that did not matter.

OVER THE NEXT FEW DAYS, one by one, the worst that some of those families expected really happened. The first wave of confirmed deaths were Christina Sacorafas, Vera Peck and her son Richard Chit of Bloomington, and Scott Sathers, who left his job at Capella University that night forty minutes later than usual. There was Greg Jolstad, who lived in Mora but worked every day on the bridge reconstruction, and Sadiya Sahal who died with her twenty-two-month-old daughter. Then Peter Hausmann, a father of four from Rosemount, who escaped from his van in the water but died as he apparently tried to help others from drowning.

Then Sherry Engebretsen, Artemio Trinidad-Mena, who had moved to Minnesota from Mexico ten years ago, and Julia Blackhawk of Savage who recently took the American Indian name Thunder Woman. Then Pat Holmes, whose wife, Jennifer, told me he loved playing baseball and wanted me to make sure we got his mitt out of the car. Paul Eickstadt, who drove the truck I saw dangling precariously on the bridge that first night, was also dead.

They came from all over the state, and from many different backgrounds and cultures. As we met their families and friends, and heard their stories, it struck me how much of our lives we spend together with strangers—in the next car on the freeway, standing next to us in the elevator or at the store. Then the common ground we share shakes and one more random rush hour turns into the moment that freezes fates together forever.

Megan and I went to almost all of their funerals and saw so many individual glimpses of humanity.

We learned about the deeply religious Hausmann, who died a hero and had lived that way his whole life, including missionary work in Africa.

At Jolstad's funeral in Mora, his lifelong friend who sat behind us began telling wonderful stories about "Jolly's" love of the Vikings. Just as the service started he smiled as a pounding guitar came through the PA playing Norman Greenbaum's "Spirit in the Sky." "That's so 'Jolly,' " he said.

At Holmes's funeral his wife, Jennifer, and their young children led the congregation out of the church, his casket carried by members of his baseball team while the organist played "Take Me Out to the Ballgame."

The Engebretsens seemed to spend most of Sherry's funeral supporting everyone else, just as they had helped others in the Family Center the night of the collapse.

Sacorafas's funeral and reception were a long, beautiful showcase for Minneapolis's incredibly warm Greek community, who made us feel like part of the family.

Eickstadt's funeral told the story of a quiet man who drove a Sara Lee truck. He never married or had a family of his own, but every month sent money to a relief program to help another child somewhere around the world. Seconds before he died, the kids in the school bus got him to honk his horn for them. Then he swerved and blocked the bus, which, intentionally or not, may well be the reason those kids didn't plunge over the edge.

THOSE DAYS ALL BLENDED TOGETHER with a rush of every kind of emotion, confused by a healthy dose of sleep deprivation. I was seeing people rise to extraordinary heights in the middle of suffering something beyond explanation. I saw hundreds of expressions of true compassion from an entire community wrapping arms around people they didn't know who came from so many different backgrounds. I was so blessed to learn about all these wonderful people. I was so completely sickened that losing them was such a complete and colossal waste.

And after the first couple of days of shock, I spent a lot of time asking, "Why?" This was not a tornado or a flood or a snowstorm. It wasn't an act of God; it was a human failure.

I knew part of my job was to call this out, but I also knew it was going to be awhile, if at all, before we could really say why the bridge fell. I would not have the luxury of tying actions directly to the cause, but I could do everything I could to prevent something like that from ever happening again.

My strongest partner on this, from the start and all the way through, was the late Congressman Oberstar, who was already at work on an infrastructure bill. Senators Klobuchar and Coleman, Congressman Ellison, and the rest of the Minnesota delegation in D.C. were exceptional. So were the members of the legislature. Political leaders from both parties, from all over, pledged their support.

One of my strongest early partners was Governor Pawlenty. We had not been allies, by any stretch of the imagination, but from the moment the disaster happened through those first days, he did everything he could. I felt it was a great comfort to a shocked community to find two political leaders who had been at odds working so closely together.

When his transportation commissioner, Carol Molnau, rushed out a design for a new bridge that I considered subpar, I objected. The governor took the unusual step of overruling her, which was extraordinary because she was also his lieutenant governor. The governor reluctantly agreed to my point that the bridge needed to be built to accommodate transit capacity, which was not a popular stand with his fellow Republicans.

A group of citizens were also encouraging me to push for more. They had been in contact with the architect Santiago Calatrava and believed they could raise the private funds to create a landmark design. It was an exciting idea, but at the time I felt I was using all my political capital to get a very reluctant governor and administration to support transit capacity, and, much as I would have loved a great design, I felt transit was more important. I have second-guessed that choice a few times, especially because the state has yet to use the extra bridge lanes for transit, but I still believe the choice will pay off in the long term.

Governor Pawlenty also made it clear to me that he, too, would do what it took to keep this from happening again. He said he realized we had to invest in infrastructure and would be willing to call a special session to provide more funds.

After several days the national media moved on to another crisis of the moment, and we went to work rebuilding lives and a bridge.

A month later, after the collapse set off a massive national discussion about infrastructure, Congressman Oberstar called me to Washington to testify before the U.S. House Transportation and Infrastructure

Committee. I told the story and proudly listened as Oberstar boldly talked about his bill to fund repairs of roads and bridges around the country.

Then I walked into the hall, surrounded by a gaggle of reporters, and the first question was, "What's it like to testify for a bill that's dead on arrival?" The media had moved on and so had many of the Washington politicians who had been so supportive when the 35W collapse was at the top of the news.

Back home things were changing too. Grover Norquist, head of the Taxpayers League, criticized Governor Pawlenty and warned him not to raise taxes. The governor, who was preparing a run for president, suddenly was saying very little about his statement to raise new money for infrastructure.

A couple of months later I called on the governor to talk about a special session and infrastructure. He said, referring to Senate Majority Leader Larry Pogemiller and House Speaker Margaret Anderson Kelliher, "Margaret needs it, and Larry needs it, but I don't really need it."

Stunned, especially remembering the commitment he made to families to keep something as catastrophic as the bridge collapse from ever happening again, I said, "Minnesota needs it."

He wasn't moved.

There would be no special session and no investment in infrastructure. Two years later, when the legislature approved the city's request to help fund the reinforcement of a bridge in far northeast Minneapolis that was in the same "fracture critical" condition as the 35W bridge, Governor Pawlenty line-item vetoed the appropriation.

THINKING ABOUT THE BRIDGE COLLAPSE today, especially when I go by the memorial we helped build overlooking the site, I have waves of conflicting emotions about a tragedy and recovery that was both horrific and deeply inspirational. I learned what happens when our common ground shakes, and I learned that common bonds are unshakable.

Every couple of months I run into one of the family members of someone who died, or one of the people who survived. One of the most exciting conversations was with the husband of one of the survivors whom I met in the days after the tragedy. When we met again last fall he told me his wife was doing great and that they had just had a baby.

One encounter sticks in my mind, however, more than most.

A month after the collapse Megan and I took Charlie to college. We dropped him off in Washington and cried like parents do when their first kid moves away.

A few days later, missing Charlie a lot and feeling really sorry for myself, I made remarks at the first day of school at Augsburg College. A young freshman walked up to me and said, "Do you remember me from the funeral?" It was Sherry Engebretsen's daughter Jessica.

As I talked to this wonderful young woman, I remembered hearing at the funeral that Sherry had been so busy helping one daughter plan a wedding and the other a move to college.

I got to say good-bye to my kid as he started college. Sherry didn't.

So many lives changed in so many other ways. And I still ask, "Why?"

## Two Campaigns

WHEN I AM UNDER STRESS, the best release for me is exercise—so being mayor meant I got in really good shape. I mountain biked and road biked, swam, canoed and kayaked, did triathlons and cross-country ski races, and, my personal favorite, campaigned.

Campaigning, to me, is an aerobic activity. Elections involve all sorts of nuance and policy, but my real joy is the physical part: door knocking until your knuckles are raw, running parades as hard as you can—then going back to do it all over again.

Election Days are the best part: starting at dawn waving your sign at cars on freeway ramps, seeing how many coffee shops you can visit, how many staircases at how many public high-rises you can climb.

There is a seasonal rhythm to it all. You see your breath as you shake hands outside caucuses in midwinter; you move outside into parks and parades in the spring and summer and then hear crunchy leaves under your feet as you door-knock those final few days in the fall. Whether my candidate wins or loses I'm always a little depressed on Election Eve as my overcharged endorphins regretfully retreat.

IT'S A GOOD THING I LIKE CAMPAIGNING because I was in one election or another for big chunks of my first two terms.

My first big campaign as mayor was Howard Dean's presidential run in 2004, which came along at a perfect time. After a few years in office, locked in way too many meetings, I was itching to get back out there. I agreed strongly with Dean's unapologetic opposition to the Iraq war. I also loved the pragmatic, tough management he showed as the governor of Vermont, which was starting to be a lot more important to me as I was spending so much time getting Minneapolis out of its financial hole.

More attractive than anything about the Dean campaign was the wide-open grassroots campaign that skipped the big endorsements and top-down directives. Internet organizing put power into the hands of activists who were moving way ahead of the formal campaign by organizing meet-ups in coffee shops.

I was one of the first big-city mayors to sign on, but all that meant was I was able to work alongside other activists. The inmates were in charge, which felt very familiar because it was so much like my first campaign.

Late at night, after a long day, I would send emails to other activists. On weekend afternoons after a few mayor events, I would show up at a Dean Meetup. Some weekends we would bring a van of activists to Iowa and door-knock whole towns.

Dean lost in Iowa and, in a few months, lost the nomination to John Kerry. But Dean, whom I still stay in touch with, showed Democrats that they should stand up more strongly for their values. I called him "the doctor who helped us find our backbone."

MANY OF THE ORGANIZING AND TECHNOLOGY ADVANCES the Obama campaign perfected four years later were pioneered in the Dean campaign. In fact, having worked in both, I honestly don't think Obama could have won if not for the unorganized but empowered base of activists laid by Dean.

The summer after Dean lost, Barack Obama gave the keynote address at the 2004 Democratic National Convention in Boston. I didn't see it because I was flying to Boston with Grace, but when we got there all the delegates we met were talking about this unknown guy from Illinois who was going to be president someday.

We heard a lot more about Obama during the rest of the convention and when I got home and watched the speech online, I understood why. A few months later I read his book *Dreams from My Father,* which was deeply moving to me. His background living on an island halfway around the world, which some still use to raise doubts about his citizenship, seemed a huge asset to me as America struggles to adjust to a changing world. His work as a community organizer in Chicago, the work Sarah Palin ridiculed as work "with no responsibilities," gave him a unique perspective about how to bring unheard voices to the table. Like a lot of people, I read the book and thought he should be president. Unlike most people, I thought that should happen right now. Democrats were desperate for inspiration and my experience with Dean's grassroots campaign showed me there was a network of activists just waiting to be tapped.

Sometime later Obama came to Minneapolis to speak at the annual Democratic-Farmer-Labor Party fund-raiser, and Mayor Chris Coleman and I were invited to meet him. In a room at the Hilton, Charlie, Grace, and Megan got to shake his hand, then Mayor Coleman and I sat down at a table with him, along with our chiefs of staff Ann Mulholland and Tina Smith.

We exchanged about a minute of niceties and then I blurted out, "You should run for president." Everyone else shifted uncomfortably.

"I'm serious. You should run for president. This year."

"Well, Michelle and I are raising little kids, and we would be going up against a pretty formidable Clinton team. This might not be the right time."

At this point I could have left it, and Tina was giving me a look to cool it, but I felt this was my best, and probably only, chance.

I told him, "It isn't often that a single person with a single act can change the world, but you can."

"Wow, that's heavy," he said. "Your eyes are really intense."

Apparently I was staring a hole in him and Tina was right, now it was time to cool it. We talked awhile longer, I'm not sure what about, but I left convinced that in spite of giving it my best shot, his running was just probably not going to happen. I still didn't want to give up.

Unauthorized, unorganized "Draft Obama" efforts were springing up around the country and going with all my grassroots impulses from my own campaigns and Dean's, I joined right in. Every few months I was part of a national call with Obama activists and I used to love the introductions that showed how much this was a ragtag effort in pure community organizing: "I'm a realtor from Stowe, Vermont," "... a stay-at-home mom from Walla Walla," "... an accountant from Lawrence, Kansas," and then, equally random, "... the mayor of Minneapolis."

A Draft Obama effort also sprang up in Minneapolis with a great group of activists who, at that point, were unknown to most in the party: Paul Provost, Carl Holmquist, Roseanne Hope, and Kim Bachand.

About eight months after the first Obama meeting I wrote a post in one of the national Obama blogs: "Barack Obama is a great man, but this is not about Barack Obama. It is about setting off a grassroots effort that can change our politics."

The next day my assistant Janna Hottinger came into my office looking stunned. "Barack Obama is on the phone," she said.

I picked up: "Hello, R.T., it's Barack . . . Obama."

I laughed. "Yes, I only know one Barack."

"I read what you wrote yesterday and I think we see this the same way . . . I don't need an ego trip but I see this is not about me. I happen to be in a position to set off a movement."

He said he had been traveling the country with his new book, *The Audacity of Hope,* and getting an overwhelming response.

"Do you mean you may actually do this?" I asked, genuinely surprised.

"Yes, I'm thinking about it. And if I do I would like you to help."

That's how I got to be the first mayor in the country to endorse Obama.

The Obama campaign took up almost every minute of free time I had when I wasn't being mayor. I explained it like this: Most people have a hobby. Some golf. Some paint. I try to elect a president.

I campaigned all over the state and for the weeks before the Iowa caucus took busloads down each weekend to door-knock all over the state.

Among the hundreds of amazing moments, a few really stand out. I remember standing in the Des Moines Convention Center, just after we learned Obama won the caucus, and the announcer said, "And now the next first family of the United States of America!" When the Obamas walked onstage, you could actually feel the entire crowd take a breath as we got our first real look at a remarkable family that didn't look anything like almost anyone who voted in the caucus. I turned to my family and could only say, "This is exactly what politics is supposed to be about."

I remember how shortly before the Minnesota caucuses, I spent a day campaigning with Michelle Obama, and she was superb. As she left, I gave her a hug and wanted to say something like, "Next time I see you, you'll be in the White House." Instead, what came out of my mouth was, "I'll see you in the Lincoln Bedroom," which was inappropriate on at least three levels. Almost immediately, she was whisked away, and I still wonder what she told Barack about her visit with that odd mayor in Minneapolis.

Obama activists from all over the country poured into Minnesota before the caucuses and they were working around the clock. But you can't call people on the phone during the Super Bowl so we had a group of them over to our house and we made them what may have been one of the few home-cooked meals they would have in months. We really came to love all these earnest people who were giving up huge chunks of their lives, and as we drank beer, watched the game, and they each told bizarre, funny stories of what was happening on the road in this campaign, I thought, "I never wanted to run away with the circus but I see how it happens." (Today many of them are working in the White House or in other big jobs in Washington. Mike Blake, who lived for a week on a cot in our basement, is now a state legislator in New York.)

A memory that will always stay with me concerned the day before the inauguration. There was a mass concert at the Lincoln Memorial with one great musician after another. Bettye LaVette was the most moving as she and Jon Bon Jovi sang the old Sam Cooke song, "A Change Is Gonna Come," about a far-off time when all the Civil Rights fights would finally pay off. Then Barack Obama stood up to speak where Martin Luther King gave the "I Have a Dream" speech. At that moment I have never been more proud to be an American.

I have stayed proud during President Obama's two terms in the White House and feel more strongly than ever that we finally got the president I was waiting for all my life. I write this in spite of how painful it has been to watch the level of hate directed at him, including the letter I received at my house from an Arizona address that showed doctored pictures of Obama looking like a monkey. If that is coming to my house, I can only imagine what kind of hate mail arrives every day at the White House. Every politician has enemies, especially when that person is president of a very divided United States, but the level of anger directed at him, and the tone, went beyond anything I would have predicted. (Did Rick Perry, the governor of Texas, really stand by and chuckle when Ted Nugent called the president "subhuman"?)

President Obama never forgot my support and has gone out of his way to thank me in public and private. At one appearance in Minneapolis. he said, in an appreciated gross exaggeration, "R.T. knew I was running before I did. . . . When Michelle gets mad at me for ever running for president, I just say, 'Blame R.T.' "

The many people I met in the Obama campaign were spread throughout federal jobs in Washington and that was very helpful as I was able to keep Minneapolis in a good position during the federal stimulus and when cities were chosen for programs like the Promise Zone effort that would eventually help fund the Northside Achievement Zone. Over the years the Obama administration also invited me to a good number of political and social events at the White House and in other parts of Washington.

One of the strangest meetings I went to was in the transition office right after the 2008 election. Three other mayors and I were getting a briefing on the shocking meltdown of the economy. We listened, slack-jawed, as Larry Summers, who would later lead the National Economic Council, clinically described the likelihood that the economy as we knew it was about to collapse into a place we had never seen before. As we were trying to get our heads around the kind of calamity we were about to face, the door burst open and in stormed Rahm Emanuel, who would become chief of staff. Intensely pointing his finger one by one at each of us mayors, he warned about the strings that would be attached to federal dollars to cities in the upcoming stimulus package. "If you f——ers think you are going to get any f——ing money from D.C. without strings attached . . . We're gonna be on your asses every minute to know where Every. F——ing. Cent. Is. Going!" Then just as quickly, he walked out the door, and Summers, without acknowledging what had just happened, picked right up on his passionless, professorial assessment of the economic disaster about to happen. Welcome to Washington.

In 2011 the president's political director Patrick Gaspard called to offer me the position of vice chair of the Democratic National Committee. This came out of left field, especially considering I hadn't been able to get the endorsement of my own party when I ran for mayor the first two times. The volunteer job gave me the chance to work on campaigns around the country, mostly on weekends. I told the DNC I especially wanted to go to red states so I could help rally Democrats fighting the really hard battles on issues such as voter registration. This got me speaking to party conventions and meetings in places like Salt Lake City, Asheville, North Carolina, and Jackson, Mississippi, where I found a surprising number of Democrats. During the 2012 campaign I was sent to early caucus and primary states, like Iowa and New Hampshire, where my job was mostly to give the Democratic response to the many Republicans running against the president. Part of that involvement included doing a lot of national media events.

The most unenviable job I got was to be the Democratic surrogate in Paul Ryan's hometown of Janesville, Wisconsin, the day the local hero had a huge send-off to go to the national convention. I felt like the only Democrat in town that day, until we did a rally at the local Democratic headquarters, where there was a big crowd of volunteers who eventually helped Obama–Biden beat Romney–Ryan in Ryan's hometown.

One of the most moving moments on the road for the DNC was also one of the most embarrassing.

In the months before the 2012 election the Ohio secretary of state was trying to end Sunday voting. On the face of it there should not be a big problem cutting a day or two of voting, until you know that in Ohio, and many other places with African American populations, Sunday is "Souls to the Polls" day, when the tradition is to go to church and then to early voting. We saw that the move to cut off Sunday voting was in fact a blatant attempt to depress black turnout, and attorneys for the DNC were helping to fight the legal and political battle that eventually kept the polls open on Sunday.

This made it especially moving the Sunday before Election Day 2012, when I arrived in a largely African American neighborhood in Cleveland on the DNC campaign bus with California Attorney General Kamala Harris, singer John Legend, and DNC attorney Will Crossley, who worked the phones all day defending against last-minute attempts to stop voting across the country. As we pulled up in the bus all we could see was smoke. The door opened, we went outside hearing loud music, and saw there was a massive street party going on; the smoke was coming from grills cooking chicken. As far as you could see there were lines of African Americans, mostly dressed for church, waiting to vote. As we walked along the lines shaking hands I innocently said to one elderly woman, "It's cold out here." She shot back a defiant look and said, emphatically, "I'm not leaving till I vote!" That woman, and the lines of people, knew what was really going on when the secretary of state tried to shut down Sunday voting, and they were going to stand there all day until they could beat him.

That's the inspirational part of the day. The embarrassing part came when we walked to the top of a grand staircase of a nearby church to address the crowd. John Legend, just as he had at stops earlier in the day, finished his remarks by singing "Wake Up Everybody." At each of our earlier stops, he got the crowd to sing along, and each time we all sang it loud and proud because we were so happy we had kept the polls open. So as I stood behind John Legend on top of those church steps I sang that song with all my heart. By about the third verse I realized that, unlike all those earlier stops, no one else was singing along. I'm sure going home that night some people in the crowd were thinking how inspiring it was to hear John Legend, but why did he have to get that white guy as a backup singer when he can't carry a note?

# Two Campaigns of My Own

DURING, and especially after, the Obama campaign people didn't just ask me *if* I was going to take a job with the new administration. Their main question was, "When?"

I told people from the beginning that I was staying right where I was, and became increasingly frustrated when so many people didn't believe me. I also quickly tried to squelch any thought that I would run for Congress when Martin Sabo retired, or for the Senate against Norm Coleman. As excited as I was about Obama becoming president, I had no intention of moving to Washington.

I'm a Minnesotan. When it snows I want to cross-country ski at Theodore Wirth Park; when it's hot I want to swim in Lake Calhoun. Minneapolis gets cooler every day. My family and Megan's family are here. I really loved my job.

The idea of running for governor was a different story. For many months I went back and forth about whether I should run.

I thought, and still think, that being a mayor is about the best job in the world, so I wasn't looking for a promotion. And wasn't I just starting to get the hang of being mayor?

Peter Wagenius made the case one afternoon that if I ran again for mayor, I could use the third term to take on a couple of big projects we hadn't gotten to, most notably building Minneapolis's first modern streetcar line. That had a lot of appeal, and so did working more directly on schools, which definitely needed my help.

I TRIED TO THINK ABOUT where I could get the most done for the things that mattered. I had spent seven years seeing how much damage a governor could do to my city and knew how much I could do to fix that. I could work on a streetcar as mayor but as governor I could move an entire state transportation plan.

Most people I talked to about that very quickly said that being governor I could get dramatically more done. The impact on transportation, schools, equity, the environment . . . on every measure it seemed I could do more, usually a lot more, if I were governor.

I went back and forth, back and forth, and finally decided to run for governor. The decision was hard; the strategy was even harder.

THE GOOD NEWS was that early polling showed I was in a strong position: Mark Dayton and I were ahead of everyone else. I know enough to not put a lot of weight on early polls because they overvalue name recognition, but it was a good place to start.

The bad news is that it seemed every Democrat in the state was running, including natural allies like Chris Coleman and Margaret Anderson Kelliher, Minnesota's Speaker of the House. Her campaign was the most complicated for me, in part because she came from the same part of Minneapolis. She also would have strong support from the many people who wanted to elect Minnesota's first woman governor, and from legislators, all of whom were Super Delegates.

The final consideration was, after so many years with Governor Pawlenty, I felt Democrats had to win. I didn't think the state could take another four or eight years. I'm as competitive and self-absorbed as the next politician, but I also realized the growing scrum of candidates needed to do everything possible not to have a divisive race that would hurt the chance that one of us would win.

To me that last point meant we couldn't have a bloody primary in August. We all had to go for the endorsement in May and support whoever won.

That wasn't good news for me because I have always had more success directly with voters than with delegates at conventions.

After long talks with the people around me, we decided the only way I could win an endorsement would be to do it almost full-time. This meant not running for mayor.

That was the plan for several months as I tried to get done as much as I could and come to terms with leaving so much unfinished. Then in

September, less than a month before I was going to announce I wouldn't run for mayor again in order to run for governor, the economy collapsed.

Almost overnight thousands of jobs were being lost. State and city revenue plummeted. The economy was in free fall and we had no idea what it would mean for the city, except that we were certain it was going to be bad. Really bad.

Two weeks after the collapse, I called department heads together to talk through what the situation would mean. I stayed calm but didn't sugarcoat the fact that we were in uncharted territory. I reminded them that we had learned over all these years that taking immediate action to cut spending meant we could be spared even more difficult cuts caused by waiting, so each of them should start planning immediately.

As we talked for around an hour I looked around the table at people who had navigated through some remarkably tough times together. Unlike the rookie mayor who years ago came into these meetings surrounded by skeptics from a previous administration, this was my team. They trusted me and were looking to me to lead us out of another big mess.

As I walked back to my office it became absolutely clear something had to change. I went into Tina's office and said, "I just can't walk out on these people. I don't know what this means for the governor thing, but we just have to figure it out."

So we hatched plan B: I would run for mayor again, keep running the city while running for governor, and let the chips fall where they may.

I look back on that now as one of the best decisions I made as mayor. No matter who came in to replace me, it would have taken months to build the team and get up to speed. With a team intact that had been in near-constant budget cycles for seven years, we knew what to do and eventually steered ourselves out of one more mess.

I couldn't have known it then but some of my best work was still to come, and none of it would have happened if I hadn't run again.

ELECTIONS FOR A THIRD TERM are notoriously hard for mayors. Many lose them, in large part because over a couple terms the bad calls start to pile up and the list of people mad at you keeps growing. A lot of mayors running for third terms are out of ideas, and some just don't campaign that hard. I had plenty of barnacles and I had plenty of people unhappy, but I also had plenty of ideas left and loved jumping into another campaign.

I worked most of the day and then phone-banked and door-knocked most nights. Then got up and did it again. There were a few candidates, but none mounted much of a challenge.

The much bigger challenge was the budget, which was quickly getting worse. Governor Pawlenty delivered tough news for the state and—no surprise—passed off a lot of the pain onto cities. This meant we had to impose more cuts and start over budgeting for the coming year with a much bleaker set of numbers.

The bright spot was President Obama and the federal stimulus, which delivered millions to the city for basic services like police and fire, bridges, and other infrastructure.

The stimulus helped but everywhere you turned things were so much worse than even six months earlier. The situation was bad everywhere, but nowhere as bad as north Minneapolis. As the saying goes, when America gets a cold, north Minneapolis gets pneumonia. Almost immediately fore-closures shot up and kept going up until block after block was pockmarked with vacant and boarded houses. Eventually our housing team would use federal dollars for a collection of interventions to help get vacant property back on the market and provide significant new money for homeowner-ship, but in those early months after the collapse it was very bleak.

I had my hands very full but managed to win a third term comfortably and, shortly afterward, announced I was running for governor.

Looking back it seems crazy to be trying to lead the city through a finan-cial crisis while starting a campaign for governor, after having just finished a campaign for mayor and after playing a major role in the Obama cam-paign and, now, the transition. The strange part of it was that I had gotten so used to having a campaign on the side it actually seemed almost nor-mal. Almost.

I spent most days locked in meetings, most nights calling delegates and contributors, and most weekends traveling around the state.

Our campaign had a lot of the energy of my first run for office. Team Teal, named after my campaign color, had a few veterans such as Tina Smith and Julie Hottinger, but it was a really young, very fun staff to be around: Andy Holmaas, Steve Hogan, Scott Anderson, Matt Steinrueck, Alex Falconer, Lauren Robb, Anja Kresojević, Clarice Tushie-Lessard, John Anderson, Grace Hanna, Sarah Helgen, Andrew Nilsen, John Sylves-ter, Mike Quadrozzi, Jamie Makepeace, and Abou Amara. They developed a reputation for being the least conventional team in the race, and the wife of one of the other candidates dismissively called them "hacky sack players," which I suppose was intended to be an insult; they loved it. To me Team Teal was an incredible source of joy, maybe the most committed and refreshing political team I've ever worked with.

We made a good run, but after fourteen hours and six ballots at the convention in Duluth, we lost to Margaret Anderson Kelliher. As promised, before the last ballot was announced, I went to the stage, withdrew, gave a speech asking all Democrats to support Anderson Kelliher, and did not run in the primary.

Usually the winning candidate has the best party of the night. I can't say how good Margaret's celebration was, but I'm certain the best party in Duluth that night was the one we held at Carmody's Irish Pub on Superior Street with Team Teal and a few mayors like Duluth's Don Ness and Dave Smiglewski of Granite Falls. A stage dive off the bar was involved. Early the next morning I walked back to the hotel with Megan and Team Teal, admittedly not in a completely straight line, as I closed that chapter and went back to the job I love.

I would be facing a new reality at City Hall because the strong team that helped bring me through my second term was breaking up. Tina left my office to run the campaign, and went on to be Governor Dayton's lieutenant governor. Jeremy Hanson Willis became chief of staff and John Stiles, who had a long political résumé, became communications director. Steven Bosacker, who did so much to make the city work so well, left on a yearlong around-the-world trip but, planning ahead as always, helped me recruit the talented Paul Aasen to replace him as city coordinator. I brought on a new city attorney, Susan Segal, who became one of my closest advisers.

As all this change was taking place around me, there was one person at the center of all of it: while people with the biggest titles usually get the most credit, the one making things work for me was my assistant Janna Hottinger. No matter what drama or chaos was swirling around her, Janna kept cool and just got things done. She eventually became deputy chief of staff and, to so many people in the know, such a part of my success that when, years later, I called my mother to tell her I got my job at Generation Next, her first question wasn't "What will you do?," "How much are you getting paid?," or "Where is your office." Her first question was "Is Janna coming with you?" Fortunately, she did.

All that churn as I returned to City Hall showed me that we had built a great team in that second term but it ultimately wasn't about any one or two people, including me. We had built a culture of competence in a place that wasn't always known for that. And now we were ready for our best work.

# More Than Point A to Point B

To MY PARENTS, freedom meant having a car. To my kids, freedom means not having to depend on a car. That simple thought explains pretty much everything you need to know about why in my lifetime American cities dramatically changed for the worse and are now changing dramatically for the better.

It explains why it was shockingly easy in the 1950s and 1960s to rip out the heart of city neighborhoods, like the integrated one where my family's drugstore was, to build freeways to newly paved former cornfields. It explains why corner stores like my family's, in neighborhoods with shrinking populations, competing with big-box chains sprawled on cheaper suburban land, eventually went away and left empty storefronts along once-vibrant urban commercial streets.

That simple thought explains why cities, and eventually schools, became more segregated and neighborhoods struggled in places like north Minneapolis, which were carved up and separated from the rest of town by impenetrable highways. It explains why, when more jobs went to the suburbs, and we couldn't, or wouldn't, build public transit to growing numbers of jobs in all those scattered office parks, the economic gaps widened.

That simple thought, especially the part about our kids wanting freedom from cars, also explains why so much of that is changing for the better. It explains why almost every neighborhood in Minneapolis has seen some kind of renaissance as a new generation, starting with mine and rapidly accelerating with my kids', chooses a lifestyle that doesn't require spending all day in a car. That explains why billions have been invested in restoring house after house, reopening corner stores and restaurants in those vacant storefronts where stores like my family's used to be. It explains why a stronger residential base is making some city schools better. It explains why, in the year I left office, downtown Minneapolis (population 35,000) finally recaptured all the population it lost in those anti-urban decades since the 1950s.

This isn't happening just in Minneapolis. The tech boom of the 1990s led to sprawling suburban campuses in the Silicon Valley south of San Francisco and Microsoft's campus west of Seattle. Today's tech boom sees Google spending a fortune on daily buses from San Francisco where workers are willing to ride an hour and a half each way so they don't have to live in the suburbs. Facebook and Uber are now in San Francisco itself, where their employees can take a short transit ride to work from walkable, vital neighborhoods. And this isn't just happening in big cities: You see this same rapid urbanization in places like Boise, Chattanooga, Bethlehem, and Youngstown.

That simple idea also explains why I never thought our transportation strategy in Minneapolis was about transportation. It was about more than getting from point A to point B; it was about building the kind of city we wanted with the most effective tools any city has to shape its future: the road, the bus, the light rail, the bike, the sidewalk, and, I hope someday in Minneapolis, the streetcar.

There were so many issues on which my thinking evolved dramatically in office. Transportation was different; my views were fully formed before I ran, and the only change after twelve years was that I had become more committed to accelerating the change as quickly as possible.

I wasn't alone in thinking this way, and, if I had been, we never could have gotten done what we did. We got hundreds of millions of dollars from Washington, especially during the federal stimulus, in large part because of two Minnesotans in the U.S. House of Representatives:

> Martin Sabo of Minneapolis, whose mastery of the budget process helped him reliably deliver the key funds for streets, bridges, buses, and light rail; and

> The late Jim Oberstar, whose district started about 100 miles north but whose key position on the Committee on Transportation and Infrastructure helped deliver for almost every transit project in the city, most notably millions for cutting-edge bike infrastructure.

There were also two players I worked with more closely, who were two of the savviest transportation thinkers anywhere, both named Peter, lived in the same part of town, worked across the street from each other, had almost identical views of how we could reshape cities with innovative transportation, and, frankly, usually didn't work very well together:

> Hennepin County commissioner Peter McLaughlin, who played a major role in every regional transit project and helped form a coalition of counties that controlled a sales tax–generated transit fund; and

> Peter Wagenius, my senior policy aide, who came into office with relatively little background in city budgets and transportation but mastered both, and spent time on the first (because we really needed him there) so that he could spend time on the second (which was his passion).

The person charged with implementing all the visions from me, and all these other complex personalities, was Public Works director Steve Kotke. In the many times when there was a sudden change from one of our partners, or a conflict broke out with the very large personalities who often were in the room, he calmly went back to his office and somehow, time after time, made it all work. He often played Mr. Spock to my Captain Kirk, as I gave him one more out-there idea that did not seem "logical" to him at first but that he eventually turned into reality.

The final partner was an exceptionally active and organized network of advocacy groups and activists whose power was unmatched anywhere between here and Portland. They made it significantly easier to go out on a limb knowing they had my back, like the time one of the council members made the mistake of trying to cut a bike coordinator out of my budget, only to run into a buzz saw of opposition from transit activists.

Unlike so much of our work—where budget challenges, economic downturns, and the hostile Pawlenty and Bush administrations made it seem the deck was stacked against us—this infrastructure of empowered transportation supporters made it possible for us to move far more than we could have alone.

Like so much of the city building I wanted to do, we had few opportunities to affect transportation planning in the early years. Heading into a budget crisis wasn't the right time to announce a major transit initiative, but from our first capital budget to the last one twelve years later, we invested as much as we possibly could in building out an infrastructure that made bike commuting a potentially viable mainstream option. Some of the bike ideas Wagenius and I talked about our first weeks in office were in the first capital budget and some, like connections to the University of Minnesota, were in the twelfth, but every single one of those budgets had at least one and usually several key investments for bike routes. The operating budgets often funded the "software" to make the physical improvements better, like Safe Routes to School and an additional bike planner. Usually the main impediment to investing more, especially in capital, was that we had to wait a year or two for a federal match, but even that got easier when Representative Oberstar delivered a multimillion-dollar fund to Minneapolis, and only two other cities, for bike innovation.

All this was helpful to those who were already interested in bikes, but as the years went on we looked for more ways to attract more riders who were not the typical Lycra-wearing, hardy, twelve-months-a-year bike commuters. We began hearing how bike sharing was attracting nontraditional riders in Europe, but every time I got another email from an advocate saying, "Bike share works in Paris," I thought, "Poodles in restaurants and berets on men work in Paris but not always in Minneapolis."

We got a break in 2008. Humana, the Louisville-based health insurer, wanted to do a temporary bike-share promotion during the national political conventions and sent a team here to see if Minneapolis and St. Paul would be interested during the Republican convention. I jumped at the chance and, with a great deal of assistance from Humana's Nate Kvamme, used the temporary promotion to help sell the idea to potential long-term sponsors.

We hired John Munger and Bill Dossett, who helped launch the City of Lakes Loppet, to develop a plan for permanent bike share and they came back with good news and bad news. The good was that there was a real path to make it work, but the bad was that it would cost $3 million, about $2 million more than I thought I could ever possibly patch together. It cost so much because an extensive network of bike stations was needed to cover enough ground so that bike-share riders would know there would be a station near where they wanted to leave the bikes. The only bike-share system then operating in the United States was in Washington, D.C., and it was failing in part because the program didn't have enough stations and didn't cover the logical routes where people were going. To give people that confidence, we could not start with just a few stations, like I wanted, but, instead, had to build a network with many stations.

Humana did the same promotion during the Democratic Convention in Denver, and when it was done I talked to John Hickenlooper, then mayor of Denver and now governor of Colorado. We agreed bike share was a great idea, that it cost dramatically more than we thought, and that each of us would look a little less like a fool if we failed together. I told him, "I don't mind looking like an idiot, but it's nice not to be a lonely idiot."

Mayor Hickenlooper raised his money in Denver, and I went to Blue Cross Blue Shield, one of those sponsors Kvamme and I brought to that trial run in Minneapolis during the Republican National Convention. We asked Blue Cross for $1 million to start the program; to my amazement the company eventually said yes, and that leveraged $1.5 million in a fund delivered by Oberstar. I got the rest by tapping a convention sales tax fund used to attract visitors. Right from the start the system, called Nice Ride, was a success both in overall ridership and in attracting the kind of irregular bike riders we were after. Nice Ride and Denver's B-Cycle showed other U.S. cities the idea could work and it inspired bike-share systems around the country. Today Nice Ride has spread to St. Paul and cities around Minnesota, and, still led by Dossett, is often cited as the best system in the country.

A year later I was doing a press conference in Minneapolis with Janette Sadik-Kahn, the truly visionary transit planner who was doing groundbreaking work against great odds in New York City. After we finished I was handed a note saying Minneapolis had been named America's Number One Bike City. Sadik-Kahn, who had every reason to feel her city was deserving, was gracious enough, but I could see her head was about to explode. In Portland, which had won the best bike city title year after year, all hell broke loose and the mayor called the award a fraud. Remembering my old *Star Tribune* office on Portland Avenue, I shot back with "Portland is just a street in Minneapolis." That became a popular bumper sticker sold in our city's bike shops. (In reality, much of our innovative work could never have been happened if not for the pioneering efforts in Portland.)

Proving all this wasn't a fluke, in 2015 Minneapolis was the only U.S. city on the list of best bike cities in the world, and the authors said we were "quickly becoming the go-to city in America for building bike infrastructure."

* * *

BIKES PATHS, for recreation and commuting, have gone a long way toward helping people become less dependent on cars, even in the winter where Minneapolis is the number two bike-commuting city in the country. This is a remarkable statistic when you think about the kind of conditions our bike commuters face in the winter. But if you want to dramatically move the dial in getting people out of cars, if you want to significantly increase the city's population without creating gridlock, you need significantly more transit options.

Sabo, Oberstar, McLaughlin, Mayor Sayles Belton, and many, many others were key players in getting the first light rail line under way. Another key player was then-governor Jesse Ventura, whose advocacy helped overcome the fierce opposition of conservative Republican legislators. I was around to help cut the ribbon, but had little to do with that first line. I can say two things: The system was built primarily in reverse, which I know because I heard the *beep-beep-beep* of trucks backing up for a full year working on the tracks right out my office. Second, it was a huge success, which made it possible to move ahead on the next lines.

The challenge with building any more lines was the lack of sustainable funding, and Governor Pawlenty was adamantly opposed to any tax dollars being allocated for transit. Early in my first term, at the first meeting of the business coalition Itasca Group, Mayor Randy Kelly and I made an impassioned pitch to CEOs that they were the only ones who could significantly change transit because they may be the only group that wanted more who had any influence over the governor and Republican legislature. Eventually, enough key business leaders who had written campaign checks to the governor were willing to make the case to build transit, but they couldn't move him. Ultimately, enough of them would help push other legislators so that Governor Pawlenty's veto of a transit-funding bill was overridden.

This breakthrough opened the door to more transit planning, and the next light rail line to be built was the connection between Minneapolis and St. Paul via the University of Minnesota. The line also went through Frogtown and other lower-income neighborhoods in St. Paul where many residents are dependent on public transit. Unlike the development of the first light rail line, when opponents stripped much of the money to help integrate the line with surrounding neighborhoods, the second light rail line could be coordinated with planning in the surrounding blocks. This happened in large part because we attracted several million dollars for community building along the line from Living Cities, a coalition of major foundations based in New York committed to investing that creates equity in cities. (I am now a senior adviser to Living Cities.)

A key, and complex, decision along the way was how many station stops there would be, which was critical given that the existing bus stopped at almost every block. If the light rail didn't have enough stops, those transit-dependent riders would actually be worse off than they were before the line.

Transit decisions such as this did not have much impact on federal funding until President Obama got elected because previously the federal government gave no points to lines that create economic development and community impact. The Obama administration changed that, saying transit was also about community building and equity, a critical change for these neighborhoods because it meant we could get credit for—-not be penalized for—-adding stops that helped low-income neighborhoods grow. With this change Mayor Coleman and I joined advocates in this neighborhood to add three more stops in the transit-dependent communities along University Avenue.

Today that makes the ride from Minneapolis to St. Paul slower and less attractive to some commuters. I would still argue that it is better than the alternative, which would have been to have transit-dependent low-income people walking many blocks in the snow with their groceries or on their way to work as they watched passing trains serving the higher-income people wanting to shave a couple of minutes off their commute.

The third light rail line to be planned was to the southwest suburbs, and from the very start I had a significant disagreement with Hennepin County. The view of McLaughlin, Commissioner Gail Dorfman, and the county staff was we should take the route that could be completed the fastest; that route would connect the suburbs along the Kenilworth Corridor skirting the western edge of Minneapolis. The corridor had rail traffic, but the county said that could be relocated so there would be enough room to keep a very popular and important bike trail through a park-like setting along the edge of Lake of the Isles and Cedar Lake.

I wanted the route to go through the heart of the city, in the vacant existing right-of-way next to the bike lanes on the Midtown Greenway. My argument was that this would cost more but attract dramatically more riders in the dense neighborhoods of Uptown, Lyn-Lake, Midtown, and Phillips, as well as connect to the bus rapid transit network we were building along I-35W. It could also be a critical catalyst for increasing development at the Greenway and Nicollet, where we continued to look for ways to create more market demand to make it possible to fund reopening Nicollet Avenue—fixing the single worst planning disaster in Minneapolis history.

Routing the light rail line along the edge of the city, and avoiding these dense neighborhoods along the Greenway, would be, in my mind, as disastrous as the decision to leave Georgetown out of Washington's Metro. In fact, it would be worse because avoiding the Greenway route would mean there might never be a way to connect the low-income residents of the center of Minneapolis to high-paying jobs in the suburbs.

Hennepin County, and some Minneapolis representatives, including council member Robert Lilligren, who represented many of the Greenway neighborhoods, battled with Wagenius and me for several years. Many equity advocates were against us, too, saying the Kenilworth route would give more service to low-income residents in north Minneapolis; I reminded them there are also plenty of low-income residents in south Minneapolis near the Greenway.

Our plan to route the line down the Greenway had a challenge because it was tough to get downtown: tunneling under Nicollet Avenue was expensive, integrating in some way with the 35W bus rapid transit was complex, running down the extra-wide Park and Portland Avenues was slower for suburban commuters. Chicago Avenue, which was being rebuilt, may be too narrow. All these options were compared with the cost of the cleaner options along Kenilworth, and each time Kenilworth came out on top in their rankings. Unfortunately, in spite of our urging, they did not take into account the potential of complications. In coming years, as Kenilworth's costs and controversy soared, it became clear to me that there never had been a clear comparison of the true costs and that Greenway alternatives would have made more sense.

Eventually we lost and I said I would get on board because it was critical to build the line. I went to the very disappointed Kenilworth neighbors and made the case that, even though there may not be a stop in their neighborhood, the benefit of another regional light rail line outweighed the drawback. A bonus would be that the county committed to moving the existing rail traffic. Some neighbors still wouldn't buy it, but enough did that we began partnering with the county and the Metropolitan Council on planning the line along the route skirting the city to the west.

After the planning was well under way, the railroads, which have virtual carte blanche to do what they want in this country, changed their minds and decided they didn't want to move the Kenilworth trains after all. Hennepin County couldn't deliver on its promise. Now the already reluctant neighbors, whose agreement we worked hard to get, felt duped, and routing light rail and the trains together created a whole host of problems.

Hundreds of trees would be cut down, it could be necessary to build a tunnel in this environmentally sensitive (and very soggy) wetland, where a single misstep could damage the fragile Chain of Lakes, Minneapolis's crown jewel. Kenilworth's park-like setting would be radically altered, and, with the North Dakota oil boom showing no sign of slowing, there was no guarantee that the route would not be jammed nonstop with trains carrying potentially dangerous cargo nearby, or under, the Chain of Lakes.

Let's just say it didn't go over very well. Like the Kenilworth residents, I felt duped, and for my final years in office it got worse, jeopardizing key projects and relationships.

ALTHOUGH THERE WAS FAR MORE DRAMA around light rail, one of the most significant transit improvements came in bus rapid transit, and it did, in part, because we put together an unlikely coalition that included some of the state legislators who were fighting light rail. The key partner to make it happen was actually George W. Bush. That came about because a group of people who had fought for years agreed to focus less on what we didn't want and more on where we had common ground.

This played out along 35W, the site of decades of bad blood between suburbs, which wanted expansion to speed car commuting, and neighborhoods that never wanted another inch taken after seeing their communities decimated by the original freeway construction.

Wagenius and I knew from the start that something had to give and we knew that in places like Bogotá, Colombia, bus rapid transit was being elevated to a new level that made it possible to attract almost as many riders as light rail. Opponents of transit funding heard the same thing but drew a different conclusion: if they could prove the far less expensive bus rapid transit worked, it could take some of the momentum away from building more light rail.

Early in the first term we began talking to suburban mayors and regional officials about a vision for bus rapid transit on 35W. This gained some momentum because it would connect a bus rapid transit line being built in the far suburbs of Eagan with downtown jobs. Meanwhile the same discussion was taking place between one of the most liberal members of the legislature, Representative Frank Hornstein from my neighborhood, and one of the most conservative members, Representative Mary Liz Holberg of Lakeville. We all agreed on probably only one thing: it was in all our interests to get a bus rapid transit lane on 35W.

We joined a group of city and suburban officials to sign an agreement that, for the first time in decades, actually said what all these people who were *against* something were *for*. Key suburban mayors like Edina's Jim Hovland and Richfield's Debbie Goettel played important roles in getting the consensus. So did council member Lilligren and the politically savvy Scott Benson.

All sides agreed that we wanted more people using the corridor, but not by physically expanding it. There was really only one way to do that, and it was to add transit—which made us city people happy—but we agreed that the transit we would add wouldn't be light rail but bus rapid transit— which made the suburban anti–light rail transit people happy.

We added another wrinkle by saying that we were open to having toll lanes, which, until then, had been supported only by some of the suburban groups. This was a controversial topic with many of our city constituents, who saw it as privatizing public roads. We saw it differently, maintaining that if we could get the toll money used to fund transit on the freeway we were finally finding a way to get drivers to subsidize more mass transit, and not the other way around. "Don't think of them as Lexus Lanes," I told a group of south Minneapolis activists. "Since they are redistributing the wealth from car drivers to bus riders, think of them as Lenin Lanes." (Don't try this argument outside south Minneapolis or a Bernie Sanders rally.)

This unlikely coalition of urban and suburban, pro-transit and anti– light rail, Republicans and Democrats actually stayed together. It hit rough spots, including when the city of Minneapolis held up its municipal approval of the expansion of the adjacent Highway 62 until we forced funding for a bus rapid transit station. The coalition was effective enough that we convinced the Pawlenty administration to apply for a federal pot of money called the Urban Partnership, which would bring $100–$150 million to implement this new vision for remaking a traditional highway.

Getting that federal money was a real long shot until we were presented with an unusual opportunity in the wake of the 35W bridge collapse, about a half mile from where our 35W improvements were being planned. The day before President Bush came to inspect the bridge damage, the federal

Department of Transportation told us to put together a request for what we needed to rebuild the bridge. We wrote a document describing the specific needs for the bridge itself but incorporated the details of an Urban Partnership request to add bus rapid transit capacity to 35W.

When we were flying to the bridge collapse site with the president, he asked what the city needed to rebuild. I told him we needed funds to rebuild the bridge with transit capacity for the future. Then I added: "We also applied for an Urban Partnership grant for 35W so the transit capacity on the bridge could just flow right down the freeway."

I knew linking the bridge collapse and the freeway improvements was a real stretch but, to my surprise, President Bush didn't hesitate. "If that's what you think you need," he said, "you tell me that in the meeting we are about to go into."

After touring the destruction at the bridge site the president and I went into a nearby building for a high-level meeting that included Transportation Secretary Mary Peters, representatives of a variety of federal agencies, and branches of the military. The president turned to me and asked, "Mayor, what do you need to rebuild?"

"We want to rebuild the bridge right, with transit capacity for the future. And we want to use the Urban Partnership grant to keep that transit going right down 35W."

The president turned to Secretary Peters: "We can do that, can't we, Mary?"

I thought I saw her turn an intense shade of pale, which I interpreted to mean they had no intention of awarding Minneapolis–St. Paul the Urban Partnership grant.

"We can if you want to, Mr. President."

"Well, I want to!" he shot back. As he spoke, the Texas drawl, which used to drive me crazy when he was talking about invading Iraq, began to sound, well, *downright homey.*

A few days later we got word that the federal government had awarded us $130 million to build a lane for express buses and carpools on 35W. That helped pay for dedicated bus–carpool lanes and to support a bus rapid transit station at Forty-Sixth Street. Most significant, this grant also funded a completely reconstructed Marquette and Second avenues downtown to serve as transit corridors to dramatically speed express buses in and out of downtown. Marquette and Second, long downtown's ugly-duckling streets, now serve more transit riders than a light rail line and are tied to a big vision that will eventually expand bus rapid transit in every direction. President Bush was no friend of mass transit, but he did a big favor for Minneapolis.

As big visions for light rail and bus rapid transit started to become real, it was also becoming clear there were two significant problems. The first problem was that we were running out of downtown streets to convert to transit: after the four light rail lines being planned were built, the current right-of-way would be at capacity and there were no obvious streets that could be converted to transit without creating major gridlock.

The second problem was that for the foreseeable future the major transit investments would be between suburbs and downtown, often on routes bypassing city neighborhoods. Generally, getting suburban workers to the city, and vice versa, is a good thing, but it meant that a city we wanted to grow might not have any major strategy to get cars off the road in our communities for at least a decade. Our goal was to add 100,000 people to the city without increasing traffic, and the only way to do that was with a significant new transit strategy. That's how we began thinking about streetcars.

Modern streetcars are nothing like the creaky, slow streetcars that rumbled down Minneapolis's streets decades ago. Today they are sleek, faster, and extremely successful in adding vitality to neighborhoods in places like Portland. It is also important to remember that they serve a different purpose than light rail and bus rapid transit, which are best for moving large numbers of people with relatively few stops (think, for example, of suburban park-and-ride lots for commuters going downtown). While people often talk about these three ways of getting around as being interchangeable, in reality streetcars are used best where population is denser; they stop more, can move more flexibly, and can share street lanes with cars.

Streetcars solve our dilemma of adding more transit without taking more streets out of commission for cars. More important, because they stop so often, streetcars are exceptionally good at building communities and small businesses. This is why in cities like Minneapolis that grew up around streetcars, every few blocks you see neighborhood-scale retail buildings to serve people who wanted to grab milk or dry cleaning on the way home. My family's drugstore was an example of a business that grew up on an intersection with an old streetcar stop.

If you doubt that a city like Minneapolis could expand its population with streetcars, remember that when the original lines were in operation in the 1950s, the city's population was 500,000; after the lines were torn up and the freeways built, the population plummeted to 325,000. All we wanted to do was to rebuild the streetcar city, with the population increasing by 100,000, without putting more cars on the road. Minneapolis could do it again because we had done it before.

Streetcars were a passion for both Wagenius and me, and we worked on them in one form or another almost my entire time in office. Our public works team devised long-term plans, task forces helped prioritize lines, community organizations built those plans into their long-range visions, and consultants vetted alternatives.

Big ideas are great but the problem is paying for them: there was far less federal money for streetcars than for light rail; the state, county, and metropolitan governments all said they would not fund them. We explored a bunch of ideas for privately funding them but never turned up a possibility that seemed viable. If we were going to build streetcars we were on our own, and with the city struggling most of those years with very lean budgets, it seemed the streetcar visions would remain visions.

The idea that finally worked was to pay for a first streetcar line by promising that it would create more development and, in turn, more property taxes along the route. We believed building a line would lead to significantly more development, and if we could capture some of that new tax revenue that wouldn't have come to the city without the line, we could find enough to pay for construction.

It made sense to think a new line would generate more growth when you realized the development potential of that first line. The plan was for the streetcar to start on Central Avenue in northeast Minneapolis, a neighborhood in the beginning of a comeback that clearly would be accelerated if residents could take an easy streetcar ride to a downtown job. It would cross the Mississippi, near the neighborhood surrounding the University of Minnesota, over the dramatic Hennepin Avenue Bridge. Entering downtown the line would run down Nicollet Avenue, the main street about to be redeveloped in a design by the architect of New York's High Line. Leaving downtown through the Loring Park neighborhood, which had tremendous development opportunities, it would run south along the vibrant "Eat Street" section of Nicollet, which was already a major attraction and poised for more growth. The final few blocks had the most potential of all: as the line approached Lake Street it would cross the Midtown Greenway and run along a newly built part of Nicollet currently blocked by an ill-fated Kmart. Surrounding that site today are several blocks of underdeveloped property that would, in my mind, clearly have new growth if there were a new streetcar line.

This was only one route. We imagined even more: along Washington Avenue, down Broadway in north Minneapolis, Chicago in south Minneapolis. Building even one line would be a massive stretch, but it was, to me, a far better way for the city to help increase its tax base than an individual subsidy to an individual project.

There was a catch with our scheme to fund the streetcar with taxes from growth along the route: it was illegal. State law prevented cities from using those funds for transit. The only way to make it happen was to get the legislature to give us an exception, and the only way to make that happen was to convince the House Taxes Committee chair, Representative Ann Lenczewski, who was the state's single biggest opponent of taking any land off the tax rolls.

Representative Lenczewski is known for being tough, but I also knew her as fair, and she agreed to at least meet. The case I made was that the state would be better off if we built the streetcar because, when it was finished, we would be creating more economic development and, eventually, a lot more revenue for the state. She didn't really seem to be buying the argument, so I asked her to get in my car and drove her the whole route of the proposed first line. In detail, on almost every block, I walked through how land would be more valuable if the line were there. At the end of the drive she had a very different view and eventually helped us pass a state law that essentially made it possible to raise about $30 million of the $90 million needed.

Once we had a way to pay our share, doors that had been closed to us opened almost immediately. Hennepin County officials started early talks about helping and the chair of the Metropolitan Council talked positively about streetcars in her State of the Region speech.

The window of opportunity that opened for streetcars would slam shut in the last half of my final year as the city's relations with these partners deteriorated during the Southwest Light Rail Transit controversy. One of my major disappointments in my time as mayor was getting so close only to leave office wondering if the opportunity would ever come again.

While that bitter disappointment soured my last year, those final months also had a more positive development on Twenty-Ninth Street in the Uptown neighborhood.

In my last few years in office it became clear that Minneapolis still was not breaking enough ground for pedestrians. We launched several efforts in the last couple of years, including expanding Safe Routes to School, where adults helped children create "walking school buses."

The biggest physical improvement planned for pedestrians was to create a walking passage in the car-dominated Uptown neighborhood. The first few blocks were already in place as a redevelopment of the Calhoun Square shopping center started a pedestrian alley behind the complex that later developments extended two more blocks to an art-filled plaza next to the Midtown Greenway. The pedestrian experience stopped abruptly at Twenty-Ninth Street, a butt-ugly pothole-filled sad excuse for a street that runs just above the Midtown Greenway. The Public Works Department proposed repaving the street but council member Meg Tuthill and I didn't want to pave over a mediocre status quo, so we transferred that money to a new account funding a plan to convert the street to a pedestrian way.

In my last month in office I worried that this idea would fall through the cracks so I brought property owners along the route together with the newly elected council member Lisa Bender. Almost all of them got the idea immediately, and in the year after I left office, Bender, a trained city planner with a great eye, worked with the community to make the idea even better than I had planned. The butt-ugly street is on its way to becoming a great place for pedestrians and we hope it will start a new era when the people who leave their cars behind and walk get the rock star treatment in Minneapolis that they deserve and that bikers already have.

# *The Next Generation*

---

T WO KIDS ON A PLAYGROUND come down the slide, one after the other, then go to the sandbox, where they each build a castle.

Most adults watching assume the children are playing together, but many times they are in totally separate worlds creating separate realities right next to each other. "Parallel play" happens all the time on the playground, and a lot of times it happens with adults as well.

Nowhere in politics does that happen as much as it does with mayors and the people who run city schools. They are in charge of the most important institutions that affect the lives of people in cities, but in many cities like Minneapolis, they have existed in parallel but separate universes. That's in large part because in Minneapolis, and many other cities, the mayor has no formal control over what happens to the kids getting an education in the city the mayor is supposed to lead.

I knew we couldn't have a great city without great schools, but I also knew I had no authority to make schools better. At first I dealt with that reality by creating a tidy separation of responsibility: the schools were in charge of making kids' lives better when they were in class, and I was in charge of making their lives better the rest of the day. I didn't get involved in what happened in the school building and focused, instead, on helping kids before they were old enough for school, on activities when they were home at night or during breaks, and on building a school-to-career pipeline we came to call the "Minneapolis Promise."

It all sounds logical but in retrospect, it was a serious miscalculation and as the years went on I began to change my strategy and get more deeply involved in education. Largely because I had no formal control, some of the strongest alliances I would build would be in education, and most of the best work happened largely out of public view.

In my early years I didn't need to get too involved in education because Minneapolis had a strong superintendent: Carol Johnson. But a couple of years into my term she announced she was leaving to become superintendent of schools in Memphis. It was a bigger blow than most of us realized at the time, and it was worse because she took with her some top talent that included future Minneapolis superintendents Bernadeia Johnson and Michael Goar, as well as future Minnesota Education Commissioner Brenda Cassellius. Her deputy David Jennings, a former Republican legislative leader who had been doing a very good job, was an obvious replacement but immediately faced a small but vocal opposition and withdrew.

After a national search the school board surprised almost everyone by picking a person almost no one had heard of: Thandiwe Peebles.

In those days I was up to my eyeballs—sometimes in over my head—with the crisis of the week, but I reached out to the new superintendent and told her I wanted to help. The meeting was pleasant enough, but from the start I privately questioned if she was the right person for the job. I wasn't alone. Very quickly word started coming back to me that there was dissension at the district offices and, almost as quickly, with many parents.

As the controversy over Superintendent Peebles grew, I realized I had made a serious mistake. The charter may not give the mayor power over schools, but they are too important to stand back when kids' education is at stake. I began to realize that working on out-of-school time, safety, summer jobs, and all that was great but I needed to do a lot more.

As Peebles was being removed many of us came to the chilling realization that because so much talent had left with Superintendent Johnson, there was no heir apparent. After what we were going through, there was no appetite for another national search. Minneapolis was also developing a reputation for being a troubled district that was very hard to lead, so there was growing concern we could not find a skilled person willing to be hired.

Unlike my first years in office, I began working with key school board members. After some very troubling weeks, Bill Green's name surfaced. A professor at Augsburg College and former school board member, Green was not a classic superintendent but he was respected and level headed. As a consensus began to develop to appoint Green, I began working the phones with community leaders, impressing on them how serious the situation was and how I thought Green could be the right person at the right time.

I met with him as I had with Peebles, but this time I was a lot more blunt. I said Minneapolis schools were in trouble. They weren't all bad, as the cartoon sometimes painted of them tried to portray. In fact, having been in many of them many times, I knew many students were getting a good and sometimes great education. The problem was that the schools were uneven and the key to the crisis was that the kids being served the least were those who needed help the most: kids who were poor, and especially, kids of color. As I had with Peebles, I told Green I would back him but added, "as long as you don't wimp out." Do tough things, make the necessary changes, and I will run as much interference as I can. "I will take on people who take you on," I said. "I will be the most loyal supporter you can find, but if I see you pulling punches because you're afraid of the consequences, I will call you out because we don't have time to waste."

He didn't wimp out, and we formed a very strong partnership as he rebuilt trust in schools. He also rebuilt the leadership team, including bringing Bernadeia Johnson back from Memphis. A strong new school board also came in that included Pam Costain, Peggy Flanagan, and Tom Madden. Green and the board developed, for the first time I remember, a strategic plan with vision, calling for more autonomy for high-performing schools and major changes at those that were failing.

After four years, Green left and was replaced by Bernadeia Johnson. Johnson grew up in a very different world than I did. As an African American going to school in Jim Crow days in Selma, Alabama, she saw firsthand what it meant to have separate and unequal schools. As the granddaughter of Minneapolis's first African American principal, she also had insight into the fact that inequity in education wasn't confined to the South.

Our experiences were different but we became extremely strong allies and, for both Megan and me, she became a very close friend. I told her the same thing I told Green: "I will be the most loyal supporter you can find, except if you wimp out."

I also gave her a paperweight from my desk that said "What would you expect to do if you knew you could not fail?" David Fey had given it to me during my first term and it always reminded me that when you get into jobs like this you sometimes have to build a wall to block out the doubters, including yourself, and just visualize what deep in your heart you really believed would make the changes that are needed.

For Johnson that meant executing that strategic plan and not accepting failing schools. Two of the high schools with the strongest histories were Washburn and Edison, but both were underperforming. The superintendent's solution was to "fresh start" both, which meant a new program, and

all teachers and leaders had to reapply for their old jobs. This was controversial at Edison. It was even more controversial at Washburn, where it
led to a walkout by the students. Johnson didn't wimp out, and neither
did Carol Markum-Cousins, the tough-as-nails principal she appointed.
I had tough conversations trying to convince some very skeptical parents
and students to support the plan but today Washburn is a far better school
in large part because of tough work there by Johnson and Markham-
Cousins, and the teachers and families who dug in to make change.

I gave Superintendent Johnson lots of political support, but she proved
to be a pretty skilled politician in her own right, using charm and intel-
lect to build support for actions that only a few years earlier would have
been unthinkable. A great example was the partnerships she built with the
Harvest and Hiawatha schools. Both high-performing charter networks
had been seen by Minneapolis schools as the opposition, not welcome
to compete to use empty school buildings and not welcome partners.
Johnson built a new alliance, allowing them to use former schools and
develop teacher-learning exchanges to help import best practices into district classrooms.

Unlike the early years in my term, I was spending more and more time
on schools, and, unlike issues in City Hall, I was learning a different part
of leadership in which I was not out front. I gave advice and helped build
support with other elected officials, foundations, and influencers. I also
convinced Johnson to give a major address outlining a vision for where the
schools needed to go next, and my communication director, John Stiles,
and education policy aide Victor Cedeño were part of weekly meetings
with the superintendent's team to develop the "Shift Initiative." This new
vision for Minneapolis schools included moving resources out of the district office and into schools, and injecting more flexibility into underperforming schools.

Meanwhile I was spending more and more time on the Minneapolis
Promise, which was really three initiatives creating a career pipeline for
kids: College and Career Centers, the Step- Up summer jobs program, and
the Power of You, a program to give high-performing, high-need students
two years at local community and technical colleges:

The College and Career Centers, started with a major grant
from former Medtronic CEO Win Wallin, created privately
funded one-stop centers in each high school where students

could meet with counselors, get information about college and financial aid, and explore career options.

STEP-UP had grown from its early days and by the end of my term had placed twenty thousand students—80 percent kids of color, 90 percent living below the poverty line, 30 percent from immigrant families—into high-quality summer jobs. Each year we would get hundreds of stories about kids whose lives were changed by the program. One of my favorites is the Vang family, Hmong refugees who came from Thailand in the 1980s. One of the four boys, Teng, was at Edison High School in 2004 when I announced the program, He became part of the first group and, after college, is now in technology at Wells Fargo. Two of his brothers now also work at Wells Fargo. A few years later their nephew Xee was in another assembly at Edison where I talked about STEP-UP and, after four years in the program and college, now also works at Wells Fargo. Wells Fargo, alone, has hired more than 160 people who worked in STEP-UP.

The Power of You is a joint program of St. Paul College and Minneapolis Community and Technical College that I helped launch in 2006. Hundreds of students have now gone through the program, and those who get these scholarships and academic support are more than 10 percent more likely to graduate.

Each of these parts of the Minneapolis Promise was growing on its own, but together they formed a clear path for our students, and for my last seven years in office I held a major assembly in each Minneapolis high school telling students to go to the College and Career Center, apply for STEP-UP, and find out about the Power of You.

I also took questions at those assemblies, and the students were brutally honest about problems in their neighborhoods, especially with crime. At first I did my best to relate to the students, trying to talk about music or some cultural reference that would send a signal I wasn't an old geek in a suit and tie. In retrospect I must have sounded a bit like one of those dads in my era who would show up at his kid's party in a Nehru jacket talking about the Grateful Dead. Claudia Fuentes, one of my education policy aides, helped convince me this was the wrong approach. So many of these kids were coming out of poverty facing all the deep challenges of race; they didn't have the privileges of the people they would be competing with for jobs. They didn't have any margin for error and couldn't afford to act the wrong way, say the wrong thing, or even send the wrong message in a job interview. I realized my job was to be a person in authority who believed deeply in them but raised expectations and taught them some of those intangible things kids with more privilege got by osmosis. I eventually made every one of them shake my hand, knowing this was going to be key to the first impression in an interview they couldn't afford to blow. I was especially blunt about the fact that they were just too young to have kids and that any boy in the room who felt he was a man because he got a girl pregnant was really a boy.

I also told them something that was usually a surprise: that they were the most valuable generation we have ever raised. They usually looked at me as if I were another politician saying what they wanted to hear, but then I proved how valuable they were by asking, "How many of you speak a language other than English?" "How many of you have family members who were born in another country?" As hands went up around the room you could see the look of recognition on the faces: students who had spent most of their lives hearing how far behind they were, were realizing that they had something special to contribute. It also became clear that our city, which has welcomed immigrants for decades, was sitting on a gold mine of cultural fluency at a time when every company is competing in a global economy. That's the value of immigrants, but then I talked about the skills African American or American Indian kids develop navigating in a world where they aren't part of the majority culture, building the skills I didn't have when I went to China and Japan and was thrown when, for the first time in my life, I wasn't part of the majority culture.

Every year, at every high school, for many years I delivered the same message and, today, about every month, I run into a young adult who tells me he or she remembers me coming to their school when they were in ninth grade and were in some part of the Minneapolis Promise, usually STEP-UP. Today they are employees of our best companies, med students, teachers. I'm certain that someday some of them will be mayors.

These ongoing talks with students, and the success of the Minneapolis Promise, especially STEP-UP, gave me real reasons to believe our kids were going to be successful. But the data showed that we still had a serious problem. In spite of all the progress, we still had massive gaps that fell along racial lines; kids of color were far behind white students in school, and more than in almost any community in the country. More than a decade earlier I had been elected mayor of a city with one of the largest racial achievement and opportunity gaps in the country, and after all the work we had done, that gap was actually growing.

That weighed heavily on my shoulders, so I was receptive when a group from the African American Leadership Forum asked me to help start a version of the Strive Initiative, which built a coalition in Cincinnati that had begun to close that community's achievement and opportunity gaps. I became part of the founding board of Generation Next, a coalition of most of the region's major foundations, businesses, and community groups. The idea was to align the hundreds of individual initiatives in the community into a focused, powerful plan to finally close these gaps.

This work, which was not on my agenda when I came into office and for the first few years, now meant more to me than anything else I was doing. More than anything else it was also convincing me that I had a lot more work to do, and, as the work continued, I began thinking the best idea was to run for a fourth term and focus on finally giving all children in Minneapolis the chance they deserve.

# Tornados Real and Imagined

SUNDAY, MAY 22, 2011. Looking west from Loring Park across the Walker Sculpture Garden, I could see the sky had suddenly turned an eerie greenish-black.

Almost immediately my phone went off, and the city's emergency operator told me a tornado had hit north Minneapolis. I ran to my car and drove north on I-94, then followed a fire truck to a corner near Folwell Park.

It looked like a scene from a post-apocalyptic movie: massive trees and rubble were scattered across streets, utility wires were down and setting off sparks, the streets were filled with dazed and scared people.

In one direction a tree had fallen on a demolished car, which we later learned was how Floyd Whitfield was killed. I turned the corner and found a terrified elderly woman barely able to move and still in her pajamas.

"What are you doing outside?" I asked.

"My house is ruined and it smells like gas. I'm afraid it will explode."

I helped her around the corner and found a woman standing on her front porch. I approached her and asked if she could let the elderly woman sit on her porch until we found help.

"She will not sit on my porch," the homeowner said bluntly.

I hate to admit what went through my mind. I saw the black homeowner and the elderly white woman and thought, "Even at a time like this people just can't get over race." I am so happy to say I sold the woman, and north Minneapolis, short.

The homeowner repeated: "She will not sit on my porch. She will sit in my living room."

The image of the homeowner welcoming the stranger in need into her living room stayed with me in the coming weeks. In neighborhoods where already people had very little, and in the middle of massive devastation, the people of north Minneapolis reached out to each other over and over again. Like the bridge collapse nearly four years earlier, the worst of times showed the best of people.

As I walked back into the chaotic street scene, Don Samuels called. He was half a mile south and said I had to get there because there was so much damage. Then Barb Johnson, who was half a mile north, called to say it was worse where she was. I told them both nothing could be worse than where I was. We all began to realize the destruction was way beyond what we could have imagined, and was far worse even than what a major tornado had done to south Minneapolis two years earlier.

North Memorial Hospital offered its helicopter for Barb Johnson and me to get a sense of the damage. Heading north over Theodore Wirth Park, we saw the once-beautiful trails were cluttered with rows of flattened trees. A magnificent canopy that I cross-country skied through in the winters was now an open field.

Wirth Park, possibly my favorite place in Minneapolis, was a mess, but it seemed trivial when we saw what was happening to nearby homes and people. In the neighborhood above the park roofs had been ripped off and huge downed trees crisscrossed the streets. We didn't know it at the time, but as we were flying over that neighborhood Rob MacIntyre was getting ready to leave his house with a chainsaw. As he helped clear his neighbor's property, he died of a heart attack.

Looking out across north Minneapolis you could see homes and trees mowed down in a straight line, as clearly as you can see the line where a mower had gone over an overgrown lawn. Every few blocks it seemed the tornado had jumped—only to come down even harder.

Having worked in north Minneapolis for so long, I had become used to seeing maps showing how the same blocks have the biggest disparities. Look at maps showing the biggest gaps in income, health, education out-comes, public assistance—whatever the disparity—you'll see that every map shows the same red splotches on the same blocks. Viewing the area from above, it was uncanny to see that the tornado had hit exactly those same blocks. The places where people were already hardest hit got hit the hardest.

As the helicopter reached the city limits we saw a scene over the river that symbolized everything. The trees on an island in the Mississippi were completely flattened, and a swarm of Great Blue Herons were circling and calling out frantically. Their rookery was gone and so were their eggs and young chicks.

By the time we landed the streets were already filled with fire trucks, ambulances, and massive trucks from the utility companies and our Public Works Department. Almost as quickly, salespeople for construction and cleanup companies—some legit and some scam artists—were going door to door. Dozens of streets were completely blocked by trees.

Traffic was snarled as gawkers and people with real needs crammed the few streets not blocked by downed trees. Emergency and repair crews faced tremendous challenges getting around.

We imposed a three-day 9:00 P.M. to 6:00 A.M. curfew, which also helped unclog the streets. This helped with traffic, as well as with an even bigger problem.

With trees on so many houses, and windows and doors damaged on so many others, we now had hundreds of unsecured properties. Many people whose homes were now uninhabited—or who were understand-ably terrified—stayed somewhere else. Many of the businesses had bro-ken windows and doors. Put all this together with the city's highest-crime neighborhoods, now filled with people who had immediate and desperate needs, and we have a perfect situation for looting.

I slept very little the first couple of nights, checking in many times with police about what was happening. Nothing did. The neighborhoods stayed calm. Once again people were underselling north Minneapolis.

THE EXPERIENCE the city team had from the bridge collapse tragedy sharpened their response, and quickly housing inspectors joined police and firefighters going door to door. An emergency family center was set up in the Army National Guard Armory across the river in northeast.

For the next couple of days council members Barb Johnson, Don Sam-uels, Diane Hofstede, and I went block by block. Each time we talked to each other we shared more stories of serious destruction.

As with any calamity people react in many different ways, but overall I was struck by how many people were staying calm in spite of how serious the situation was. One example was the woman I approached in her front yard to see how she was doing.

"We've got some damage to the house, but we can probably manage it," she said. She took me around to the back of her house, and I saw that what she characterized as "some damage" was in fact a massive tree that had fallen on her house and partly ripped off the roof.

I knew that if this had happened in another part of town, one not as used to daily challenges, the response would have been more extreme, more panicked. Here in north Minneapolis, where people had been battling crime, poverty, and a host of other serious issues for many years, this was one more setback. Clearly there were deep impacts and dire consequences, but it was also clear that this part of town just had more grit than almost anywhere else I could imagine.

After a few days it became obvious to those providing services, especially the social services in Hennepin County, that it was too great a hardship for so many people from north Minneapolis to go all the way downtown for those services. We made the decision to open a relief center in the heart of the destruction at Farview Park where we would concentrate as many services as we could.

The next morning, an hour before this one-stop center was to open, there was a line halfway through the park. But there was trouble inside. The Internet connections weren't working and social workers couldn't access their records. The hour passed and they still couldn't get online. Then more time went by, and the center still wasn't open.

I kept walking up and down the line, making conversation, trying to keep people calm, but the crowd kept building and the heat and humidity were making people even more impatient. Angry words started to get exchanged. When one man tried to cut into the middle of the line he got pushed, and he pushed back. Others in the line began to yell, and it appeared the lid was about to blow off.

I got up onto a picnic table and tried to get people's attention. Explaining how hard people were working inside, I added, "Look around. There are TV cameras and reporters everywhere. What do you want on the news tonight? One more story about another problem in north Minneapolis, or a story that even a tornado can't stop north Minneapolis?"

"Won't matter to us," someone yelled, "because you can't watch TV without electricity."

Somehow that struck enough people as funny that it broke the tension. A few leaders stepped up from the crowd, helped calm down the two people fighting, and the rest of the line got back into place.

They finally got the center open, but standing in that line I heard some horrible stories. An elderly woman said her grandson always stayed over on Sunday night, but he didn't this time and the tornado blew the air conditioner through the window and smashed it into the bed where he normally sleeps. Deeply traumatized by the image of that air conditioner smashing into her grandson, she said, with horror in her eyes, "I never want him in that room again."

It was also clear that those seriously in need weren't the only ones hurting. In many cases people who were just holding on to the middle class were seeing that this latest setback might mean their precarious grasp on a comfortable lifestyle would slip through their fingers.

I asked one middle-aged woman how she was doing. She turned away for a minute, turned back, and said haltingly, "I am just one step away from losing it." She began to cry but caught herself; began to cry, then caught herself again. She told me she had two houses: one where she lived and one she rented to her mother. She had a catering business, and a big job was coming up in just two weeks that amounted to a huge part of her annual income. When the tornado had ripped the roof off her house all her cooking equipment was ruined, and if she didn't do the big catering job she may not be able to pay the mortgage on either house. Where would she and her mother go, and how would she make a living if she couldn't afford to replace her equipment?

The good news was that we had just opened Kindred Kitchen, a community cooking facility a few blocks away. I called there to get her in, and she was able to do the big catering job.

Most people's problems were much harder to solve. Cars were smashed, and if people couldn't get to work they would lose their jobs. Over and over we heard about problems with landlords who already rented substandard housing; some were now refusing to make any repairs. In many cases we couldn't tell who owned a piece of property.

We also knew we weren't getting to everyone who needed help. The crowd at Farview that first day was almost all African Americans, although we knew there was also a significant Hmong community in the tornado's path. We sent around flyers that had been translated into Hmong and sent door knockers into neighborhoods were we knew they lived.

In talking to people, it also became clear that food was starting to become an issue. Three days after the electricity went out some people hadn't opened their refrigerators, fearful the food would spoil, and those that had been opened were no longer cold. In many other neighborhoods people would have simply bought another bag of groceries, but many of the people I met at the park said they usually had just enough to buy only enough for each week. They had no money to shop again.

I called my friend Scott Anderson, who was working for a program that provided nutrition aid to Africa, and he brought a truck full of food relief packets to Farview Park. Nearby New Salem Missionary Baptist Church set up a barbeque. Impromptu cookouts started up around north Minneapolis, and Cub Foods gave out groceries. It was clear, however, that this sort of assistance couldn't last much longer because now we were dealing with massive damage and, increasingly, real hunger.

It would be extremely hard in any part of any city to clean up this kind of damage. Going door to door and standing in that line at Farview Park were showing me starkly that the response would be significantly harder because it hit people who already faced such deep needs. Months later, when we analyzed who we helped, we found that about 80 percent of the people who needed tornado response help were already receiving public assistance; those who were working were spending an average of 70 percent of their income on housing; and around 40 percent of the families helped listed a single woman as the head of household.

People with almost nothing now had a whole new list of expenses to confront. How could they manage with the little money they had, given all the added demands? Do they buy tarps to cover holes in the roof, or supplies to clean the dirt and mud blown in through broken windows? Do they buy groceries to replace the food rotting in the refrigerator because there's no electricity, or replace damaged personal items like toothbrushes, toilet paper, and shampoo? Do I trust this person going door to door with a chainsaw to get this tree off the back of my house—and if not, how would I even start to do it myself? What will insurance cover, and even if I get something, can I afford to pay anything out of pocket and wait for reimbursement?

Grassroots community needs called for a grassroots response. The Northside Community Response Team was formed within a few days. Funded by the Minneapolis Foundation and the United Way, and led by Louis King of Summit Academy, it included leaders of a broad range of organizations, including Urban Homeworks, Emerge, Pillsbury United Communities, NorthPoint, and the Urban League. In normal times a group of leaders claiming to represent the community would quickly run into a buzz saw of criticism. This time almost everyone put aside their competiveness and past histories, and the Community Response Team played a critical role in getting short-term resources to people for basic needs and, in the longer term, helped local, minority contractors get more of the construction work.

Rumors were circulating that individuals would be reimbursed for personal costs by the Federal Emergency Management Agency. FEMA, I learned, was now a household name, thanks in large part to Hurricane Katrina. This knowledge was a major problem, because in the few days after the north Minneapolis tornado people were buying things they couldn't afford and even staying several nights in hotels, assuming they would get reimbursed, which most of them didn't.

All the work on the 35W bridge collapse response gave our team tremendous experience securing reimbursement dollars, and almost immediately we had a group working on state and federal aid. President Obama called and assigned a point person in the White House to coordinate all federal aid. Senators Amy Klobuchar and Al Franken, and Representative Keith Ellison were all on the scene almost immediately, and stayed focused for weeks.

We had the right players and strategy in place, but it was clear almost immediately that the federal government had a high bar for aid to individuals. My job was to help state and federal officials see that ours was a distinctive situation because of the personal toll and particular needs of a neighborhood already hard hit before the tornado. That was also the job of the mayors of scores of other cities with disasters, including those in southern Minnesota who hadn't gotten individual aid for the floods a year earlier.

With President Obama in office I now had dramatically better access and almost immediately the president's team assigned a White House liaison to set up a cross-agency team coordinating the response. The meeting laid the groundwork for tens of millions of dollars to help rebuild public infrastructure, create new housing, and make small business loans for the people in north Minneapolis.

The big disappointment was that we did not receive individual aid. We also got a good education about how many other communities with real needs didn't reach the bar for individual aid. The north Minneapolis tornado, like Katrina, showed how more needs to be done to recognize that disasters require a disproportionate response where people already have disproportionate needs.

* * *

BACK IN NORTH MINNEAPOLIS, it was remarkable that almost all the streets had been reopened in a few days—and just a few days later, most of the electricity was restored as well.

Rebuilding homes took much longer and was made more complex by the challenge of finding out who owned many of them. When the economy collapsed in 2008, property values in north Minneapolis plummeted, and owners of many underwater properties simply walked away. Renters also fought with owners about who had responsibility—a significant challenge when one-third of the 3,700 properties damaged were rentals.

A year later, more than 90 percent of the damaged properties had been either repaired or torn down. Some look better than before, but many don't. Thousands of volunteers were part of mass cleanup of debris. Hundreds more were part of paint-a-thons and team home rebuilding. A group of architects volunteered their expertise regarding home restorations.

North Minneapolis, often disturbingly turned into a cartoon of dysfunction on nightly news shows, demonstrated the remarkable resilience of a community that has overcome tremendous obstacles. And the residents of north Minneapolis, who often talk about being left out and forgotten, got the chance to have caring people from all over wrap hundreds of arms around them.

Along with all the massive work of reconstruction, we started a small effort that should send a nice message over the years: we replaced some of the damaged trees with crab apples, cherry, and other trees that bloom in spring. We put an ongoing item in the city budget to keep planting flowering trees—and if that continues, a few years from now the anniversary of the event will be marked by hundreds of trees flowering just at the time when the tornado hit.

WHEN SCHOOL STARTED AGAIN after the tornado, I spent time in many classrooms and on many playgrounds hearing from kids and their teachers. Teachers talked about some children whose behavior changed dramatically after the storm, and they worried about the kids who never came back to school. School nurses said every time clouds got dark or there was a bad storm, their offices were filled with kids who said they had stomachaches.

Much of north Minneapolis has been rebuilt, but it will take much longer to fully understand the damage that can't be seen.

# Minneapolis–the Brand

THERE ARE THREE WAYS for a mayor to have an impact. The most obvious is to do the job, fulfill the job's basic responsibilities: present a budget, oversee departments, make appointments, sign stacks of documents, and so on.

I learned during my second term that the Itasca Group and the Regional Council of Mayors, and other partnerships, could broaden my impact into a wider arena.

The third way to have an impact is the most abstract, but it also was the most natural to me: a mayor can be the brand-builder-in-chief. As the most visible elected official in a city, as the person most associated with the image of the city, the mayor has the potential to be the personification of a place.

It's easy to dismiss this brand-building role as superficial, but a city's image has a tremendous impact on its economy. Talent is mobile and, increasingly, jobs are too. The cities that thrive are usually the ones that create a compelling narrative about themselves—the ones that tell the story about why you want to stay there, move there, or visit there.

Even as a kid, I played spin-doctor for my hometown. All those cheery Barbara Flanagan columns I was reading gave me great material. I was always armed with the names of great people born in Minneapolis, some new design award given to the Nicollet Mall or the IDS Center, some new "first" in the city that, of course, was being underreported in the national press. This tendency always came in handy on our annual visits to see our cousins in San Francisco—the height of cool in the 1960s—when I had to make sure everyone knew I wasn't from some cow town.

I ramped up this determination even more during my time at Boston College when I felt it was my personal responsibility to use my four years there to convince the entire East Coast that somewhere out on the plains there was this shiny city on a hill called Minneapolis where maybe, just maybe, if they were really lucky, they, too, could someday live happily ever after.

When I started running for mayor, I was so frustrated that whenever people around the country were writing about great cities they rarely mentioned Minneapolis. I started using an awkward phrase that all the same meant a lot to me: "I want Minneapolis to regain its collective swagger."

Part of what I wanted was aspiration: a city with so many assets should be reaching higher, risking more, taking on tougher issues, innovating more because, of course, no one could do it better.

The other part of what I wanted was for people not only to believe it but also to *say* it. There's an old adage about someone being born on third and thinking he hit a triple. It seemed people in Minneapolis knew we were born on third but only talked as if they hit a single so people wouldn't feel bad. That's a polite way to act at the neighborhood potluck, but it's not what's needed when cities are in a dogfight for global talent and recognition.

THERE IS NOTHING about any of this in the job description of "mayor," but right from the start I decided to make it a big part of my work. I had been around some form of sales most of my career, and now I appointed myself a shameless brand champion and huckster for an amazing product called "Minneapolis."

"Wait, there's more! If you act before midnight tonight, you also get the beautiful, historic capital city of St. Paul!"

The time I spent working with John Pellegrene, the legendary Target marketing genius, taught me that building a brand requires a sharp narrative. You have to tell the story, and I saw Minneapolis as having some great stories to tell: the most beautiful urban environment in America, where hyperactive people get outdoors and move; one of the country's great arts capitals; a midwestern city using immigration from around the world to become a global city; America's number one volunteer city; a city that works.

We are, of course, an understated people, but this is the one part of me that isn't Minnesotan. Maybe because my mom was from California, maybe because my dad was a super salesman, I have never been like most of the rest of the people from my state who try to avoid calling attention to themselves. (This probably comes as no surprise to most.) An illustration was the groundbreaking for Norway House on East Franklin Avenue. I went up onto the podium under a small tent to speak and looked out on the crowd to see that not a single person was seated in the ten rows of chairs. All the people who were gathered were standing, outside the tent, because, of course, self-effacing Norwegians all wanted to let someone else have the chair. I started to speak and it began to rain. The Norwegians in the crowd, many wearing those three-hundred-dollar Norwegian sweaters that get ruined when they get wet, motioned to each other to take the chairs under the tent and then, every one of them, kept standing in the rain. Finally I had to stop speaking, jump down from the podium and literally push them inside to get out of the rain. I love these people but I am not one of them.

MINNEAPOLIS WAS AN AMAZING PRODUCT to sell but there was, of course, the weather. So I went on a mission to embrace winter. "Frozen Tundra" became a "Theater of Seasons" where there was something wonderful, and ever changing, all twelve months of the year. In making that case, my nose only grew six or seven months of the year. "Minneapolis gives you a 'Theater of Seasons,' where there is something exciting in spring, summer, fall, and winter. If you want Kabuki theater, where nothing ever happens, go to San Diego and, just like *Groundhog Day,* you wake up every day to the same old thing."

Overcoming winter ultimately takes a lot more than a slogan. Winter after winter, year after year, national weather reports reinforce just how cold it can get. That's almost impossible to counter—so if you can't beat it, just go with it. We had to convince people that winter was an advantage, but as hard as I tried, we weren't having much success.

Then, a year after I got elected, we got an unplanned break. Some friends and I were coming home from the Birkebeiner in northern Wisconsin, the country's largest cross-country ski race, and we noticed how many people we saw who were from Minneapolis and St. Paul. Half-jokingly, we started fantasizing about what it would be like to have a race like that right in Minneapolis, the only major U.S. city where you can ski within the city limits. We could start in Theodore Wirth Regional Park, ski through the forested trails around the Quaking Bog, somehow cross over the freeway, and then onto the frozen lakes right into Uptown.

When we got home I posted a message on email listserves for cross-country skiers and mountain bikers: anyone who wants to work on an urban cross-country ski race and creating legal mountain bike trails in Theodore Wirth should meet at the park's chalet in two weeks.

The rest, as they say, is history. The chalet was jammed. Part of the group worked with Minnesota Off-Road Cyclists to build world-class mountain bike trails in Wirth Park. The other, led by the remarkable John Munger, launched the City of Lakes Loppet, a two-day cross-country ski festival that is now second in size only to the Birkebeiner. Several years into the race—which takes that very route we first spelled out in the car—a group of volunteers began putting ice globes around the trails on Lake of the Isles, which grew into the Luminary Loppet, attracting more than ten thousand people in the dead of winter to an event many now consider Minneapolis's most beautiful night of the year. The Loppet organizers also formed a nonprofit dedicated to getting kids in north Minneapolis outside and active during winter; so far their volunteers have taught cross-country skiing to thousands of young people who otherwise would have no outside activity in the winter.

The Loppet became the centerpiece of our attempt to create a new image of winter for the city of Minneapolis. Coupled with the Pond Hockey Championship, and the work Mayor Coleman was doing with events like Crashed Ice to revive the St. Paul's Winter Carnival, there were now a series of big events reinterpreting Minnesota winter. We could actually say with a straight face: Visit Minneapolis–St. Paul in winter. We also told those thinking about moving here that the place didn't just go into hibernation five months of the year.

THE LOPPET HELPED TEACH ME how I could use my position and visibility as mayor to build the Minneapolis brand. It also showed me—in a time of extremely tight budgets—that I could, without city money, use the job to leverage free media, attract sponsors, and recruit key volunteers.

I wrapped all these new initiatives and events into the larger brand of "Minneapolis: America's Most Active City." Almost every weekend I was doing some active sport: a triathlon, biking, swimming, cross-country skiing, kayaking, paddleboarding, a "polar plunge" into an icy lake. I was promoting the city and building a brand, but the reality was that I probably would have been doing it anyway. As long as you are giving up huge chunks of your life to be mayor you may as well be having fun.

I was also leading a city with amazing cultural assets, and Megan and

I had always loved the arts. We went to our share of events at the Guthrie Theater, the Walker Art Center, and the Minneapolis Institute of Art—but we tried hard to also use our visibility to help emerging cultural groups like Open Eye Figure Theatre, Illusion Theater, and Mu Performing Arts. We also started Mosaic, an arts festival focused on using performance to bridge cultures.

The biggest cultural crisis I faced was the closing of First Avenue night-club. When people describe the club they often say it's where Prince got started—which is true to a degree—but First Avenue has been far more important than even that. It has been the centerpiece of live music in Min-neapolis for decades, a key part of American music history, and hallowed ground for people like me who spent several nights a week there in the 1980s. The closing of First Avenue was a major blow to Minneapolis's nightlife—and image.

I worked hard to help reopen the club, worked with the new owners to allow a revenue-producing billboard on the roof, and talked behind the scenes to potential investors. I even made a public promise that if it reopened I would stage dive on opening night, which, thankfully I even-tually had a chance to do.

After the club reopened it was hotter than ever and occasionally I would end up onstage, including playing bongos for the reunion of the Suburbs. I reprised the stage dive a few times, the most memorable being right after Duluth's mayor Don Ness and I introduced Trampled by Turtles. The band started to play and I convinced a reluctant Mayor Ness to join me in leaping into the crowd. I didn't realize that when I took off first the strong people in the front row would carry me, leaving no one around for Mayor Ness. As I bobbed over the top of the crowd I heard someone shout: "Mayor Ness is down!" Thinking he was shot, I jumped down, but when I found him it was a lot less dramatic. Don had jumped into the crowd, which had caught his top half but never got hold of the lanky mayor's bottom half. He just kind of jackknifed to the floor, pretty much unharmed. Never could convince him to do it again.

My secret weapon in all my music work was Andy Holmaas, who was an aspiring musician before he got into my campaign and then my office. Andy knew he had carte blanche to interrupt a meeting to hand me a note saying something like "Remember to tweet that Doomtree's new album comes out this afternoon" or "Dessa is doing an in-store at the Electric Fetus."

Andy, a home-brewer, was also a key to another big brand-building campaign during these years: I always liked beer but I truly loved the independent, rebel vibe around some of the new breed of local brewers like Surly's Omar Ansari, the team from Fulton who built a major brand out of a beer first brewed in a garage in my neighborhood, the true craftsmen of the nuanced Belgian brews from Boom Island, and so many others.

I loved the local beer scene even more because it was creating jobs, and I was really astonished when I saw all the hoops in state law these brewers had to jump through. Most absurd, I thought, was that they couldn't sell their product out of their own breweries. When Ansari said he was going to challenge that law I was all for it, and was taken aback when I saw how much resistance there was at the legislature. Shortly after I came out publicly for changing the law, a lobbyist who works in the field pulled me aside and told me I was taking a dangerous political stance and that we would lose. Wrong on both counts: a few brave legislators got on board and the Surly crowd led a broad coalition in a social media campaign that helped create the support to change the law.

The signing of the "Surly Bill" made it possible for Surly to break ground on a massive "destination brewery" in Minneapolis, and for a while it seemed another new brewery was opening every week. As I bounced from one brewery opening to the next, my Twitter feed started to look like I was spending more time drinking beer than anything else. In reality, I am pretty much a lightweight who usually only drinks a beer or two, but pretty quickly I developed a taste for the richer, hoppier beers coming out of this new crop of breweries—Indeed, 612, Dangerous Man, and Harriet.

While Minneapolis was increasingly at the center of the growing local beer movement, it also became a center for local food. Our friend Julie Ristau was way ahead of this movement, and right after I got elected she tried to convince me to start a campaign to promote a homegrown food economy. I wasn't ready then but finally got on board in my third term after Megan wouldn't stop reading me quotes from *The Omnivore's Dilemma*, Michael Pollan's bible of local food.

Led by Megan and Julie, with significant help from council member Cam Gordon, we worked with the Health Department to start Homegrown Minneapolis, a game-changing initiative that got the city government on the same side as grassroots food efforts by urban gardeners and farmers, chefs and restaurants, public health officials and healthy food advocates, and neighborhood and local food activists. The effort led to an Urban Agriculture Policy Plan and Food Council that helped create more than two hundred community gardens; Homegrown Minneapolis also inspired successful Kickstarter campaigns for local food projects by the Beez Kneez and Honeybee Mobile Market and for building on-site growing capacity for Gandhi Mahal restaurant. The effort led to ordinance changes legalizing market gardens, market stands, and mobile markets in the city, and funding to create marketing support for the central farmers' market and an effort to have the city help neighborhood corner stores buy refrigeration cases and other equipment for stocking more fresh produce. Compost rule changes laid the groundwork for the urban farms and community gardens by tripling the allowable size of backyard compost piles and building into law best practices for composting.

The effort also made it possible to create fifteen urban farms with hundreds of subscription members, including Bootstrap Farm, whose scattered plots include a large one that today takes up most of our own back yard. A customer who ordered a dish with tomatoes, basil, or kale at Riverview Wine Bar may not have known it, but those foods may have been grown in the mayor's back yard.

Megan also recruited Bertrand Weber to take over the food service for Minneapolis Public Schools. He had an almost immediate impact, reintroducing salad bars and building new kitchens so that schools would have alternatives to prepackaged and mostly processed foods that were the only choices before he arrived. Weber also formed partnerships with some of the best local restaurants to create school menus and began buying from sustainable farmers to provide healthier options for the kids while supporting the growing alternative farm movement.

Megan not only led all my food work but also helped me identify early on that an emerging "makers movement" was giving new life to heritage brands like Minnesota's Red Wing Shoes, Faribault Woolen Mills, and J. W. Hulme leather goods. I saw that part of my job was to use my brand—through social media, ribbon cutting, or whatever was needed—to help businesses develop their brands. There were also tangible ways I could help, including getting local vocational programs developed to produce more professional craftspeople for their projects.

Minneapolis was a hotbed for some of these businesses, but the state remained behind where it should be in technology business start-ups. I didn't want to go down the road of many cities that invested time and great effort in incubators that produced little; I didn't think a facility run by a city or some other public entity could ever be spry enough to respond to rapidly changing needs of tech entrepreneurs. Instead, we did what we could to promote private efforts.

My favorites example of that was when CoCo, a local group developing coworking spaces, came to me for advice on a downtown location. I took them to the historic Grain Exchange, one of the most inspirational spaces in the city. Today the former trading floor, with its three-story windows and trading pit, is a CoCo space where start-ups develop their businesses. I love the idea that the Grain Exchange has become the Brain Exchange, where the space that a century ago housed traders turning tiny riverfront mills into companies like General Mills and Pillsbury is now a hothouse for the next wave of the city's economy.

VERY QUICKLY all these efforts started to converge into a single brand through-line, from local beer to local music to local food to local art to local business. The Minneapolis Brand was rapidly being honed into the image of an independent, creative capital where we didn't have to follow other cities. We weren't the "Mini-Apple." We created our own.

This, in turn, accelerated our rise in the growing lists of city rankings, about which I had a very simple rule: if Minneapolis was ranked high I would call it a very scientific survey, and if Minneapolis was ranked low I said I never paid any attention to city rankings. In one two-week period we got three "first" rankings in a row: America's Most Fun City, Most Literate City, and Best City for Sleep. A reporter asked me what that all meant and I said, "If you put them together it means we have a fun time in bed . . . but we're reading."

After we got the Most Fun City designation, CNN had me debate Las Vegas mayor Oscar Goodman. Outraged that his city had been passed over for, of all places, Minneapolis, he asked me how I could possibly say it was more fun than Vegas. You could see steam coming out of his head when I said I couldn't tell him "because what happens in Minneapolis stays in Minneapolis."

A critically important tool in all this was my engagement with social media. I had worked in the Internet before becoming mayor and was always comfortable with tools like email listserves—but in the early years in office, I could never send out emails fast enough to counter whatever image was coming out of the mainstream media. Then came Facebook. Then came Twitter. Now I could reach thousands of people in an instant, and create an echo chamber that could craft our own message without an intermediary.

Someone wrote on Wikipedia that I was the first U.S. mayor to use Twitter, but I can't believe that's true. I also never reached the "Superman" heroics of Newark's Cory Booker, who used his Twitter feed to find which snowbound resident needed him to deliver food or which burning building he could run into. I did, however, quickly develop a base of fifty thousand followers and intentionally bounced from lightweight tweets about a local beer or musician to a serious policy stance and then back again.

People assumed a staff person wrote my tweets, but with the exception of some prompts from Andy, I wrote them all. If someone else had written some of the inane comments I tweeted, I probably would have fired them.

Social media was a great way to promote a new brewery or restaurant or give recognition to someone who would otherwise go unnoticed. It helped me define the city, but in a larger sense, it allowed me to define myself. For years I was frustrated that no matter what I said or even felt, it would only get to people through a reporter's filter. (Poetic justice, perhaps, for a former reporter.) When it snowed I also began tweeting poems to remind people to move their cars from the streets so the plows could get through. Here are some of my favorites:

> Snow plows are putting
> Blades to our streets
> Move cars off emergency
> Routes—Toots Sweet

Or:

> On snow emergency routes
> Here's your motto:
> By nine o'clock tonight
> Please move your auto

Or:

> Here in Fun City
> Rock out, wine and dine
> But from snow emergency routes
> Move your car by nine

I didn't want people to assume they shouldn't move their car until I tweeted, so I did this one:

> You ain't so groovy
> You ain't no playa
> If you can't move your car
> Without a poem from da Maya

At one time or another I made most of my staff, and others around me, nervous with an overly blunt tweet or Facebook post. But more than ever, I was able to simply and honestly tell people what I had on my mind. I was speaking directly to people in real time without a media outlet as an editorial filter in the middle. In an era where the most diabolical political weapon was authenticity, it was an enormous advantage to have a way to just be myself.

And the most natural thing in the world was to project that image of myself onto the city I led, and vice versa.

# The Big Bang

D URING THE TIME I WAS MAYOR I heard rumors that there were
people living somewhere on the planet who actually worked five days
a week. They reportedly enjoyed something called a "weekend" and—get
this—had "Nights Off." None of this, of course, was confirmed, but it did
sound appealing.

There were rare Friday afternoons when the weather was beautiful, I
had nothing on my calendar, and it actually appeared as if I could learn
what this "weekend" thing was all about. One of those was a spectacular
May afternoon in 2010 when I was sitting on my front steps in the sunshine
thinking about gardening, bike riding, and everything else I was going to
do after a very long week.

Then the phone rang. A state legislator whom I was friendly with called
to tell me about a conversation he overheard. He thought it would alarm
me.

He was right.

The conversation was between two legislative leaders who knew that
the bonds on the Minneapolis Convention Center, supported by sales
taxes in Minneapolis, would be paid off in a few years. These legislative
leaders were talking about using that sales tax to help pay for a new Vikings
stadium in Arden Hills. In other words: money generated in Minneapolis
would be used to move a business out of our city and leave Minneapolis
with a white elephant called the Metrodome.

My open weekend ended quickly and I spent the next few days on the
phone playing enough defense in hopes that time would run out on the
legislative session before anything could happen. When the session ended
it was never clear how serious the idea had been, but it was clear to me
there was finally movement on the long-simmering debate about a new
stadium for the Vikings.

It was also clear the Minneapolis sales tax was very much in play. I thought it was pretty outrageous that this money would be used elsewhere, and it was also a problem because we needed some of that money ongoing to keep the Convention Center competitive.

I hoped future legislators would understand that Minneapolis's convention business is a cash cow for the state, which already collected most of the sales taxes generated in the city. I also knew that wasn't guaranteed: I was a reporter covering the debate in the 1980s about funding the current Convention Center and knew then—and still do today—that there was an expectation Minneapolis should carry most of the cost, even though a convention of any size fills hotels well beyond the city's borders, especially in Bloomington, and generates millions in sales taxes for the state.

We had to do something to protect those sales taxes, and we had to do something to not get stuck with an empty Metrodome. The challenge was that I did not want to get involved in a Vikings stadium deal, *at all*.

I may have only a few years left as mayor. If I was going to work on any big issues, I wanted them to be education and north Minneapolis. If I worked on any big infrastructure issues I wanted them to be redoing Nicollet Mall or building a streetcar line. If I was going to get involved in any sports facility it was going to be Target Center, home of the Timberwolves and Lynx.

TARGET CENTER'S MARKETING had improved, but it still struggled financially as it competed with the newer Xcel Center in downtown St. Paul. A deal made before I came into office also paid Target Center's debt service out of the general fund, meaning every year its payments are equal to about a 2 percent property tax increase. That deal required the city to keep the building "competitive," which it increasingly wasn't, but we had no way to pay for the estimated $100 million it needed in improvements.

Council president Barb Johnson and I had been working with the Timberwolves' owners on a remodeling plan. That was way more money than we had, but it was at least a lot more practical than the $300 million Orlando spent for an entirely new arena.

Johnson, Timberwolves president Glen Taylor, and I announced this "practical" plan and were practically laughed out of the press conference. The reporters knew what we also knew: the city didn't have the money and the legislature had refused to do anything to help the city get off the hook, even though Minneapolis taxpayers were supporting what we thought was a statewide facility.

So we had no money, an arena in need of $100 million, and a Convention Center whose bonds were going to be paid off but that still needed ongoing investments to stay competitive. Now we could add to that mess the threat of being left with a white elephant Metrodome while a major chunk of our hospitality business was taken out of the city . . . with money from Minneapolis sales taxes.

President Johnson and I saw that the threat was real and decided it was better to play offense than defense. We needed a plan to bring to the legislature, but to figure out what to propose, we had the staff spend the next few months answering four key questions:

- How much could we expect to generate in sales taxes in the next two decades?
- How much would it cost to keep the Convention Center competitive?
- What would it cost to renovate Target Center and take it off the property tax rolls?
- What would it cost for the city to be part of a Vikings stadium deal?

The result would be perhaps one of the most complex financial deals in Minneapolis history. It would solve many of those problems in front of us by bringing a stadium to Minneapolis, fixing another, and a lot more. But this would not come easily.

FOR A WHILE it looked like the city wouldn't need to play a role in the stadium planning at all. While we were sorting out all the city's stadium issues, we started hearing rumors that a number of Hennepin County commissioners were working on a deal to build a Vikings stadium across downtown from the Metrodome on the site of the Farmers Market. It was great news that the county could step in and help solve the problem, like they did when they funded the new Twins stadium a few years earlier. Their plan, however, had some problems.

Johnson and I, and most council members, thought that was the wrong place for a stadium. Why demolish the Farmers Market, a Minneapolis institution, and build all-new infrastructure while leaving the Metrodome empty across town? We thought it would be much less expensive, and better city planning, to replace the Metrodome and use the infrastructure already there. The idea of a "sports district" with the Twins and Vikings playing next to each other sounds good on paper, but it loses its appeal when you think about traffic when there are two games on one day. It's even less appealing when you remember that these are very large buildings, and even ones with the best designs have long dead spaces. Back-to-back buildings with that many dead spaces make for a poor pedestrian experience.

I met with Commissioner Mike Opat, who confirmed that he was working on a stadium plan. I told him about our concerns, but he was unmoved and said the county was going ahead, with or without us.

Johnson and I stepped back, but our team kept working on a plan B just in case the county plan fell through. We had to do this without our longtime financial director Pat Born, who had left at that point to run the Metropolitan Council. Born was an exceptionally clear thinker with a cool head. He patiently mentored me through a multiyear course in public finance as we steered the city through the many tough decisions we needed to make to get Minneapolis back on solid financial ground.

Losing Born was a major blow, but the new finance director, Kevin Carpenter, brought a whole new group of skills. He had spent years in private finance and was very comfortable developing complex financial deals. Right after coming to the city he helped me develop a budget that opened up ongoing money for an extensive paving program.

Like the game "Rock, Paper, Scissors"—in which each player is stronger at different times—Born had been exactly the right person early on to lay the clear path out of a financial hole, and Carpenter was exactly the right person now.

When Carpenter took the job two years earlier we talked about the fact that city streets were deteriorating rapidly at the same time the economic collapse had lowered interest rates. I asked if this might be the time for us to rethink the very conservative financial strategy we had taken to this point to find a financing strategy that could free up money for a long-term paving program. Carpenter came back with a great strategy to fund miles of paving, and for the first time in at least two decades, Minneapolis's streets were finally improving.

The next problem we put in front of Carpenter was far more complex. He led a team that developed a way to fund the city's share of a new football stadium, renovate Target Center, and ensure ongoing maintenance of the Convention Center by proposing that the state give the city more control of the sales taxes collected in Minneapolis. Current law let the state take back more of our hospitality sales taxes in 2020 when the bonds on the Convention Center were paid off. According to Carpenter's calculations, if the city could keep those taxes for thirty more years, we would have enough for all three buildings.

Once Johnson and I agreed that the plan worked, we were ready when, without warning, the county abruptly pulled its plan off the table. The Vikings' owners, Mark and Zygi Wilf, and Governor Dayton weren't. All three liked the idea of a new stadium in suburban Arden Hills. The Wilfs, who made their money in real estate, especially liked the idea of being able to control development in the area around the suburban site.

One thing virtually everyone except Johnson and I agreed on was that a Vikings stadium on the Metrodome site would not attract new development. The governor, the Wilfs, most legislators, most downtown business leaders—everyone except us, it seemed—said the Metrodome was surrounded by empty parking lots and the new stadium would be, too. The Vikings also hated the idea that they would have to play at the University of Minnesota's TCF Stadium while the new stadium was being built.

There was already tremendous controversy concerning the stadium, but the one thing nearly everyone seemed to agree on was that the plan Johnson and I were shopping was going absolutely nowhere. There was also an almost universal belief that no matter what we presented we would never get the support of the city council. Privately, Johnson and I wondered about that, too.

After several months, the Vikings management finally agreed to at least talk to us. The meeting didn't go very well, but they understood it would be tough enough to get any plan through the legislature so they agreed to at least help us develop our alternative.

The Vikings made it even harder when they said they needed about two thousand parking spaces attached to the stadium for their high-end ticket holders—and they didn't want to go anywhere if there wasn't any other development. They didn't know at the time, and we were only beginning to figure out, that the parking requirement would actually make it easier to attract development.

On the face of it I thought the parking issue was a colossal waste: spend a bunch of money so very wealthy people could walk across the street to a game. But my time writing about development and at the Downtown Council had given me years of experience seeing how the mega-ramps operated on the other side of downtown next to Target Center and the Twins stadium. They weren't empty on non-game days. Because they were next to the core of downtown, workers filled them on weekdays and generated significant revenue. In many ways those ramps had been key to the development of the Warehouse District.

Building ramps next to the stadium, in a part of town with so much undeveloped land, could attract development. If we could put development next door to these mega-ramps by the new stadium, daytime parkers could fill the otherwise empty stalls and generate a lot of money.

I set up a meeting with Mike Sweeney, chair of the board of the *Star Tribune,* and Mike Klingensmith, the paper's publisher. The paper owned five blocks next to the Metrodome that they had been trying to redevelop since I worked there decades earlier. The only nibble I knew of in all that time was when the Wilfs had a purchase agreement a couple of years earlier. At the last minute the Wilfs pulled out, which I assume they really regretted later when they saw how things turned out.

I told Sweeney and Klingensmith something they clearly already knew: this was the best chance they would ever have to sell the land. I also made the case that the ramp could potentially make this a much better deal. They agreed and began working with Ryan Companies on development.

A few weeks later the leaders of Wells Fargo came to visit Johnson and me. Several decades earlier they were saviors in south Minneapolis when they moved their mortgage division into the vacant Honeywell headquarters. Now they had outgrown that site. They would keep employees there but needed another campus, and, since, they said, there was no land for that in the city, they were informing us that they were looking in the suburbs.

We told them there were definitely places for them in the city: the Upper River Terminal, the Bassett Creek Valley, and the area near 35W and Lake Street, where we wanted to reopen Nicollet Avenue. The other option, we said, was the *Star Tribune* land—which had the added bonus that it would have a major ramp built for the stadium next door.

We told the Wells Fargo leaders about my meeting with Sweeney and Klingensmith and connected them to Ryan Companies. Together they developed an exciting plan that had the bank's campus facing a "Central

Park"–style open space next to the stadium. The park was great, but it was almost impossible to find a way to fund our part of the stadium without now adding this additional cost.

After a series of talks with Ryan we agreed they should move ahead with a plan for Wells Fargo, but we told them that they could not ask for city money and the property had to stay on the tax rolls. (This meant no tax increment financing.) I said we would work on the park part but only if we could find a way to fund it through some kind of user fee, like Wells Fargo employee non-game-day parking fees for the ramp.

Wells Fargo's growing interest would have given us a major boost at the legislature, where there was substantial concern that the new stadium would sit in a desolate part of town. But the bank also did not want to get dragged into the stadium controversy, so for months we had to keep our mouths shut while almost daily we were being told the stadium would never attract development.

Support for the stadium, however, was slowly starting to grow at the legislature. Part of that was because Vikings fans were making themselves known in emails, calls to legislators, and, most visibly, by showing up at hearings in their game-day purple and gold.

During those days at the Capitol there would be the normal frenzy of deadly serious lobbyists combing the corridors—and then the occasional beefy guy in horned helmet, sword, and shield. Moving between the Capitol's classical columns, the decked-out fans looked like barbarians storming Rome.

After a few weeks some Vikings fans added another element of theater by pulling up an RV in front of the Capitol and tailgating. This meant whenever it got too nutty inside the building I could go outside and hang out with the saner crowd wearing fur vests and purple-gold face paint. Every so often someone would pull out a flask.

The Vikings fans provided comic relief during a pretty tense time. They ended up being some really wonderful people, but since they were always in costume I wouldn't recognize almost any of them if I passed them on the street. The one you couldn't help remembering, though, was Larry Spooner, a warmhearted self-proclaimed "Super Fan" whose over-the-top testimony proclaiming blind love for the Vikings took the edge off the hotly contested debates.

Up until this point, almost every issue I had worked on at the legislature had been partisan. Transportation funding, aid to cities, and marriage equity mostly involved working with fellow Democrats against most Republicans. Stadium politics are very different: they are as highly charged as you get, and they jumble the political landscape.

Some Democrats supported the stadium, notably Governor Dayton and Tina Smith, who had gone from being my chief of staff to his. But the two authors were Republicans: Senator Julie Rosen and Representative Morrie Lanning. Both were veteran legislators widely respected at the Capitol. Both were also getting torn apart by segments of their party caucus, much as I was.

A few months into the session, I was in Senator Rosen's office waiting for her to come back from the Republican Senate Caucus down the hall. The door to that room was open, and, unintentionally, I heard them ripping her up one side and down the other. I felt bad for her, but there was a certain comfort in knowing that eviscerating supporters of stadiums was a bipartisan activity.

I didn't really know Senator Rosen and Representative Lanning before we started working together but I ended up having a tremendous respect for both of them, and we left the battle as friends. It was also refreshing, for once, to be working across party lines. Both parties were badly split, but the upside was that this meant many traditional coalitions had broken down and many legislators were deciding an issue on its own merits. What a novel concept.

The issue began to move at the Capitol, but the toughest question Johnson and I had to answer was whether we could get the support of the Minneapolis City Council.

For many months the only other solid supporter we had on the city council was Don Samuels. He had represented north Minneapolis through the worst of the recession, had seen how many of his constituents lost jobs and how many had lost their homes to foreclosure. To him this was a straight-up jobs vote, and we would never get a chance to put so many people to work on construction as well as once the stadium opened. Many of those jobs would go to his constituents, he said, and I saw that for myself when I met with a group of stadium concessions employees and saw how many were from Samuels's ward in north Minneapolis. Hearing him give one especially fiery speech about this issue made me realize the rest of us were not making a strong enough case that we would be putting thousands of people to work.

Working with unions in the trades and the hospitality industry, we put together a press conference at the Metrodome. Our focus was to tell the story of real people in these industries who had been out of work; what it was like for the family of a construction worker who hadn't had a job in fifteen months; or what a job at the Metrodome meant for an immigrant.

That press conference—which put a human face on what we were doing—was the turning point. It definitely wasn't easy before that and it definitely wasn't easy after, but we had finally offered a strong counterbalance to the argument that this was just a way to put government money into the hands of billionaire team owners and millionaire football players. It was also about putting people to work in the middle of the roughest economic conditions since the Great Depression.

People tried to dismiss the number of jobs we were creating by saying they weren't "permanent" jobs. Technically, yes, a construction worker would only be working on the stadium until it was done, but unless you are building something like the pyramids that takes lifetimes, that's the way the construction industry works. Keeping construction workers employed means building a pipeline where people can go from one project to the next—and when the pipeline slammed shut during the recession, the families in this industry were hit harder than almost anyone. People tried to dismiss the jobs inside the stadium as "not good jobs," but tell that to the immigrant who uses such employment to help raise a family.

It helped to know that if the stadium was built it was increasingly likely to attract the Wells Fargo development, as well as set off a development boom in East Downtown. It sure didn't help, however, that we still couldn't say anything about that.

Near the end of the legislative session, with the stadium bill still short of votes, we faced another challenge. Johnson and I were insisting that any stadium plan had to include a way for us to pay off the debt on Target Center.

This was a deal breaker to many of the legislators we would need to pass the bill. In a tense meeting with key legislators in the governor's office, Johnson and I were told we were endangering the bill. They wanted us to drop Target Center from the bill, and said it could be taken up separately in the coming years. If we didn't drop it, then they weren't sure the votes were there—and, basically, Johnson and I would be responsible for the entire package falling apart.

We didn't flinch, even if it meant the whole thing would fall apart. We could only be a part of this if it included paying off the Target Center debt.

Minneapolis could not take on another stadium without solving the problems already on our hands. We had been making the case for our involvement in the stadium by saying it would give relief from Target Center
payments, which currently were coming right out of the pockets of property tax payers.

Taking it out of the bill now would be one more turn in Target Center's
rocky relationship with the state. Unlike every other stadium in the region,
Target Center started as just the thing people always say they want: a stadium where the rich owners pay for the building. Marv Wolfenson and
Harvey Ratner were Minneapolis kids who grew up to make a fortune in
real estate. They repaid their hometown by bringing back NBA basketball,
buying the franchise, and paying for the arena.

Everything changed during the savings and loan crisis in the mid-1990s.
Wolfenson and Ratner's financial partner, Midwest Federal, collapsed, and
they no longer had the resources to fund the team and the arena. The city
could not get state help, and, with very few options, it finally created a plan
backed by city property taxes. The situation got worse when the state then
funded the Xcel Center in St. Paul, which cut dramatically into revenue for
Target Center.

For many years the city had been trying, without even a whiff of success,
to get state help for what we saw as a statewide facility. This new Viking
stadium legislation was the only way we could fix Target Center.

Johnson and I ended the meeting in the governor's office by reiterating
to the legislators that we could only support a bill—and could only get the
votes on the city council—if Target Center were included. But we offered
another idea: Don't ask anyone to take a vote on Target Center. Simply
give Minneapolis more control over more of our sales taxes, and we would
create our own plan to use them for Target Center debt relief, the ongoing
costs of the Convention Center, and our share of the stadium. No legislator
from outside Minneapolis would have to take an unpopular vote on Target
Center; just give local control (a very Republican idea) to Minneapolis (a
very Democratic city).

They eventually said yes, and that broke the roadblocks at both the Capitol and City Hall. Some legislators, certainly not all, saw this as Minneapolis using its own funds to solve its own problems without getting the
state involved in Target Center. Some, certainly not all, council members
began to see this as a mega-deal that could solve several problems at once.

We got even more support from council members when we showed them our financial projections. Sales taxes over the past decade, including during the Great Recession, had grown by 2.7 percent. If ours grew at only 2 percent, we would have enough to fund our portion of the stadium, pay for modest ongoing upgrades at the Convention Center, get Target Center off the tax rolls, and fund a modest renovation for it. It got better when we included a clause in the legislation that said the city got to keep about half the excess if revenue came in above 2 percent. This clause ended up being a very good deal; in the first year, revenue grew by 5 percent.

After a bruising fight at the Capitol, the stadium legislation passed.

After a bruising fight at City Hall, the stadium package passed.

After the city vote—which so many doubted for so long was something we could win—many of those same costumed, face-painted Vikings fans congregated in my office. Like those days in the RV during the legislative session, an occasional flask came out. But they were only in my office for a few minutes. We were tremendously relieved to be done with the rough battle at City Hall, but we were in no mood, and no position, to celebrate. There were lots of challenges ahead.

The council members who helped us narrowly pass the agreement— Samuels, Kevin Reich, John Quincy, Meg Tuthill, Diane Hofstede, and Sandy Colvin Roy—all had taken one of the most controversial votes in their careers. The council members who voted against the agreement included a few longtime, very loyal allies and relationships on all sides were left badly strained. Council member Goodman was especially angry, giving an emotional speech about being ashamed to be part of the same Democratic Party as people like Governor Dayton and me. This was especially problematic because we would need her support to put together the package we knew was coming for Wells Fargo and the park.

The city was as split as the state, and that didn't go away quickly or easily. Some of the wounds never healed.

As the debate went on, it was clear that this was one of those issues where a lot of people saw things in black and white. Many, many people were simply not going to be swayed by any argument; they just opposed public involvement in professional sports.

I didn't blame them and—on many levels—I agreed with them. Pro sports economics are sick. They are based on shockingly inflated salaries and owners with monopolies. If the choice in front of us had been only about whether to help build a stadium, I probably would have voted no. But the choice to me was about more.

In my eyes this was not a vote on a stadium. It was about whether we understood realistically that this was going to be solved one way or the other—and the city would be dramatically better off if we shaped our own destiny.

If we had not gotten involved, the likely result would have been that a city in which hospitality was a $1 billion industry would lose one of its top attractions. And from there:

- A stadium would be built in Arden Hills with no clear alternative for reusing the Metrodome, and with other, newer buildings competing with Target Center for events.
- Surrounding the empty dome would be a sea of vacant parking lots.
- The legislature would not help the city get Target Center off the tax rolls and the city would have to find another way to honor the part of our contract that required tens of millions in renovations.
- There would be no plan for funding ongoing renovations of the Convention Center.
- It was likely the sales tax paying off the Convention Center bonds would be used for another purpose out of the city, possibly to build that Arden Hills stadium.
- Wells Fargo would probably expand in the suburbs.

Instead, by getting involved and working to shape our own destiny:

- We got a $1 billion stadium built downtown, helping to fill our hotels and restaurants with Vikings fans, and people who attend other events, including the Super Bowl and the Final Four.
- The city got the funding tools to pay for the renovation of Target Center and give property tax relief because we no longer had to pay arena costs from our general fund.
- Wells Fargo and Ryan built a $400 million development downtown that, because we did not use tax increment, went immediately onto the tax rolls. In its first year the

project was estimated to generate about $6–7 million
when completed. In the first year the city of Minneapolis
would receive about 35 percent of that (likely more than
$2 million), with the remaining funds going to Hennepin
County and Minneapolis schools. The value of the project
can be expected to grow significantly, so property tax revenue for the city, county, and schools can also be expected
to increase.

• By early 2015 another half billion dollars in new development was under way, including hotels, housing, office
buildings, and a grocery store. That expansion could be
bringing in several million more in annual property taxes.

• The ramp built for the stadium, which would have been
empty on non-game days, is next to the new Wells Fargo
headquarters and the resulting revenue used to fund a
two-block park.

• The clause we put in the legislation giving the city part of
the hospitality taxes over 2 percent meant the city got a
windfall of an estimated $1 million in the first year alone.

An indirect benefit is that the *Star Tribune,* which has struggled like all
newspapers, made tens of millions off the sale of its land that could be used
to keep the paper growing. The paper now has a new headquarters in the
heart of downtown.

Another long-term impact of the deal was the redevelopment of Block
E, the underperforming entertainment complex across the street from Target Center. While Johnson and I were putting this deal together, we heard
that the Timberwolves were working with Mayo Clinic to locate a sports
medicine clinic with the team's workout facility at the Mall of America.
We made it very clear that we would not do all the political work on Target Center unless this project was downtown. Today the failed Block E has
new life as Mayo Clinic Square, which includes the clinic and the Timberwolves workout facility.

WHEN I CAME INTO OFFICE, the only qualification I felt I had for the
job was that I knew economic development. For the past decade, while
working on finance, public safety, and so much more, that was the one

skill I hadn't had a chance to use. Now, in one fell swoop, I was leading the redevelopment of an entire side of downtown.

Getting all this done wasn't pretty. It meant throwing myself into the center of enormous controversy. It deeply tested the lesson I learned in my first reelection about the difference between love and respect: on a matter this controversial, on which most people had an opinion, would people really support my taking stands based on what I thought was best instead of what was popular?

To me this was one more in a series of highly imperfect choices handed to me for a decade in which we didn't get to pick what was put in front of us. I didn't get to pick the problems. My job was to try to solve them.

# The Way He Looked at His Son

W HEN I FIRST RAN FOR MAYOR I spent a lot of time talking about the environment. That was seen as a little flaky in 2001, but over the years it became an increasingly more mainstream cause and with each year the work got broader.

We started with a straightforward agenda: clean water, green transportation like bikes and transit, fighting airport noise. From there, one cause simply led to the next one. Converting the Riverside Generating Plant led me into environmental justice. Learning that on rainy days raw sewage was flowing into the Mississippi River led us to work on water management, including putting green roofs on City Hall, the Central Library, and Target Center. Then Megan convinced me to take on the local food work that would become Homegrown Minneapolis. Winning a lawsuit against airport noise put $130 million into energy-saving retrofits for thousands of homes across the southern half of the city.

The Great Recession that began in 2007 led us into another expansion of our environmental work: green jobs. Our biggest inspiration was the environmental advocate and civil rights activist Van Jones, whose work in Oakland was showing that "green jobs" weren't just for highly educated, affluent workers involved in deep research but, increasingly, were about rebuilding a new working class with skills in hands-on work like energy retrofits. Jones became a valuable adviser, coming to Minneapolis to help our team truly understand the intersection between a new attack on climate change and a new attack on inequity.

We knew the city government of Minneapolis could not, alone, build a new green economy, but we began to invest in retraining workers for the kinds of green jobs for which Van Jones had been advocating. Cathy

Polasky, who led our economic team, also started the Green Jobs Task Force with a remarkable group of entrepreneurs who were all thriving in the middle of an economic calamity because they understood this new green future. This included companies like Vast Pavers, which made paving materials out of old tires, and Wood from the Hood, which repurposed wood from diseased boulevard trees into cutting boards and building materials.

Great people were on that Green Jobs Task Force, but the biggest personality by far was the infectiously enthusiastic Reuven Rahamim. His company, Accent Signage Systems, was pioneering green production strategies from its facility in the Bryn Mawr neighborhood. Accent was pioneering work in other areas, most notably the innovative integration of Braille into signage that won this small Minnesota business contracts around the world, including a major contract for the Olympics in China.

In August 2012, when we heard that Francisco Sánchez, the U.S. under secretary of commerce, wanted to see examples of small businesses involved in exemplary exporting practices, we knew we should take him to meet Reuven Rahamim and his team at Accent.

Reuven didn't disappoint us. He took Sánchez, Representative Keith Ellison, me, and a large entourage on what was supposed to be a short visit. Then he wanted to show us one more thing. Then one more thing. One more. One more. Then one more thing. I could see the rest of the day's schedule blowing up before my eyes—and I couldn't imagine what this was doing to the under secretary of commerce's and the congressman's schedules—but Reuven was so-over-the-top excited about every single thing happening at the company, he was just irresistible.

Then, just as we were about to leave, he asked me to take a picture with his son Sami. As proud as Reuven was of every single thing in the company, you could see in his eyes he was twice as proud of Sami. We took the picture, we heard about all the great things Sami had done in high school, and we heard about his college plans. I left knowing a *lot* about Accent and its phenomenal work, but the thing I remember most from Reuven that day was the way he looked at his son. That look would come back to haunt me at a horrific time.

A MONTH AND A HALF LATER, on September 27, I got an urgent call from Sherman Patterson that there had been a shooting at Accent. In the quick information I received it was clear it was bad, and when I got to the scene Deputy Chief Kris Arneson told me the gruesome details. A worker who had been fired that morning came back into the business with a Glock pistol and shot at least five people, including himself. At least two more were seriously injured.

I asked Arneson for names, and one by one learned that Reuven and almost every person we met on that tour a few months earlier was either dead or in critical condition. Also killed was Keith Basinski, a beloved UPS driver for the neighborhood. I heard the details of what happened, about what the other employees saw, about what officers had to do as they entered the building. I heard about how Reuven's wife was told. Then I asked, "Where's Sami?" When I heard he was on a bus to Madison to look at the University of Wisconsin, and that a family member was driving there to tell Sami the horrible news in person, all I could see in my head was the way Reuven had looked at his son earlier that summer. I was almost paralyzed by that image and could only listen, saying nothing for what seemed like a long, long time.

A crowd, mostly neighbors, began to gather. After being at so many tragedies on so many corners, I knew that it is best to move away from the crime scene, so Council Member Lisa Goodman and I led the neighbors to a small park a couple of blocks away. We lit candles and held a short press conference. I drove home in a daze, feeling about as hollow as I have ever felt.

The funerals over the next few days were powerful. We heard about Reuven's journey from living on a farm in Israel with no toilets, leaving school in eighth grade and fighting in the Yom Kippur War to, now, owning a multimillion-dollar company exporting work around the world. We heard about Rami Cooks, one of the top managers at Accent, whose family had been killed by the Nazis at Treblinka. We heard about Jacob Beneke, who spent the day at his production job in the Accent shop but on off hours was a promising artist. We heard about Ronald Edberg and Eric Rivers, both important members of the Accent team. And we heard about Basinski, the UPS driver who just happened to be making a delivery at Accent when the shooting occurred.

Thankfully, we did not go to the funeral of John Souter. The operations director at Accent had been shot and was in critical condition but finally recovered and eventually returned to work.

I had met Souter, and his wife, before because our sons were going to school together, and got to know them much better over the coming months as we appeared together at events trying to find ways to pass laws that would have made it harder for a shooting like this to take place.

The other person who became active in trying to find ways to prevent this from happening again was Sami Rahamim. Sami gave powerful testimony around the country about why more needed to be done to prevent these mass shootings. He seemed to grow with each speech, even when sometimes faced with hostile questioning, in press conferences in Minneapolis and at the Capitol in Washington, D.C. And I like to think somewhere, Reuven still had that look in his eye as he proudly sees his son.

# "No Más"

W HEN I RETURNED to our house on the night of the Accent shooting, Megan asked me, with real concern, "Are you okay?"

She had been there when I came home from so many different tragedies, and she had seen me speak about them on television many times, but when she saw me on the news at the Accent scene, she knew something was different.

She said my face was "a mask of grief." She knew me well.

When Deputy Chief Arneson was standing outside the crime scene telling me the grisly details, and as I heard, one after another, that so many of Accent's employees whom I had met earlier that summer were dead, when I thought about Sami innocently riding a bus to visit a college and then hearing that his father had been murdered, I felt like an anvil had been dropped on my head. I had been through death many times before, and I knew what I was supposed to do. But at that moment I recognized this was just more than I could carry.

I knew right then that I couldn't run for mayor again.

This feeling of being overwhelmed by grief had been building for a long time. There was Tyesha Edwards, there was Brian Cole, there were so many other kids who had died. The 35W bridge. The tornado. Paying condolences to an elderly woman whose husband went out to walk the dog and was killed by a car in a police chase. One tragedy on top of another on top of another for years.

Things calmed down for a while, and finally I was able to spend some months away from so much tragedy. But a few months before the Accent shooting, after a steady drop in crime for several years, we had a two-week period when three young people were shot in north Minneapolis. Speaking at a street corner vigil near North Commons, I began calmly asking for help from residents to stop the flow of guns to kids. As I talked I could feel the blood rushing into my head as I got more and more enraged that adults had played a role in getting guns into the hand of children. I began, louder and louder, to demand, "Who is arming our kids? Who is arming our kids?" Then I just abruptly stopped and walked back into the crowd. Father Michael O'Connell, whom I deeply trusted during my years as mayor, pulled me to the side and asked me if I was okay.

All I could manage was "I am nowhere near okay." Seeing so many people go through so much pain, only to have more people enable this kind of violence among children, was almost more than I could take. I walked around the neighborhood for a long time before I got into my car, acknowledging that I was losing the resilience that had once helped me rebound from so many traumas to be ready for the next one.

Accent was the final straw.

Over the years I knew there was a consequence to throwing myself so directly into so many situations filled with so much grief, but it always paled when compared to what the families of the victims were experiencing. They had lost a child or a spouse, and I'm supposed to feel bad because I have to go to a funeral?

I also believed I had the capacity to engage with these situations more because, starting at a young age with my father, I had built up an immunity to death. I thought I could take on some of the weight for others because I thought I had acquired enough of an emotional shield. Now it was clear that doing this over and over without a break—knowing it could happen again at any moment no matter how normal everything seemed at the time—was not sustainable anymore.

Making this all more difficult, our family was living through a very painful tragedy as our beloved thirteen-year-old niece Shannon was dying of cancer.

I KNEW I COULD NOT SUSTAIN another four years immersed in almost nonstop tragedy, but that was not the only reason I did not run for a fourth term. I was emerging from the years when most people are saving for retirement and had very little in the bank. I also knew there were many ways for me to make a difference in people's lives besides being mayor.

But the other part of my mind was leaning more and more toward running again. I saw how many of the things I had wanted to work on for so long were just getting started, especially the Nicollet Mall, streetcars, a series of downtown parks, a big plan for the upper river, and other city building projects. Another major factor in wanting to run again was that I could see I was finally having an impact on schools, and another four years partnering with Bernadeia Johnson would make good progress toward closing the achievement gap, especially now that Generation Next had started.

For months I had been going back and forth, unable to decide if I should walk away when things were running so well.

Accent made it all much more clear.

After the Accent shooting, the *Star Tribune* posted a photograph taken about an hour after the incident as Deputy Chief Arneson was telling me the details. As I looked at the picture, I saw the look on my face that had Megan so worried. I knew exactly what I had been thinking. Plunged back into what seemed an endless series of tragedies, this was the crystallizing moment when I knew I had to stop. I felt a lot like champion boxer Roberto Durán, who seemed tough enough to take on anything, then abruptly walked into the middle of the ring, in the middle of the fight, and quit. Like him, I finally had to say, "No más."

As this bizarre boxing match shows, my promotional strategy was "There's no such thing as 'Over the Top.'" If you could do stuff like this day after day, wouldn't you? Photograph by Jerry Holt.

Jimmy Carter and Walter Mondale joined me in building Habitat for Humanity homes in Hawthorne EcoVillage in north Minneapolis. Photograph by Richard Sennott.

Prioritizing dinner together kept our family close, but more important were the many evenings Megan managed life at home when I was out in the community or on the road. Photograph by Stormi Greener.

"By the power finally vested in me, by the laws of the people of Minnesota . . ."
I pronounced Cathy ten Broeke and Margaret Miles legally married in the first
same-sex wedding at City Hall. The happy couple was upstaged by their five-
year-old son, Louie. Photograph by David Joles.

Al Giraud and Jeff Isaacson were the first men we married on the historic night
of August 1, 2013. Forty-six couples would tie the knot before we finished at
6:45 A.M. Photograph by Stacy Bengs/AP Images.

The shootings at Accent Signage so completely filled me with grief that I knew immediately I could not run for mayor again. Photograph copyright Reuters.

Sami Rahamim was an inspirational young man who channeled his massive grief after his father's murder into a courageous campaign to prevent others from being killed with guns. Photograph by Jerry Holt.

President Obama was always kind to me. I think that's because I never asked him for anything; it was enough for me to get the president I had been hoping for all my life.

I didn't believe my eighty-year-old mom when she said, a few months before the 2012 election, that she wanted to stage dive. But minutes after Obama was reelected and the anti–gay-marriage amendment failed, she said, "Let's go!" Photograph by David Joles.

The vacant Sears Building on Lake Street would become the headquarters of Allina and one of the county's best examples of immigrant and entrepreneurial success: the Midtown Global Market. Photograph copyright Mark Mahaney.

With me at the beginning and as I began the end, my family joined me at my announcement that I would not seek reelection. Along with Megan, Grace, and Charlie are my mom, my sister, Georgeann, and her daughter, Tori. Photograph by Jeff Wheeler.

No matter how hard I was working, my team knew I would recharge my batteries by being around kids, which I enjoyed even more as our own kids left home for college.

I was always energized by school visits, like this event at South High. In the background is one of my heroes, Hussein Samatar, founder of the African Development Center and member of the Library Board and School Board, who died my last year in office.

Grace and Charlie showed the poise of seasoned veterans who grew up in public at this press conference after my heart attack. Photograph by Jeff Wheeler.

A social person who is also very private, Megan was usually the one with the firmer grip on reality. She made our lives work.

# My Favorite Year (Part 1)

A LL THOSE YEARS AGO, as I was about to announce that I was running for mayor, I lay awake all night and worried I was about to ruin our family.

All these years later, as I was about to announce that I wasn't running again, I had the indescribable satisfaction of knowing that it hadn't happened. The job hadn't ruined our family. We were coming out the other side—and in so many ways, my time as mayor made our family even stronger. So, of course, we waited until Charlie was home for Christmas break to make the announcement. We started this as a family and I wanted to start the end with all of us, too.

We held the press conference at the Midtown Global Market, one of my proudest accomplishments. As I was about to start I looked over at my sister, Georgeann. I thought about how she had been with me every step of the way, including taking months off from work to volunteer in that first campaign. As usual, she wasn't saying anything or asking for anything except just standing at my side. After giving all that, the only thing she asked for during my twelve years as mayor was to have three proclamations for her daughter Tori's skating club. People overuse the term *humbled,* but at that moment, when it was so clear that I got to be the celebrated guy at the mike because so many people like Georgeann stood quietly by my side, I was, in fact, very humbled.

I didn't set out to say anything too memorable, and I accomplished that. I did admit it was hard to step aside from my dream job, but I also got across that I had no intention of being a lame duck who takes up space for the next year. I was going to run through the finish line. "I believe in delivering taxpayers a good value for their money," I said, "so in the next year the people of Minneapolis are going to get four years of work out of me."

It was a throwaway line, but it ended up being absolutely true. I said I would get done everything still on my plate or it would kill me. As it turned out, *that* almost ended up being absolutely true.

I DIDN'T THINK the biggest problem would be getting all the work done. It was staying relevant—which, of course, makes it harder to get the work done. In an election year, when everyone is looking forward, the sitting mayor starts not to matter as much. People also begin to perceive that you aren't as engaged.

To physically show I had no intention of coasting through the last year, we filled a giant whiteboard in the office with everything we were going to get done, sorted it into priorities, and invited in the media to see, in detail, that we had a concrete agenda. My staff wasn't nuts about this idea, which they saw as limiting our options. That was actually my point: let's make it crystal clear, in detail, what we were going to do and hold ourselves accountable. Doing that also helped make it undeniable that I fully intended to be a full-tilt mayor for every minute of the year I had left. That whiteboard filled with my plans was very crowded. It included:

- finishing development deals for Target Center and what would become the Wells Fargo development near the new football stadium;
- putting in place financing for the first streetcar line;
- developing a financing plan for luring businesses to north Minneapolis;
- significantly expanding car share programs; and
- making sure there were long-term strategies for two of my favorite projects, the Midtown Global Market and the STEP-UP jobs program.

I gave as many interviews and speeches about my agenda as I could to make it clear I was not coasting. I mixed into those conversations, about tangible actions, some wilder ideas that had been percolating in my head. I knew I wouldn't get to them but hoped to spur a champion in the mayor's race or on the next city council who could finish the job.

One of my favorite wild ideas was to capture more of the steam from the downtown garbage burner to heat the core of the city. "If we did this right," I told the Downtown Council, "Nicollet Mall could be its own out-door micro-climate. It could have palm trees." As I was saying that I could see every head in the room full of prominent business leaders turn halfway to the side, like a dog does when he looks at you and has absolutely no idea what you are talking about.

I could have repeated all this in my annual State of the City speech, but that speech had always been my chance to speak to bigger visions for Min-neapolis and I didn't want to just focus on my few months left. I didn't want to be seen as just talking about the past. Instead, for the first ten minutes, without explanation, I gave the State of the City speech as if it were 2025.

I started by talking about a "current" debate (in 2025) regarding building another high school in north Minneapolis. I picked this scenario because if there actually were such a debate, it would mean three things that mat-tered deeply had happened: our population was growing; more people were sending their kids to the Minneapolis public schools; and growth was happening in north Minneapolis.

I assumed after this start to the speech that people in the audience would look confused about why I was discussing a debate happening in the year 2025—but in a humbling moment that showed a politician just how little attention people pay to these big speeches, no one seemed to notice that I was talking as if it were a decade later.

So I kept going. I talked about hundreds of people hopping on the streetcar after working in the northeast brewing district along Central Ave-nue, riding the streetcar across the river into downtown, and continuing south on Nicollet Avenue to the "Eat Street" district and several blocks farther south to the part of Nicollet Avenue where the Kmart used to be.

AFTER THAT SPEECH I hit the road to sell my final year's agenda, going one by one through the checklist from my whiteboard. One of the earliest checks was next to car share: after a year of work we passed an ordinance that expanded the two existing services and launched 250 new smart cars for Car2Go. Within a year they had 500, and other car share groups in the city expanded too.

Not everything could happen that quickly, and this was especially true of the Wells Fargo development. Starting in January, and for much of 2013, we had at least one meeting a week in my office negotiating between the developer Ryan, our city team, and, occasionally, the Minnesota Sports Facilities Authority. We had a couple of major constraints. Unlike almost every other project like this, we weren't going to use tax increment financing—all the new tax base would go back into the city. This was a dramatically better deal for taxpayers, but it also made things dramatically more difficult. We also weren't going to fund any office space; city money would only go to public space in the two-block park connecting the Wells Fargo development to the new stadium. Money for that would come from the parking ramp revenue, just as I had hoped when I first talked to the *Star Tribune* and Ryan about this two years earlier.

That park had great potential, but also great complexity. My hope was that it could bring needed green space to a part of town with mostly concrete, and could attract more multi-unit housing. There were already several downtown parks, including Gold Medal Park a few blocks away, which were beautiful but restrained. I saw this place as much more lively, a simple, flexible green space that was aggressively programmed to be the most active urban green space in the country: playing fields could accommodate daily and nightly volleyball, soccer, lacrosse, and touch football; in the winter, all the snow cleared from the streets could be dumped there to create a giant sledding hill. Residents moving out of single-family homes to live in nearby condos and apartments could use this like they had their back yards, so I started referring to it as the Yard. (After I left office it got the official name the Commons and got a more formal design that is beautiful but very different from the original idea.)

To get all this done we needed to build support on the city council. Normally this would be fairly easy, as the development would make for the largest office relocation into the city in Minneapolis history, without tax increment—but Wells Fargo did not want its name used until the deal was final.

THIS PLAN WAS ALSO ESPECIALLY COMPLEX because it was coming just after the bruising fight over the stadium had split the council and left bad blood on both sides. Something like this needed a new coalition, and the people who were adamantly opposed to the stadium would now need to support the project next door.

Complex as it all was, we solved these issues one after the other—in large part because between each meeting, the Ryan team or the city team—and usually both—knocked down one wall after the other to keep things moving. At almost every meeting I looked around the room at our team—Kevin Carpenter, development vet Chuck Lutz, city coordinator

Paul Aasen, and Susan Segal, the city attorney whom I had come to trust deeply—and thought about how much I would miss working with them.

If it had been just up to Ryan and the city, we would have had tough but successful negotiations. But because we were using money from the ramp, and funds that were originally intended for a much smaller stadium plaza, we had two other partners to deal with: the Minnesota Sports Facilities Authority and the Vikings. Both wanted to reserve major chunks of time in the Yard for Vikings and stadium events, as well as put major restrictions on who we could raise money from. I was not going to allow a public space—paid for because we negotiated a remarkable development deal no one anticipated—to become privatized. We had hour after hour of negotiating with the MSFA and the Vikings, week after week, with very little progress. They didn't budge, and neither did I.

ALTHOUGH THE WELLS FARGO DEVELOPMENT was the most time-consuming project during my last year, the most complicated initiative was expected to be the streetcar. After we got the legislature to give us the taxing authority we needed, we began negotiating with the Metropolitan Council and the Hennepin County Regional Railroad Authority to have them pick up other parts of the cost. By late spring it actually seemed possible that we could get a streetcar funding plan in place before I left.

Then, just as quickly as it started coming together, it fell apart due to the controversy over the proposed Southwest Light Rail Line. A few years earlier, the HCRRA and the Met Council had chosen a route for the line over my strong objections. Instead of my preferred route through the dense Uptown and Midtown neighborhoods, they chose to skirt most of the city population and route the line through parkland and the middle of the Chain of Lakes along the Kenilworth Corridor. After losing that battle, I grudgingly got on board and helped sell reluctant Kenilworth neighbors on the plan. Then, in spite of earlier promises, the Met Council and the Regional Railroad Authority did an about-face and declared that the Kenilworth Corridor would also have to take freight traffic. They acknowledged they had promised it wouldn't go there, but also explained that they had no authority to stop the railroad from moving freight. In any case, residents went nuts, we felt duped, and the coalition that had worked so hard to get the line this far blamed the city for delays. The mess ended any chance of regional partnership for the streetcar line, and suddenly a new, very complex issue was crowding out my whiteboard to-do list.

* * *

THERE WAS ALSO A NEW CONTROVERSY. Contract negotiations were breaking down at the Minnesota Orchestra and had quickly became hostile. The board finally locked out the players—and the town split into camps. In the middle of the fight, the orchestra was nominated for a Grammy for its recording of Jean Sibelius's First and Fourth Symphonies. Longtime orchestra patron Judy Dayton and I thought this was a good opportunity to bring the sides together. She helped fund a special concert to play the works conducted by orchestra director Osmo Vänskä. Judy and I thought this could remind everyone what was being lost by the impasse and somehow thaw the tensions. It was a great concert but it had no impact and the impasse went on. I did my best in private to keep channels of communication open, but people from both sides alternately told me to mind my own business and criticized me for not resolving the situation.

WHEN SUMMER CAME I held a press conference to call attention to the 40 percent increase in spending for street repair, just as crews started work on fifty-five miles of repaved roadway. Just a few years earlier, local ice cream shop Sebastian Joe's had created a flavor called "Nicollet Avenue Pothole." The flavor, chocolate with some marshmallows and nuts, was delicious but it embarrassed me to order it because I knew our streets were a mess. A couple of years earlier, during the budget speech in which I had announced the start of new paving funding, I ended by inviting the crowd across the hall to sample the flavor that Sebastian Joe's renamed, in a nod to Prince, "The Flavor Formerly Known as Nicollet Avenue Pothole." Now, in my final summer, and as I showed off the newly repaved, pothole-free Nicollet Avenue to the press, I was so excited that I lay down on the asphalt, suit and all, and rolled down the smooth-as-silk pavement.

That summer I also put together my final budget, which delivered more money for paving and ongoing funding to build a diverse farm team of new employees to replace part of the rapidly retiring workforce. Best of all, after years of having to make up for massive cuts in state aid (down $60 million a year since I took office), I finally got to do something I had wanted to do for a long time: I delivered a budget with no property tax increase.

In spite of all the work on my plate, I didn't want to miss my last summer of parades, especially the three big ones: the Northeast Parade, the Aquatennial, and, biggest of all, Gay Pride. For each one, Andy Holmaas organized a team of volunteers to whom we taught dance routines and strange cheers. As usual, I ran all the parades, going back and forth across the street on the hot nights, trying to shake every hand I could.

I knew I would miss the parades when the year was over, so I milked every ounce out of them. But at the end of each of the three, I felt a lot more winded than I had in the past. I wondered if it just wasn't in me anymore. About six months later I would understand that while I still had the desire, I didn't have the heart.

# Big Night in the Summer of Love

---

*We interrupt "My Favorite Year" to tell about one wonderful night, six months before I left office when, for the first time, every Minnesotan had the right to marry.*

DURING THE TOUGHEST PERIOD of my family's life as I was growing up, a wonderful man came into our lives.

Lyle Harris met my parents when he was a salesperson for a drug company and periodically would come by to sell pharmaceuticals to my parents' store. When my father had a stroke and was very sick, Lyle became more than just a salesperson who came into the store. He became someone my mother could lean on when she was in real need of support.

On the Sunday morning when my dad died, before we knew what had happened, my mother dropped us off at church. It seemed a little odd that Lyle picked up my brother, sister, and me, and took us bowling afterward. When he brought us home we understood he had been keeping us busy while my mom had my dad's body moved from the house and prepared to tell us that he had died.

Over the next couple of years, as we all adjusted to life without my dad, we spent a lot of time with Lyle. He took my mom out to dinner every Saturday night, and he came to our house for a big dinner every Sunday—but the highlight was every Friday night. That's when Lyle would take my mom, my brother, my sister, and me on a family activity: bowling, roller-skating, a movie. He took my brother and me on Boy Scout campouts. One weekend he took all of us kids to Chicago on the train while my mother stayed home and, I imagine, had one of the very few times to herself in years. He talked my mom into getting Sonny, a Scottie dog we loved.

Every once in a while we would go to Lyle's house, an immaculate one-story rambler in suburban Edina that he shared with two other men, including his best friend, Jim, who was also incredibly kind to us.

After losing my dad and seeing my mom go through so much, we had suddenly, magically, come into what I still see as possibly the very best part of my family's life. Lyle was incredibly nice to all of us and kind to my mom. They weren't into big public displays of affection, but I did come into the living room a couple of times to find them kissing, including one time when they were on the couch smooching while the Association's corny hit "Cherish" played in the background. That kind of thing makes adolescent boys cringe, but it seemed normal enough to have your mom dating, especially someone who was so great to our family.

THEN, ABRUPTLY, Lyle wasn't there. He was gone for a couple of weeks. Then he was back. Then, gone for good.

A few months later Chuck Mesken came into our lives. Chuck, who owned real estate in the neighborhood around our store, had an office next store. My mother started dating him and we settled into the same Friday, Saturday, Sunday routine we had had with Lyle. Chuck eventually married my mom and became very much like a father to all of us.

Over the span of a few months after Lyle left, my mom let us in on a series of details about their relationship, and finally had an honest talk with us explaining that Lyle was what we then called a "homosexual." Without going into too much detail, she got across the fact that he was a wonderful man but that she and Lyle were not going to be a good match. A year or so later I was walking out of the barbershop Lyle had once told us about and there in the doorway, on his way in, was Lyle himself. In one of the moments I regret most in my life, I saw him, looked away, only after seeing his face full of hurt, and walked past him without saying a word. I just didn't know what to say but I know how hard my lack of response would have been for him.

The first gay person I knew in my life had had a profoundly positive impact on my family—so when a couple of decades later right-wing groups started targeting gay people for ruining the country's moral fabric, one thing was clear to me: Lyle Harris had given me one of the best lessons in family values I ever could get.

HAVING BEEN INTRODUCED TO GAY PEOPLE in such a positive way, I never had any of the negative prejudices that have made this issue so complex for so many. In some ways that experience helped me think about the issue more like people my own kids' age, who overwhelmingly tend to approach this issue by being baffled why people made it such a big deal.

But when I first started hearing about "gay marriage," it seemed both odd and almost beside the point. If someone wanted to do it, I thought, I guess that's fine but all the other issues of equal rights for gay people just seem a lot more important—bullying, job discrimination, benefits, adoption. When I was elected mayor, I planned to focus on those issues and not waste time and capital on the fight for marriage.

Back in those early years in office David Fey helped me navigate through the issue when Mayor Gavin Newsom started performing weddings in San Francisco's City Hall. The experience taught me that David and his partner, Michael, didn't have the same rights I did. In later years I would see the same inequity with my chief of staff, Jeremy Hanson Willis, and his partner, Sam, as well as with my communications director, John Stiles, and his partner, Javier.

A few years later the gay marriage issue came to life once more when a group of Republican legislators again proposed the constitutional ban. It was never overtly said that there was a motive, but it was pretty clear to many of us that they were following the lead of conservatives in other states who found putting an anti–gay marriage amendment on the ballot could bring more of their voters to the polls.

On a hot and sticky spring night in May 2011, crowds from both sides of the debate filled the State Capitol. I stood for hours alongside amendment opponents—including many same-sex couples and their children—in the corridors where the temperature was becoming increasingly unbearable. As the night went on and it became clearer that we were going to lose, reality sank in: my state was about to take a vote on whether one group of residents should have fewer rights than another. I saw it as though voters were being asked whether we should write discrimination directly into the Constitution.

When the vote was announced the exhausted, sweating crowd around us was in chaos. Among the many families trying to explain all this to their kids were two women from St. Paul who were sobbing with their six-year-old boy. I leaned down to him and told him I knew this felt bad today but that just meant it would feel all the better when his parents finally did get the chance to marry . . . and they would. I would meet them again in the same place two years later in much better circumstances.

While most at the Capitol that humid evening had been fairly certain the amendment would pass, my gut told me differently. I told a few people this could be a gift: the proposed amendment seemed to be so extreme that it may be further than even marriage opponents were willing to go. That meant it would be harder to pass, and, if it went down, maybe that would create a climate in which we could actually turn around and pass marriage equality.

I wondered whether my optimism was blinding me to a much worse reality, but I was certain either way it was going to be a brutal year and a half filled with months of television commercials saying the worst possible things about gay people.

That ended up not being true. The campaign to beat the amendment was one of the best-organized grassroots efforts Minnesota has ever seen, and the bulk of the commercials came from the far-better-financed amendment opponents. They humanized the faces and stories of gay people simply wanting to live their lives like other Minnesotans.

Equally important, organizers rejected advice from people like me who said the message shouldn't take on the broader language of marriage equity for gay Minnesotans. I felt it would be more likely to win if the case were made that, no matter what you felt about gay marriage, we should not be using the Constitution to limit rights.

I'm glad they didn't listen to me because the campaign ended up being a referendum on gay marriage and, in many ways, on the wider question of whether we were a state that would accept people for who they are. The amendment was defeated in November 2012, and many Minnesotans who had no opinions came away with a much better understanding of why marriage was needed. It's clear to me that the energy of the campaign, mixed with the extraordinary grassroots organization of the Obama campaign, was vital in electing a Democratic majority in both houses of the state legislature. At the next session in May 2013, in an about-face almost none of us would have predicted on that depressing, steamy day just two years earlier, and in the same State Capitol, the new legislature passed marriage equity in Minnesota.

STANDING THERE in the same place at the Capitol that May, trying to take in this amazing change, two women and a young boy came up to me. They reminded me that they were the same couple I had seen crying two years ago and had spoken with. The women said their son told them many times over the past couple of years about my prediction—which even I thought at the time was wildly optimistic—that someday they would get their equal rights. Then the son said, "And I *do* feel so much better." Then he held up a sign that had a picture of his two moms and him and said, "And equal rights for all . . . including us." The four of us just smiled and cried.

A few minutes before the vote was taken, while I was standing on the rotunda's second floor overlooking a massive crowd, I yelled down, "If this thing passes, come on down to City Hall and I'll marry you!"

Standing next to me was my aide Andy Holmaas, whose eyes got as big as saucers because he realized, much more than I did, that my offer was a lot bigger than I thought. "I think . . . I better . . . call . . . the . . . office," he said, stunned. He was right. Almost immediately we were flooded with calls, and when we got to around forty-two confirmed weddings and did the math on how long it takes to perform even the fastest ceremony, we had to cut it off. We probably could have done five hundred.

My team knew this would get attention, especially that first couple. This mattered a lot because, at the time, it was unclear whether other states would follow. Many people would be watching us, and we could either create an inspirational evening that led others to follow suit, or have a night that scared potential supporters away. We knew the first couple would have to be what we came to call "a Jackie Robinson couple," meaning a barrier breaker so extraordinary no one could question that they deserved equal rights.

Our answer came in the crowd on the State Capitol lawn as the governor was signing the bill just a few days later, on May 14, 2013, when I ran into Cathy ten Broeke and her partner, Margaret Miles. Cathy is the state's director of Prevent and End Homelessness, and for many years she had the same position with the county and Minneapolis. Margaret also works on homelessness for St. Stephen's Human Services. They had been together for fifteen years, were raising their son, Louie, and in my mind were the kind of extraordinary people, and extraordinary family, who said all the very best things about why this new law mattered so much. When Cathy asked, almost offhandedly, whether I would marry them, I was deeply honored. I also immediately knew we had our Jackie Robinsons.

Throughout June and July 2013, while we were trying to finish our last budget and attack the massive agenda we had set for the last year, our staff's time was now being consumed more and more by planning forty-two weddings. The work fell especially on Stiles, Hottinger, and Holmaas.

Andy Holmaas was an especially unlikely person to be planning all those weddings. A twenty-eight-year-old music- and beer-loving single guy, Andy is a musician who worked in politics, not the other way around. He cares about a lot of things—actually most things—-more than he does fashion and style, but there he was, dealing with the fussy flowers and vocals and wedding cakes. When a reporter asked him if all this work on weddings was making him want one for himself, he said, "I'd be happy just to date."

We decided to start about 11:30 on August 1, say the first vows at midnight—just as the law went into effect—and then keep going until we were done. Rightfully, people wanting to get married needed a lot of details, but the calls were coming in at a volume we couldn't handle, even if setting things up was all we had to do. Conference calls with all the participants helped a lot, but that seemingly innocent offer I made to a crowd at the State Capitol when the law was passed had created an overwhelming body of work for everyone around me.

But this massive task got easier every time we picked up the phone because so many people wanted to help. We needed flowers, so Roger Beck, an amazingly talented florist, volunteered to decorate the City Hall rotunda. We needed music, so Philip Brunelle, founder of the internationally known choral group VocalEssence, organized a group to play fanfares for the couples. Jeremy Messersmith brought in a group of Minnesota's best musicians to entertain the couples as they waited in line. My favorite wrinkle: General Mills donated spectacular Betty Crocker cakes, a decidedly Middle America touch that was exactly what we wanted to say.

The public relations company Tunheim dedicated a team to write profiles of the individual couples. That was really helpful for me as I tried to learn everything about them. We wanted our marriage marathon to be back-to-back unique, personal experiences worthy of something you remember all your life. This was not going to be a conveyor belt of love.

On the night of the ceremony I got to City Hall about 9:45. Roger Beck's extraordinary white flower arrangements spiraled around the banisters. The chairs and sign-in tables and Betty Crocker cakes were in place. Volunteers were everywhere.

Then the Gay Men's Chorus came in for their sound check. Around fifty members lined up on the broad marble staircase and started to sing "Marry Me." The group had begun performing the song years ago, and it had become an anthem for those who had fought this battle for so long. We had heard it many times at fund-raisers and at Pride Parades. It's an emotional song about being accepted, but I've always heard it as almost an "Over the Rainbow" kind of lament about some unattainable better world. For the first time it was the story of the world we were about to enter. I focused on two of the singers: David Fey, my former chief of staff, who first taught me why this issue matters, and John Stiles, who had carefully steered me through every public statement I made about the topic for the past few years. It seemed so fitting for both of them, in this building where they had worked for many years without the benefits they deserved, to now be singing about progress on that grand staircase.

Just outside the door there was a street party, complete with food trucks, and a long line waiting to get in. Once the City Hall doors opened all five floors of the open atrium quickly filled. Local singer Erin Schwab warmed up the room with a bawdy, Bette Midler–style, call-and-response version of Queen's "Somebody to Love." As 11:00 P.M. came, she moved into the Etta James classic "At Last" and the whole place seemed to sing the final lines with special meaning: "And here we are in heaven / for you are mine . . . / at last."

The place was rocking, but now we had to pivot to an atmosphere resembling something close to a wedding ceremony. So I walked onto the staircase and tried, not so successfully, to quiet the crowd. There were several speeches; Governor Dayton, who a couple of months earlier signed the legislation into law, got a huge response. Typically self-deprecating, he said, "All I did was sign a piece of paper."

Then at 11:30, Margaret and Cathy came down the staircase—looking fantastic, seemingly overjoyed, but in control. There was no escaping the fact that this may be the wedding of two people but their image would be seen all over the country, maybe the world, viewed by people who didn't quite know what to make of it. Seeing them together, clearly in love, said everything we wanted to say in the very best way.

What we didn't count on was their son, Louie. Walking his two moms down the aisle in a spiffy tuxedo, a star was born. And. He. Knew. It.

Louie took center stage on the marble staircase, in front of four hundred people, and like the poised politician I can only someday dream to be, he waved confidently to a crowd he now had in the palm of his hand.

Throughout the ceremony, Louie moved smoothly between his moms, with an occasional sudden wave to his crowd. At one minute he abruptly sat down on the stairs, put his head in his hands, seemingly bored with it all, but then, just as quickly, rebounded for another star turn wave.

We thought a lot about what words to use and chose to make the service sound as much as we could like a traditional wedding because, in fact, that is exactly what it was. We also wanted to capture the gravity of the moment, so I started with, "Dearly beloved, we are gathered here to make history in the name of love."

Joining the couple and me, and, of course, Louie, on the staircase was the Reverend James Gertmenian of Plymouth Congregational Church. A few years earlier, on the Sunday after the anti-marriage amendment was put on the ballot, when members of his church were deeply depressed, he gave one of the most memorable sermons I have ever read: "I understand your fear," he said, "but I want to remind you that this spasm of hatred is the lashing out of a dying dragon. This dragon, homophobia, is angry because it is dying. And in its anger and fear, it may seem stronger than it really is. But it is dying."

He was right. And now, on the night when the dragon died, he gave a beautiful tribute to Margaret and Cathy.

They exchanged vows and everything was moving just as we planned when I got ready to say the vows. Except we had a slight problem: everything had been timed carefully so that I would pronounce the vows exactly at midnight, when the law went into effect. And as I said the final words we had about two minutes and fifteen seconds left. I stretched out a couple of words but finally just stopped talking, let the crowd take a breath, and then, exactly at midnight, I said, "And now, by the power finally vested in me, by the laws of the people of Minnesota, we hereby declare Margaret and Cathy legally married in the state of Minnesota. And now you may kiss the bride." The place went nuts.

Now that we had married the first women it was time for the first men. Al Giraud and Jeff Isaacson came down the staircase, and Margaret and Cathy ran up to hug them. The two couples had become good friends since learning, a couple of months earlier, that they would be making history together.

Al and Jeff met years ago at a Vikings game and, as I said during the ceremony, "A lot of guys meet each other at a football game, but they don't usually get married."

They exchanged vows, and this time I ended with, "And now you may kiss the groom."

With the first two couples married City Hall broke out into a party as the Betty Crocker cakes were served.

At 12:30 it was time to get down to the business of marrying the remaining forty couples. The first, Harvey Zuckman and Phil Oxman, both in their sixties, had been together for decades. They are Jewish, so a chuppah was set up on the staircase, they broke a wine glass when it was over, the chuppah was taken down, and just like that we moved on to couple number four.

Some of the couples we were marrying I knew well, like friends R. D. Zimmerman and Lars Peterssen. Most I was meeting for the first time, but in each case we did our best to have my comments reflect them personally.

As we moved through the group, I followed a ritual up and down the staircase. The ceremony would be on the landing, halfway up to the second floor. After the ceremony I would walk down the stairs with the couple to a table where we would sign the papers. Then my aide Victor Cedeño would hand me a briefing paper with details of the next couple, which I would read as I walked up the two flights to meet them. The couple and I would talk for a couple of minutes about why they were getting married, I would compose a speech in my head as I walked down to the landing, and, a few minutes later the couple would come down to join me. In this way, one after the other, we personalized each wedding ceremony.

The pattern went pretty well for the first couple of hours, but at about 2:00 A.M., as I was walking up the staircase to meet the couple, I fell into kind of a daze and lost my footing. It wasn't too obvious to everyone around me, but as I got up I was dizzy and worried that I had bitten off more than I could chew. I couldn't imagine how we were going to keep doing this for four more hours.

The next couple changed everything. Nic and Lisa are actors. They met when Nic, who is deaf, was in a play and Lisa performed the vocals for her. I was so impressed with their story and immediately saw their extraordinary bond. When they came down to the landing for the ceremony I wasn't certain how we would navigate the vows. Then, as I started speaking, the couple began signing to each other. I have never seen sign performed so dramatically, and with such passion and, without even saying a word, their movements said so clearly to me, and to the rest of City Hall, now watching in silence, "You complete me."

As they finished Nic Zapko and Lisa Zapko shook their hands above their heads in the sign for applause, and the crowd waved back.

It was such a powerful moment I snapped back into clarity, and that gave me the steam I needed to keep going through the night.

The couples were a remarkable mix of ages. I was struck by the difference between the younger ones, like the University of Minnesota couple who met the preceding year online, and the older ones, like those who met decades earlier at a meeting trying to fight Anita Bryant's anti-gay campaign. The younger ones had such a freshness to them, almost blithely unaffected by the years of fighting to get where they were. Those who had been together for decades had both the scars, and the strength, that come from loving each other in a world that didn't accept them. I asked every one of those older couples if they ever expected this day to come and every one said no. They seemed almost shell-shocked, stunned things had turned around so quickly.

There was also a remarkably creative range of outfits. Some wore traditional wedding attire, like the men in tuxes and the pregnant bride in a wedding dress. Two men wore different parts of a three-piece suit in a simple, but profound statement that you needed both of them together to make a whole. There was a whole wedding party in tie-dye and another in Hawaiian shirts and leis. In a particularly colorful couple one of the women wore orange half-length shorts, a yellow shirt, a green scarf, and lavender knee-highs while the other woman wore a bright red shirt, lime green belt, bright red shorts, and multicolored knee-highs.

Even though it was the middle of the night, there were many children. One wedding had two little flower girls in brightly colored Barbie-style flouncy dresses sashaying down the staircase dropping rose petals in front of the couple. As another ceremony ended, just as the vows were done, a loud voice boomed from the crowd, "I love you, Moms," which, at that time, in that place, said a lot.

The goal was to finish by 6:00 A.M., which was important, not only for us to get some rest, but also because people had been waiting many hours, including those children. We were determined to stay on schedule and thought we had planned the timing perfectly to finish the forty-two weddings on time. Throughout the night Andy and Victor were giving me updates on the schedule, but as hard as we tried we kept falling behind. They tried not to look panicked, but in between each wedding they would update the schedule and had more urgency as they told me we were further and further behind. We couldn't figure out what was going wrong because even though we were completing each ceremony on schedule, without having the couple feel rushed, we still had more couples waiting than we had planned. Eventually we realized we didn't have forty-two couples signed up; we had forty-six. So we just recalculated, kept walking up and down the stairs faster and faster, and eventually got at least close to back on track.

At 6:45 the next morning, more than seven hours after that first wedding began, I looked up and saw that the line was done. I called out to see if anyone else wanted to get married. Hearing nothing I announced, "The chapel of love is now officially closed."

I WALKED OUT into a spectacular sunny morning. The sun came up like it always did. Nothing about my marriage to Megan—or any other marriage in Minnesota—had been changed because of what we just did. The only difference was that ninety-two people from incredibly different backgrounds now had exactly one thing in common: they had the same rights today that my wife and I had yesterday.

# My Favorite Year (Part 2)

---

T
HE REALIZATION HIT ME at a really inconvenient time because I
didn't want anything to distract from an incredible moment. I was on
New York's High Line with its now world-famous designer James Corner,
hearing about his design for the second phase of this incredibly popular
elevated park. I knew this was one of those moments you want to remember years later, and it was especially important because Corner was bringing some of these same ideas to his work designing the new Nicollet Mall.

The problem was that I couldn't get another thought out of my mind:
I was running out of time. I could talk to Corner about the future all I
wanted, but I only had a few months left in office. What I said to the architect for Nicollet Mall didn't really matter much because I wasn't going to
be mayor when the big decisions about the project were made.

I also was coming to realize I wouldn't be mayor for a lot of things:
building a new park next to the Vikings stadium; starting a streetcar line;
making sure new Police Chief Janeé Harteau got off to a strong start; finishing building Green Homes North; identifying sustainable long-term funding for prized projects like the Midtown Global Market and the Northside
Achievement Zone.

I wouldn't even have another year of STEP-UP.

It was also an election year and the simple fact was that the closer it got
to the end of the year, the less relevant I would become. If someone didn't
like what I thought, they could just wait me out.

I began to tell a friend that I felt like someone who knows he has only
six months to live and crams in as much as he can. As the words came out
of my mouth I cringed because I've known people who actually did have
only six months to live. No, my situation was absolutely nothing like theirs.
I realized I needed to shut up, stop whining, and double down. If I wanted
to get more done, I just had to work harder.

* * *

FOR NICOLLET MALL that meant I would need to jam into James Corner's head every fact or observation I've ever had about the street. The. Poor. Man.

When he came to town a couple of months later I did just that. We walked down Nicollet Mall and I don't think I took a breath for the first five blocks. I told him:

"People gather on the west side of the street between Sixth and Seventh but on the east side between Seventh and Eighth, except during the Farmers Market."

"Sixth Street between Nicollet and Hennepin is a wind tunnel."

"Do you see that there is surprisingly little sunlight? So that limits the trees you can plant."

"We tried that movable chair idea of yours in 1986."

"Minneapolis is where the woods meet the prairie, so don't you think we should have both in the landscape?"

"Did I tell you my parents met when my dad ran the Walgreen's at Ninth and Nicollet? . . . OK, well, let me tell you again."

BACK IN CITY HALL I was inflicting the same torture on my staff, and pretty much any city employee I could find. One punch-drunk victim after another staggered out of my office, muttering, "All I said was, 'Mayor, we don't have time for that.' "

To make matters worse, two big issues were taking up more and more time. We hadn't planned for the Orchestra lockout or the growing controversy over the light rail line, and they kept drowning out our own agenda.

The Southwest Light Rail Line was especially difficult because we had to find ways to break a deadlock over an alignment of the line I never wanted in the first place.

We had a series of meetings throughout that fall but were unable to find a compromise that worked. On one side were extremely unhappy residents, who saw this as deeply damaging their neighborhood, and on the other side were the Metropolitan Council and Hennepin County, who felt we had to move ahead in spite of the opposition or risk not having any light rail line at all.

All that time on the Southwest LRT was bad enough, but the hard feelings with the county also made it far less likely they would help us build a streetcar line through downtown Minneapolis. By midfall it was clear that the streetcar, which we had been working on in some form for years, and for which we had improbably finally gotten a funding plan through the legislature, was just not going to happen in this term. Not knowing if a new council and mayor would pick up the plan, I realized this meant it may not happen at all.

Giving up on the streetcar was a very bitter pill to swallow, but there was really no other choice. I had three whopping issues in front of me: getting approval for my last budget, and getting the Wells Fargo and Target Center approvals through the city council. This was more than I ever moved through the council in a full year, and we were trying to do it in the three months left. I couldn't afford to get distracted.

As time was running out I very reluctantly gave up so many small projects that I thought mattered a lot. I wouldn't be able to create an alumni association for STEP-UP so that we could track the twenty thousand young people in the program and get them connected to jobs as they graduated from college.

Or launch "Sign Off," a database that finally identified every single sign the city had clogging sidewalks so that we could take down about half of them.

Or get bike access to a railroad bridge across the Mississippi north of Broadway Street in north Minneapolis, which would help spark a greenway across the northern part of the city.

Or a seemingly small idea that would have been very big for bikers: start a new street-paving strategy that would have concrete from curbs spread farther into the asphalt street surface so that bike lanes didn't have two, uneven types of pavement.

These ideas seemed ridiculously detailed for someone about to leave office, and I worried about even bringing them up, but, after twelve years, I had realized that sometimes the best work in cities involves putting in place the hundreds of small things that make everyday life a little better. I also realized it had taken me more than a decade to understand the nuances behind those hundreds of small things and if I didn't get them done, they might not happen for a long time.

I did make time for one issue that wasn't a crisis but needed to happen. My predecessor, Sharon Sayles Belton, was the first woman mayor of Minneapolis, and the city's first African American mayor. She deserved to be recognized for making history, and kids growing up in Minneapolis deserved to have a significant way to remember her.

For several years I had been thinking about the right tribute, and it finally came when the Public Works staff made a budget request to repaint the bridge crossing I-94 at Third Avenue South behind the Convention Center. The eye-catching bridge was modeled after a design by Frank Lloyd Wright. Mayor Sayles Belton helped get it built in partnership with the Minneapolis Institute of Art as part of an effort to make Third Avenue the "Avenue of the Arts." It also connected downtown to a site where a proposed Minneapolis African American Museum was going to be built.

Naming this the Sharon Sayles Belton Bridge was also fitting because she grew up in St. Paul's Rondo neighborhood, which was torn up for a freeway, and later, on the city council, represented a Minneapolis ward straddling two sides of the freeway where she had to bridge largely white neighborhoods with largely African American ones.

I put the bridge repainting in the budget and added some money in the public art budget. On a chilly fall night the former mayor was honored in a ceremony reopening the repainted bridge with a lit sculpture dedicated to her. Both she and her husband, Steve Belton, gave moving speeches. Listening to them I thought about the years I spent as a reporter covering her when she started, about the tough election we had, and how much more appreciation you get for someone's work once you sit in her chair.

WE ALSO CONTINUED THE IMPORTANT WORK from that big night in the summer of love. Following the evening of marriages at City Hall, and after a few hours' sleep, our staff got back together in the mayor's office that afternoon. We were looking at the newspaper coverage and I was struck by a map that showed where same-sex marriage was legal, and equally important, where it was not. Minnesota and Iowa stood out in the center of the country, while gay couples couldn't get married in major cities like Denver, Milwaukee, Kansas City and, the big one, Chicago. John Stiles and I realized this was a gold mine for our hospitality industry, and a great way to showcase Minneapolis's values. We convinced Meet Minneapolis to place two small ads in gay papers in Chicago telling gay people there, if you don't have equal rights in your city, get married in Minneapolis, which is more than happy to take your money and show you the respect you deserve.

Stiles sent out a press release about our "Marry Me in Minneapolis" campaign to Chicago media and we scheduled a press conference. No one could have predicted the reaction: it was the main story on the front page of the *Chicago Tribune*, I was booked on every single morning television show and three drive-time radio shows, public radio, and public television. Best of all, the leader of the Illinois State Senate was quoted as saying, "Don't let a big-buck ad campaign from Minneapolis take dollars out of Chicago." He proposed moving gay rights legislation in Illinois, and it passed. We were very happy to play at least a small role in adding momentum to the stunningly fast evolution of people's thinking about gay marriage, even if we showed that sometimes it helps that money talks.

I ALSO HAD THE NOT-SO-LITTLE DECISION about what I was going to do next. When I announced I wasn't going to run I said I wouldn't talk about the next step until the coming fall, and for the most part people didn't bug me about it. But as fall arrived people on the street or at events began encouraging me to take time off, travel, rest, and not jump into something right away. These were all nice ideas, but they usually came from people who didn't know me very well. It was clear to me—and most who knew anything about me—that after a couple weeks of "taking it easy" I would be completely stir crazy. I also had a very clear idea about the kind of work I wanted to do next.

As proud as I was of all we had done, it weighed very heavily on me that twelve years earlier I became mayor of the city with some of the largest achievement and opportunity gaps for kids of color. Back then it was shocking to me that in almost no other community in the country was there a bigger difference between the academic performance of kids. It was even more shocking that twelve years later, after all our work in housing, workforce training, summer jobs and so much more, those gaps were actually worse. To me, the single most important issue in the city was the horrendous fact that you could predict the likelihood of a child's success by looking at the color of his or her skin. My work wasn't done.

I had worked on this issue in many different ways for my whole tenure, but I was spending more time on it now that Generation Next had started. I loved the idea of Generation Next, and knew we had the right people at the table to make change, but I was growing increasingly vocal at the board meetings that we weren't moving fast enough. In early fall a couple of board members came to me and essentially said, "If you think this is so easy, why don't you run it?"

The idea came out of the blue, but after thinking about it for a couple of weeks it made all the sense in the world. Even if I ran for a fourth term and focused on closing the gap, something always happens in the city to take my focus off even the most important idea. Running Generation Next would let me focus 100 percent on the biggest issue around. I took the job and made plans to start there the week I left office. In the meantime, the group had significant issues—so on top of the work already on my plate, I had a new body of work keeping Generation Next on track until I got there.

AGAINST ALL THIS was the backdrop of a wide-open city election to pick my successor and a new city council. Unlike any other election I remember, I had to stay neutral.

Like a racehorse stuck in the paddock during the Kentucky Derby, I knew it would be hard to sit on the sidelines the last couple of weeks before the election. One of the few campaign events I did was a door knock with Barb Johnson. Being out on a crisp October day, smelling fall, and hearing the leaves crunching beneath my feet brought back wave after wave of nostalgia. I didn't regret that I wasn't going to be in office anymore. I just wanted to be in the fight. To mix some metaphors, the racehorse wanted to get in the game but didn't have a dog in the fight so had to cool his jets . . . or something like that.

Luckily Megan and I knew this would happen and booked a trip to D.C. to visit Charlie and just be out of town for the final weekend before the election. I called on my friend Anthony Foxx, whom I got to know when he was mayor of Charlotte and who now was secretary of transportation. My goal was to assure him that, in spite of the news seeping back to Washington that we were in a big fight about the Southwest Light Rail Line, it was all going to come together. (I was more optimistic than I should have been.) Knowing he built the first streetcar line in Charlotte I also wanted a potential line in Minneapolis to be on his radar.

The rest of that spectacular fall weekend we spent with Charlie and his girlfriend, Ashley Lowes, seeing Washington beyond the tourist spots. Walking down a beautiful side street shaded by trees in full fall color, seeing all the great places to live, Megan and I said to each other that if there was ever a time when we were tempted to move to Washington, this would be it: being back with our son, seeing a peer of mine happily transitioning to a job in the administration, my job as mayor done.

Then we instantly agreed: we weren't tempted for a second. I wasn't going to find my next chapter by running away. I was going to do it in the only place I ever wanted to call home. And a few months later I got to prove that point to myself when I was offered a truly great job in Washington but, not even tempted, turned it down.

ALMOST EVERY ELECTION DAY, I wake up as early as I can and stand at the 46th Street freeway entrance waving a campaign sign. This time I woke up, walked to the polls, voted, and went to work. For the first time in at least two decades, I had absolutely no role on Election Day.

Most expected a very close race, but council member Betsy Hodges won by a lot. Because Minneapolis has ranked-choice voting, it took a day to know the result so the following night, the mayor-elect had a victory party at the 612 Brewery in northeast Minneapolis.

Having stayed out of the election, I didn't have a clear sense of who was involved in the different campaigns, but when I walked into the Hodges party it was fun to see a lot of the same people who had been active in my own races. I felt right at home, the mayor-elect did a great job reaching out beyond her own supporters, and I left feeling this was going to maybe be easier than I thought.

A couple of nights later Megan and I went to the annual benefit for the Northside Achievement Zone. We sat with the mayor-elect, her husband, Gary Cunningham, and Don and Sondra Samuels. Don, fresh off his own run for mayor, was obviously disappointed but seemingly at peace that he got universal praise for being the "education candidate" who focused the race on our kids.

Sondra had started the Northside Achievement Zone, which was now a multimillion-dollar operation doing exceptional work with kids and families. As we were out on the dance floor, I looked around at the hundreds of people at the dinner supporting the work; I thought about how far Don and Sondra and Megan and I had come since we met over serious crime issues in north Minneapolis.

I looked across the dance floor at Pam Costain, who opposed me when I ran for reelection because I wasn't focused enough on schools, and who eventually became one of my closest allies. She was now leading Achieve Minneapolis, the foundation for Minneapolis schools that runs STEP-UP. I saw Peggy Flanagan and thought about helping her when she was a young candidate running for the school board and who was now leading the Children's Defense Fund–Minnesota. I looked at Mayor Hodges, who was going to be launching a "Cradle to K Cabinet," and her husband, Gary, who has been involved with youth for years, including helping start Generation Next. I thought about the work I was about to start with Generation Next.

The dance floor started to look like one of those movie dream sequences where everyone you know is in one place doing the one thing you want them to—only this time it was real and all of us were going to be part of the same body of work for kids.

I went to bed that night feeling something I never predicted I would feel a few days after an election that began the end of my term: I had made the right choice and was in exactly the right place.

THE NEXT MORNING I woke up in a panic because there was so much left to do.

Getting ready to leave a job I loved, where there is a never-ending list of things to do, felt a lot like taking our kids to college: you know your time is almost up, you know there is so much more you want to tell them, but you know you have to pick your shots. I couldn't do everything I wanted, so I had to choose carefully what really mattered. I like to say there was a science to it, but, actually, I decided what to work on in those final two months by picking what would really bug me in ten years.

Using that criterion one issue shot to the top of the list: it would truly bug me, a heck of a lot, if the Midtown Global Market failed. We had saved a vacant hulk of a building that most people had given up on, and now it was one of Minneapolis' greatest attractions: all those people from so many cultures, owning their own businesses, putting out great food, attracting all those people to Midtown because of its diversity, not in spite of it. Thinking about that vibrant space being empty was just crushing. It was doing fine, traffic and sales were strong, but it had always operated with a debt. To me this was grossly unfair: almost every public market in the country had public money and few of them—in fact, none that I knew of—have so many truly local, immigrant entrepreneurs.

Our plan was to get the private lenders who held part of the original debt to forgive their loans if the city forgave its own loan. We called the private lenders in and, to their tremendous credit, they eventually agreed. Then I ran into a buzz saw.

Council member Lisa Goodman, who chaired the committee that would have to approve this, saw the situation differently. She believed the market was a private business and that the city should not be letting private businesses off the hook. She and I had an alliance for many years that supported tough negotiations with developers looking for private money. She saw this as one more tough negotiation where we could not give in to private interests. I saw Midtown Market as a public amenity that operated almost privately, and, if we should ever use public funds (even forgivable loans), we should do so when we were creating jobs for immigrants in a part of town that depended on this lively attraction.

It was a legitimate difference in policy that rapidly devolved. Goodman and I had a meeting with representatives of the market's partnership, and they were four of the most respected, distinguished people in town: public-minded banker Bill Sands, retired Allina executive and longtime civic leader Gordon Sprenger; Atum Azzahir, whose Cultural Wellness Center is dedicated to respectful community empowerment; and Mike Temali, Midtown Market's true founder, with a no-drama, all-business style.

The conversation began calmly enough, but Goodman made it clear she would not support forgiving the loan. Then she went further and lit into the four market representatives, disparaging them for asking for loan forgiveness. I reminded her that I, not them, was asking for the forgiveness. It escalated from there.

The genteel group of four sat slack-jawed as Goodman and I had an old-fashioned knock-down, drag-out brawl straight out of *Jersey Shore*, ending with my using some select words at the top of my lungs to kick her out of the office.

WHEN PARENTS FIGHT they often don't realize at the time that everyone in the house can hear. The same is true in City Hall, where a fight between two elected officials can send shock waves through the building with implications far beyond the office where it happened.

News spread very quickly around City Hall that Goodman and I had had an explosive fight, and it had widespread implications. Much of the work left to do depended on the mayor and the Community Development chair shepherding the Wells Fargo and Target Center deals through approvals. When Goodman and I were on the same page we could be a strong team, but everyone in the building was keenly aware that when she and I were at odds, there could be fireworks.

(Eventually I got enough votes from other council members, and both Goodman and I gave in a little, so we got $1.5 million in debt relief for the market, which triggered the private debt forgiveness.)

For many years Goodman and I lurched between being the best of allies or the bitterest of opponents, and the toughest part was that I couldn't always tell when it was going to abruptly shift. There is no question that, overall, she and I did exceptional work together. Right from the start we led a sweeping overhaul of the city's development structure that made it much easier to do business in the city. We also kept our promise to dramatically cut the amount of city money paid to developers, and, together, we cut in half the amount of city land off the tax rolls for tax increment deals.

When Goodman and I were on opposite sides, it usually wasn't pretty. Hard as it got, we always seemed to find a way to paste the partnership back together. In one of our last meetings we finally learned to use her explosiveness to our advantage.

Near the end of our negotiations with the Timberwolves regarding the Target Center renovation, the NBA sent in a lawyer from New York. He was, well, a New York Lawyer who was definitely not Minnesota Nice. He brought an unbending, sarcastic hard edge into what had been fairly smooth talks with Timberwolves reps. Now, the lawyer was making particularly outrageous demands in a meeting with Goodman, Council President Johnson, and me, and it was clear we weren't going to get anywhere unless he changed his tone. I asked for a brief break and Goodman, Johnson, and I left the conference room with our attorney Susan Segal for my office, where we worked out a plan: knowing firsthand how intimidating Goodman could be when she launched into one of her verbal assaults, we agreed that when I said the word "constituents" she would go off on the lawyer.

The meeting resumed and, after a few minutes as planned I said, "I don't think that will fly with our constituents."

Goodman didn't pick up the hint.

A few minutes later I tried again. "You have to remember that this has to pass the smell test with our CONSTITUENTS."

To my frustration, Goodman still said nothing.

Finally, a few minutes later, when I said "constituents" again, she sat straight up in her chair and delivered a tongue-lashing that sent the lawyer flying back across the Hudson River. The tone of the meeting changed, and we got pretty much what we wanted. You can only imagine what Goodman and I could have gotten done if we had figured this strategy out years ago.

* * *

THE MEETINGS about Target Center and Wells Fargo continued almost nonstop all fall. In early November, after a particularly complex meeting with Wells Fargo and our staff, we looked around the table and came to the conclusion that it was almost impossible to get one of the—if not *the*— most complex development deals in city history through council approval by the end of the year. We debated taking it as far as it could go but scheduling a final vote in February.

Almost immediately we rejected the idea of delaying until the next year, thinking what it would be like for a new administration and new council to get up to speed on all the moving parts of this deal when they had different agendas of their own. I also remembered what it was like in my first months in office to be distracted by trying to solve the budget the previous council had left unfinished.

We really had no business trying to get this done in the time remaining, but we also had no alternative. We plowed ahead. The Target Center passed through the council in mid-November. Shortly thereafter, in early December the budget was passed, the first in many years that did not have a property tax increase, and included funding key goals like diversifying the workforce and debt relief for the Midtown Global Market.

Finally, on December 14, in the last scheduled meeting in December, the city council passed the full package. This was an enormous relief, and I was exceptionally proud it passed unanimously. This was a great accomplishment for a council that only a few months earlier was ripped apart by the stadium debate. It also showed that City Hall was not like Congress— where a majority ran over the minority on every vote, and each issue was decided according to whose "side" you were on.

I never had a "side" or totally predictable allies on the council. In the twelve years with three councils there were never permanent voting blocs on the council. That may sound strange to a lot of politicians, but it made me very proud, and I saw it as my delivering on an original campaign promise.

When I ran for office I was critical of the fact that too many of the big decisions were made with a 7–6 vote where a majority bloc was always outvoting the minority. If those votes always held it meant a mayor could get what he wanted through a council but only if he could compromise enough to keep those seven people happy. It also meant that the six members in the minority, and, more important, the people they represented, were pretty much cut off from representation. This is what you see today in Congress, where virtually every representative sticks with his or her bloc and could essentially send in a robot to cast the vote.

I could very proudly say that after twelve years in office, with three different city councils, every council member who served with me voted with me on at least one big issue and every single one opposed me on at least one big issue. I formed an alliance with every single council member, usually many, and each felt comfortable in an alliance against an issue of mine. Some council members were far better partners than others—but, unlike some members of Congress who spent the entire Obama presidency voting against anything he did, our councils didn't let politics get in the way of good ideas.

AS I BEGAN to clean twelve years of junk out of my office, I also went to as many city offices, fire stations, and police precincts as I could so that I could say "Thank you" to those who did the work. We also threw a party for employees in the atrium and gave everyone a thank-you card listing everything we had done together. Employees who joined us for cake and cookies also got a thank-you card that showed the progress they had made. We used Results Minneapolis data to show them that since 2002 they answered more than three million 311 calls and resolved 89 percent of them; issued 50 percent more animal licenses; planted ten thousand trees; increased the number of National Night Out block parties by 22 percent; placed more than twenty thousand youth in STEP-UP summer jobs; and helped city residents produce 18 percent less garbage and decrease greenhouse gas emissions in the city by 9 percent. The value of property in the city grew by 29 percent, construction permits in 2013 hit an all-time city high of $1.14 billion; and city employment and training programs placed 14,627 hard-to-employ adults in jobs.

Crime, which had taken up so much of my time in office, was clearly moving in the right direction: since 2001 violent crime was down 6 percent; graffiti was down 31 percent; fires were down 39 percent; domestic violence convictions were up 50 percent; and the number of organized public safety block clubs increased 69 percent.

The biannual resident satisfaction survey also yielded good news about attitudes. Between 2003 and 2012, 19 percent more people said Minneapolis was moving in the right direction; 15 percent more reported that "Minneapolis government represents and provides for the needs of all its citizens"; 16 percent more said that Minneapolis government provided value for tax dollars; and 15 percent more indicated that their neighborhood was a good or very good place to be.

I DID NOT WANT to have one of those boring farewell dinners filled with speeches. Instead, we held the "Unaugural," a dance party at First Avenue with musicians Chastity Brown, Dave Simonett and some of the other members of Trampled by Turtles, Tapes 'n Tapes, and D. J. Shannon Blowtorch.

There were some pictures of my time in office projected on the big screen, but otherwise there was not a lot of looking back. It felt great to be there in the club that was reborn better than ever, with so many people who were part of the journey. It was the perfect send-off except it just felt so wrong that Charlie, who was living in Washington, couldn't be there. Right when I was feeling bad about that I turned around and there he was, surprising his dad with a great present of coming home for a very special evening.

He joined Megan, Grace, and me for a quick, fun appearance onstage and then—I couldn't help it—I stage dived.

I HAD SAVED one last thing that I wanted to be the final action I took as mayor: the state was planning a new freeway entrance into downtown Minneapolis so the current I-94 entrance from St. Paul would no longer be needed and would be turned over to the city. I put money into the budget to convert this long, wide freeway bridge into a pedestrian connection. It would link the new stadium, a nearby light rail line, and the West Bank, home to the city's largest Somali population that is now cut off from the rest of the city.

The day before I moved my boxes out of City Hall, Mayor-Elect Hodges and I announced this new walkway would be named after Hussein Samatar.

Samatar, who had died of cancer a year earlier, was one of my favorite partners. A refugee from Somalia who had to flee the war just as he was finishing his college degree in economics, Samatar came to Minneapolis speaking no English. He taught himself the language by reading books about banking at the Franklin Library, got a job at Wells Fargo, and after several years, left to start the African Development Center. At ADC Samatar helped scores of Somalis start small businesses, and he partnered with the city to get business help to entrepreneurs of the Islamic faith without violating their religious ban on usury. ADC was also a key partner in developing the Midtown Global Market. Samatar was a very good friend I deeply missed, so it was a fitting final action to know this new public space would be called Samatar Crossing to honor the path he and other immigrants took to help build Minneapolis.

AFTER A GREAT family Christmas and New Year, I sat down on New Year's Day to watch bowl games and was pledging to veg out on the couch until Megan and I went to a couple of New Year's Day parties. Someone posted a hilarious picture of a duck with a crutch on my Facebook page and almost immediately I put it up as my new profile picture. I had been reading about Rob Ford, the way-out-there Toronto mayor, who, among other things, had smoked crack, and I wondered what would it actually take for me to get impeached at this point. I tweeted: "Only a few more hours to go. Must. Suppress. Inner. Rob. Ford." Literally the second I sent the tweet my phone rang and my lame duck status abruptly changed: there had been a terrible explosion and fire on the West Bank. I threw on some jeans, a hoodie, and down jacket, and headed to the scene. When I got there the street was filled with fire trucks and hoses, the firefighters had fallen back into defensive posture as smoke was billowing out of the building. It was far worse than I thought.

An older storefront and the apartments above it were completely destroyed. The residents above were scattered, including two who were facedown in the street. All of them were East African, meaning that all the chaos of residents fleeing a fire was complicated by language and culture.

After getting briefed in the fire command vehicle, Mayor-Elect Hodges, council member-elect for the area Abdi Warsame, and I headed off to visit victims at hospitals. Warsame, the first Somali elected to the Minneapolis City Council, played the invaluable role of translator as we worked as a team, quickly expressing sympathy to families and injured residents, then leaving them to recover.

Without realizing it I had begun to download to the new leaders of City Hall some of the lessons I learned from responding at such scenes over twelve years: "Here's the right door to enter the emergency room at Hennepin Council Medical"; "Park here for Fairview University Hospital"; "Here are a few things I try to say at a press conference." It was soon really clear they knew what to do and didn't need my help anymore.

* * *

THE NEXT DAY at Mayor Hodges's inauguration I got a certain kick out
of not being the center of attention. I had been worried about how I would
react, but it was strange how normal it felt. After the mayor was sworn in,
she called me up onstage, and we took a selfie. I filtered back into the crowd
and walked out the door.

# The End, Almost Literally

THEY SAY that in politics you never really know who your friends are. That was never true with us. We made a ton of friends from our work in politics. We also knew that no matter what the latest crisis was, or even how sloppy we had become in staying in touch, we would always have this small group of friends who had been with us long before I ran for office.

I'm sure for them that having me be mayor was a source of some pride, and a bit of a novelty when they were talking to other people, but it was never the core of what we were all about. We had been there when most of the couples had first met, had children at the same time, began to see our children get married, and now started to see the others have grandchildren. We stayed up late and danced when we were younger, and now were staying up late and dancing when we were older. Their names were never publicly connected to my work, but a lot of the credit I got as mayor should go to the people who held us together over all those years. Friends like Linda Houden and Jerry Van Amerongen, Marnie and Dan Boivin, Holly Jepson, Tom and Anne Ulseth, Peter and Liz Taylor, Marc and Zina Balbo, Rob and Maria Owens, Brian Balleria and Joanie Bechtold.

So it was fitting that a bunch of us got together a couple of nights after I left office in early January 2014. In the car on the way home Megan and I talked about how grateful we were to be surrounded by people who knew us for what we were. No matter what. There would probably be some people who weren't as interested in seeing us now that I wasn't mayor. But we didn't have to worry about this loyal group of longtime friends. I also told Megan this night was the first time I have intentionally left the house without my cell phone in thirteen years.

THANKFULLY, I took the phone with me the next morning when I went cross-country skiing at Theodore Wirth Park. It was intensely cold, but we had the best snow cover in years. The Loppet was only a month away, and, anxious to catch up on the training I had missed because of the insane amount of work in December, I skied as hard as I could.

About thirteen kilometers into the ski I had a strange feeling in my chest—almost like someone put an ice pack on my heart. Knowing how cold it was I thought if I worked a little harder I would warm up and it would go away. The strange sensation was a distraction, but mostly I was thinking about how free I was: all the obligations lifted off me, all alone in the woods. I couldn't get over how perfect the snow conditions were as I went up, then down, then up again on the steep hills around Wirth's Bird Sanctuary. Climbing the last big hill I realized I had noticeably less strength than I usually had, and, by the time I got to the top, I knew something was seriously wrong. Fortunately the quarter mile remaining on the course was flat or downhill, so I glided back to the parking lot and got into my car.

I didn't really know exactly what hypothermia felt like but knowing how cold it was, I thought that might be the problem. I turned up the heat in the car, began to thaw, and started feeling better. My friends Scott Gislason and Ed Ryan, who, ironically, were in the car with me a decade earlier when we thought up the idea of the Loppet, were also skiing that day. When they passed the car, they started cracking jokes, but I told them something was wrong. "Should we call 911?"

"No, I think it's just a hiccup . . ." and then, almost immediately, I started to lose my breath. I told them to call 911. A fire truck and then an ambulance came. I was given some nitroglycerin in the ambulance and got to the hospital feeling pretty good.

Megan and Grace met me there and came with me into the emergency room. Suddenly, as I was lying on the operating table, something went terribly wrong: I crashed and just like that, I had the startling realization that I may be dying. I couldn't believe what was happening. For years I had done everything possible not to go like my dad—exercising, eating an incredibly healthy diet—but now I was about to die just like he did. I didn't want Megan and Grace to see it, so I told them "I think I have to do this alone" and asked them to step into the hall. I heard the doctor say something to Megan about a heart attack and everything went black.

Next thing I knew I was in a hospital room with Megan and Grace. I felt really great, as if nothing had happened. Unfortunately, it had been a lot harder for both of them: after I blacked out they had to watch me being wheeled into the cath lab with a team of doctors and nurses working frantically on me.

Meanwhile in Washington, D.C., Charlie had gotten a call from Megan, and after seeing a flurry of tweets about me having a massive heart attack he—for probably the first and only time in his adult life—stopped looking at social media.

It was surreal to wake up and hear what happened, to hear that media people were all over the hospital and wild rumors were spreading on social media. I calmed that down with a couple of quick tweets from the hospital bed: *My cardiac surprise / Gave me quite a start / But it proves this politician / Has a great big heart* followed with *By the way the ski trails at Wirth are awesome today.*

My mayoral staff, shocked as well, no longer worked for me but they moved into action and tried to temper the public reaction. They did their best to explain how in a two-hour stretch I could go from having a massive heart attack to tweeting rhymes and updates on snow conditions. It was clear there had to be a press conference to clear everything up. Megan was in no mood to do it, so Grace joined the hospital staff for a truly masterful performance under intense pressure, including tips for people who worry about their heart condition. Charlie flew into town and the next day he and Grace did a follow-up press conference. Their proud dad has only watched it on YouTube 1,345 times.

This would be a good time for me to advise anyone: if you plan to have a heart attack, do it around my family. The gallows humor of it all just struck us as wickedly funny, partly because all four of us were all so relieved that all four of us were there. We laughed so hard in the next few days that the nurses got mad. "You're ripping out his stitches!" They literally had me in stitches, which meant I almost wasn't. The rest of our families and a few friends came by, including Robbie Soskin, who arrived with a big enough care package from his wife Patti's restaurant Yum! that we could treat half the nursing staff.

I am incredibly grateful for the amazing care I received at Abbott Northwestern Hospital and the Minneapolis Heart Institute. Mixing that with a healthy lifestyle and a lot of luck meant I recovered with literally no permanent heart damage. I was slowed down but I was back at work in my new job at Generation Next in six days. I already ate well and exercised, so I couldn't change too much of my lifestyle, but I did have to start taking a bunch of pills. When I later complained about the pills to my mother she shot back: "Who are you to complain about pills? Your father was a pharmacist! People buying pills paid for you to go to college. You should be telling people to take as many pills as they possibly can!"

The only serious long-term consequence of the heart attack is that when I go to food trucks the entire line weighs in on whether or not my order is "heart healthy."

So The End wasn't THE END after all.

JUST AS QUICKLY as the heart attack came and went, I was at work with a huge new challenge on my hands at Generation Next. I had almost no time to think about not being mayor. I was up to my eyeballs in work that had been building up at Generation Next, and I had only a week to get ready for "Mayor 101," the class I began teaching in late January at the University of Minnesota. Almost immediately, I was on to a new life that seemed just as full as the last one.

It took a few weeks for me to catch my breath and think about what had happened, including the crazy last year and, especially, the truly crazy ending. I was struck by how strange it was that this new life seemed so normal. For most of the time I was mayor I wondered what it would be like when I finally stopped, assuming leaving my dream job would be a massive transition. The bizarre part was it felt pretty much the same.

The Generation Next work—aligning schools, nonprofits, philanthropy, and government to address the complex issues of closing the achievement gap—felt a lot like being mayor. Do whatever it takes to solve the problem, only unlike the mayor job, instead of being spread among hundreds of issues, I could go really deep on one big one. Ironically, it ended up being the most political job I have had; not in a *House of Cards* backstabbing political way, but political in trying to align all these public and private systems and players. It was also becoming clear that closing the achievement and opportunity gaps may be the most important work I would do, and, on many levels, the most difficult.

A FEW YEARS EARLIER, when I was in the middle of some of my most complicated work as mayor, I read *Angle of Repose*, a wonderful novel by Wallace Stegner about the choices we make in our lives. I loved the book—and almost loved the title's metaphor even more. An "angle of repose" is the point at which a rock, rolling downhill, comes to its logical resting place. In the book, and in our lives, it's the point at which all the exploring and experimenting leads us to the rightful place where we finally are meant to be.

As I read the book when I was still mayor I thought about how I had spent my life on a very intentional journey that was always meant to get me to one very specific place. When I reached my "angle of repose" as mayor, it was clear it was a better angle for me than I had even imagined. Being mayor wasn't a resting place, to be sure, but it was so very much the right place.

It's wonderful to have a dream about your future when you are a kid, but it's a problem when you wake up before you find out how it really ends. I knew from a very early age that I wanted to be mayor of Minneapolis, but, until now, I never thought about what came next.

I never could have imagined how completely fulfilled I was as mayor.

I couldn't have imagined the massive financial problems we would face, or that we could solve so many.

I couldn't have imagined the collected grief that came from losing Tyesha Edwards, Brian Cole, and Reuven Rahamim, or known the power of the relationships we would build with their families and the others they left behind.

I could not have imagined the horror of the bridge collapse, or the north Minneapolis tornado; but I also couldn't have imaged how inspirational it was to see that bridge rebuilt so fast and so well, and to see thousands of volunteers stream into north Minneapolis to help rebuild neighborhoods and lives.

I had seen so much but still felt I was very much the same person who started an improbable campaign many years ago. Now, for the first time in my life, there wasn't this Big Thing on the horizon. I was, for the first time in my adult life, living one step at a time.

Now, "angle of repose" meant something a bit different. I saw that until now, no matter where life was taking me, I tried to get that rock to roll back toward that one place I knew I should be. Now the rock was rolling again, and, for the first time, I wasn't trying to steer.

# Why I Wrote This Book

On a hot summer afternoon during my last year as mayor, I dove into Lake Hubert in Nisswa, Minnesota, for a long swim. Exercise has always been my refuge, especially when I'm under pressure. I really needed exercise when I was mayor.

As I swam out into the lake I expected my brain would start working over all the things I was trying to get done during those last months in office. Instead I started thinking about being a kid again, throwing a tennis ball against our house and pretending I was a star for the Minnesota Twins. Forty minutes later as I swam back to shore I had pretty much composed in my head what would become the second chapter of *Pothole Confidential*. As I got out of the water, I had this rush of other memories about the highly unlikely reality of growing up to do the Big Thing you dreamed about as a kid. Over the next few months, early in the morning or sitting on a plane, I started to write down those stories. Eventually I saw that I was writing a book.

Someone once said poets should become astronauts because the only descriptions we have of outer space are from people trained to fly airplanes. I kept that in mind when I wrote this, because most books about politics are from politicians. I am no poet but I was a journalist, and I tried to write this thinking I wasn't a former mayor writing a book, I was a journalist embedded at City Hall.

I tried to tell stories the way I heard them, sitting for hours around my mom's table growing up, and I tried to remember the lessons I learned from Jeremy Hanson Willis, my long-time aide who, more than any other person, helped me find my true voice when I was mayor.

I didn't have a clue how to get a book published, so I sent an e-mail to the first publisher I thought of—and I completely lucked out because

that e-mail went to the University of Minnesota Press. I met with director Doug Armato, editorial director Jason Weidemann, and regional editor Erik Anderson, who immediately understood what I was trying to do.
When they told me not to read another political bio until I was finished
with my manuscript, I knew I had a home for my book.

I wanted to write this myself, so that people reading it would know it
came directly from me, but Erik made tremendous contributions. He knew
when to push me to be more honest, even when it brought back painful
memories. His insight helped me understand parts of my story that I didn't
fully comprehend before. If he ever leaves his current profession (which
would be a real shame), he would be a great psychotherapist or bartender.

I am grateful to all the good folks at the Press who helped along the
way, particularly Emily Hamilton and Heather Skinner in marketing, Dan-
iel Ochsner and Laura Westlund in production and design, and Kristian
Tvedten in editorial. Mary Byers was a wonderful and attentive copy editor.

Susan Segal, Andy Luger, and Dave Hage gave up valuable time to read
an early draft of the manuscript and recommended great suggestions that
made the book better.

A special thanks to Steve Berg, a long-time friend from our days as
reporters and the most gifted journalist I know. He provided enormous
support and much needed criticism when he wrote for the *Star Tribune*
editorial board when I was mayor. He was the first person outside my family I talked to about this book idea; he gave true insight then as well as after
reading my first draft.

In this endeavor, as in so much of my work over the past decade, I
deeply thank Janna Hottinger, my deputy chief of staff when I was mayor
who now works with me at Generation Next. She was my institutional
memory as I tried to replay all this, and she spent many hours of her own
time organizing this writing as fragments of chapters flew in all directions.

I wanted to write this book so my family understood that all these
things we lived through really mattered. I wanted all the idealistic young
people I have met to understand *House of Cards* and all those cynical shows
about politics are bullshit. There is such a thing as public service: it is a
noble life's work, and you will come to know amazing people committed
to a higher calling than themselves. True, the field also has a few charlatans,
egomaniacs, psychopaths, and sleeze-buckets, but you find them in every
profession. I wanted adults to understand they can be the gift in someone's
life—like the teacher Steve Kingsberry was to me when he found a kid who

was giving up on himself and reminded him he had something to say: it made all the difference in the world. I wanted men to understand what I learned from role models like John Pellegrene, who showed me you can put everything you possibly have into your work and still put even more into your family.

And I wanted politicians to understand this: some day you will be at a ribbon cutting or gala testimonial dinner and, maybe wearing a sash, you will stride grandly to the microphone, clear your throat, and loftily proclaim: "I never could have done this without all of you." You don't really believe it, but it was in your talking points, and, now that it's coming out of your mouth, it actually sounds pretty darn good. Then in the audience someone who just read *Pothole Confidential* yells: "You're right! You never could have done it without all of us!"

# Index

*All geographic locations are in Minneapolis unless otherwise specified.*

**R.T. RYBAK** has lived his entire life in Minneapolis. Before his twelve years as mayor, he was a journalist, publisher, Internet strategist, and marketing consultant. He now leads Generation Next, a public–private coalition that works to improve academic outcomes for children of color. He is a vice chair of the Democratic National Committee, senior adviser to Living Cities, and taught the course Mayor 101 at the University of Minnesota.